Help the
Helper

Also by Dr. John Eliot

Overachievement: The New Model for Exceptional Performance
www.overachievement.com

Overachievement, the comic book
www.smartercomics.com/overachievement

The Maverick Mindset
www.nightingale.com

Help the Helper

Building a
Culture of Extreme Teamwork

KEVIN PRITCHARD
and JOHN ELIOT, Ph.D.

Portfolio / Penguin

424 4543

PORTFOLIO / PENGUIN
Published by the Penguin Group
Penguin Group (USA) Inc., 375 Hudson Street,
New York, New York 10014, U.S.A.
Penguin Group (Canada), 90 Eglinton Avenue East, Suite 700,
Toronto, Ontario, Canada M4P 2Y3
(a division of Pearson Penguin Canada Inc.)
Penguin Books Ltd, 80 Strand, London WC2R 0RL, England
Penguin Ireland, 25 St. Stephen's Green, Dublin 2, Ireland
(a division of Penguin Books Ltd)
Penguin Books Australia Ltd, 250 Camberwell Road, Camberwell,
Victoria 3124, Australia
(a division of Pearson Australia Group Pty Ltd)
Penguin Books India Pvt Ltd, 11 Community Centre, Panchsheel Park,
New Delhi – 110 017, India
Penguin Group (NZ), 67 Apollo Drive, Rosedale, Auckland 0632,
New Zealand (a division of Pearson New Zealand Ltd)
Penguin Books (South Africa) (Pty) Ltd, 24 Sturdee Avenue,
Rosebank, Johannesburg 2196, South Africa

Penguin Books Ltd, Registered Offices:
80 Strand, London WC2R 0RL, England

First published in 2012 by Portfolio / Penguin,
a member of Penguin Group (USA) Inc.

10 9 8 7 6 5 4 3 2 1

LIBRARY OF CONGRESS CATALOGING IN PUBLICATION DATA

Pritchard, Kevin.
  Help the helper : building a culture of extreme teamwork / Kevin Pritchard and John
Eliot.
    p. cm.
  Includes bibliographical references and index.
  ISBN 978-1-59184-545-4
  1. Organizational behavior. 2. Teams in the workplace. 3. Leadership. I. Eliot, John,
1971– II. Title.
  HD58.7.P7427 2012
  658.4'022—dc23
                        2012018027

Printed in the United States of America
Set in Adobe Garamond Pro
Designed by Elyse Strongin, Neuwirth & Associates, Inc.

ALWAYS LEARNING   PEARSON

For Our Parents,

for giving us the confidence to pursue our dreams

For KJ & Kendall, and Anner & Norm,

for being inspirations

For Marlene

Contents

---

*H2H is our text and twitter moniker for giving "help to helpers." We use H2H synony-
mously with the term "Help the Helper."

Help the
Helper

Introduction

If you're like most people we know, you've probably had this restaurant experience—or something like it. You've just been served your soup. In haste to enjoy it, though, you dropped your spoon. You need a replacement but your waiter is not available, having gone back into the kitchen to check on an order for another table. The dining room is very busy.

In a Good Restaurant

You grab the nearest waiter as he passes your table and explain that you need a new spoon. That server says he will inform your server. You wait. If you're lucky, it doesn't take long for your waiter to reappear.

In a Better Restaurant

The waiter you grabbed says "right away" and immediately gets you another spoon, even though he's not assigned to your table.

In a Great Restaurant

The second your spoon hit the floor, it drew the attention of a busboy, two other servers in your area, and the maître d'. While all were busy tending to their own duties, a dropped spoon—to them—wasn't your waiter's problem, it was the restaurant's problem. The busboy is instantly at your table offering you a new spoon before you can even pick up the old one.

Such coordination is a complicated feat for a small eatery, well nigh impossible for a large, multinational organization. And yet this very experience is what the world's best-run companies deliver to customers, vendors, and other stakeholders.

Their secret sauce? *They Help the Helper—the pinnacle of teamwork.*

For a combined thirty years, our careers have focused on building high-performing groups. We've crushed our friend Malcolm Gladwell's 10,000-Hour Rule (as presented in his bestseller *Outliers*), logging upward of fifty thousand hours studying separation factors that create champions and dynasties. The exhaustive testing, scouting, and evaluating has taught us that truly special teams have one immutable common denominator, independent of industry type: a willingness to do whatever it takes to help others succeed. Like the most outstanding restaurants, the best-run companies develop this willingness into a fervent, operational passion.

In basketball lingo it's called *Helping the Helper*, a phrase brought to prominence by Hall of Fame coach Dean Smith. Coach Smith used the strategy to set an NCAA wins record, earn ten-time Coach of the Year honors, tutor greats such as Michael Jordan, and capture an unprecedented wealth of conference, national, and world championships (including an Olympic gold medal). Legendary coaches Phil Jackson, Mike Krzyzewski, Pat Summitt, and Roy Williams adopted the approach in compiling their own historic stream of successes, as have hoops' hottest up-and-comers. We're going to show you how to put it to work in *your* business, just as we did in ours.

In 2006, the Portland Trail Blazers were a disgrace to basketball. They were known around the country as the "Jail Blazers"—with some of their most talented players in trouble with the law, teammates fighting in the locker room, and a front office wrought with dissent. The Rose Garden Arena was in bankruptcy. Consumers were the last thing on the organization's mind. The team finished the season at the bottom of the barrel with a woeful 21-61 record.

In the same year, the Tampa Bay Devil Rays were an embarrassment to baseball. An expansion franchise in 1998, they'd never had a winning season, finishing eleven games under .500—at their very best—and dead last every year but one. St. Petersburg residents seemed to have no interest in buying tickets; attendance was the lowest in the league, failing to reach even half that of any other MLB club (even those that also fell low in the standings). The Rays concluded the summer by notching 101 losses.

During the NBA's offseason, Kevin Pritchard—KP—affectionately dubbed "culture kid" by the city of Portland, was given the reins to handle trades and player development for the Blazers. Concomitantly, during the MLB offseason, John Eliot—the doc—then a Rice University professor (now at Stanford) who students say "changes lives," was hired by the Rays into a newly created position, director of performance psychology.

In less than three years, the Trail Blazers flirted with a .700 winning percentage, making it to the playoffs, and assessors called the outfit a model of operational excellence that other businesses should copy; the Tampa Bay Rays dropped "Devil" from their name, filled Tropicana Field to capacity every night with cowbell-ringing fans, and hoisted an American League pennant.

To explain the transformations, "experts" are quick to point to human capital analytics—the trendy and fascinating use of empirical performance data and econometrics to drive personnel valuation, procurement, and management.

Front offices in professional sports were largely void of this kind of scientific approach to leadership until the mid-1990s, when Sandy Alderson, a Vietnam Marine Corps vet with degrees from Dartmouth and Harvard Law, began innovating as the GM of the Oakland Athletics. With the A's in considerable debt when owners Steve Schott and Ken Hofmann took over the team, Alderson was tasked with slashing salaries—to the extent of having the lowest payroll in baseball, no longer able to afford the kind of beefy (literally) Mark McGwire and José Canseco roster that led Oakland to the 1989 World Series crown. Sandy is a staunchly principled competitor. Relegation to the back of the line? Accepting defeat? Not an option. Armed by the union of military discipline with Ivy League brilliance, Sandy will always find a way to battle. And if he can't beat you on your turf, he'll make you fight on his.

Enter sabermetrics, the new battlefield of baseball executives, brought to prominence by Alderson's apprentice, Billy Beane, made corporately hip by author Michael Lewis in *Moneyball*, now turned silver screen sexy by Brad Pitt. The A's leap from more than a half decade of losing to annual division-topping winning percentages, two 100-plus-win seasons, and a streak of playoff appearances from 2000 to 2006—all while staying in the bottom three of all thirty teams in total player salary—spawned a movement across sports to, as commentators enjoy phrasing it, "geek out." The profile of general managers, from

MLB to the NFL and NBA, began to shift. Scores of gut-instinct, "rub some dirt on it" scouts, who had charted a lifetime working their way up the ladder, were replaced by twenty-eight-year-old kids who were as nimble running spreadsheets as Ozzie Smith was doing backflips at shortstop. Leveraging statistics to find and develop undervalued assets became the name of the game.

So it's no surprise when journalists, reporting on the accomplishments in Portland and Tampa, talk numbers. Both were small-market teams with significant payroll limitations. Both employed wizards like the famed Vegas-beating MIT grad Jeff Ma.* Both mapped Oakland's success curve, without Alex Rodriguez/Kobe Bryant All-Star power. So they must be examples of *Moneyball* at work. Only they're not.

There's a good reason Ma's name comes up in this discussion. He knows more about mathematics than most of today's sabermetrics proponents combined. And he's a good friend of ours. Analytics absolutely played a role in crafting the Trail Blazers' and Rays' rosters; we tend to be what you call early adopters. We believe in installing scientifically tested strategies for leadership. We pride ourselves on evidence-based practice and on working tirelessly to stay on the cutting edge of emerging technologies (including presently pushing the envelope of dynamic motion capture, biofeedback, and physiometry). As former athletes ourselves, we also share a helix of DNA with Billy Beane, which we feel allowed us to quickly recognize the merits of Alderson's and Beane's pioneering efforts.

But so did Theo Epstein, the mastermind behind breaking Boston's Curse of the Bambino; R. C. Buford, the GM who assembled the class-act string of NBA titles in San Antonio; and Bob Kraft, the NFL owner consistently releasing Pro Bowl and first-pick-of-the-draft Patriots en route to three Vince Lombardi trophies in four years. Two central flaws exist in the logical assumption that statistical savvy generates champions or turnarounds:

1. By 2006, when we started making organizational changes, the Sox and Spurs, and many other league opponents—including big-market teams that could use their deep pockets to outspend in the area of sabermetrics just as they outspend in talent

---

*Jeff Ma is the mathematician-turned-entrepreneur whose story was the inspiration for the book *Bringing Down the House* and the Kevin Spacey movie *21*.

acquisition—had already implemented performance analytics staffs and strategies. First-mover competitive advantage was gone. Chimes one of the most respected sports economists, Andrew Zimbalist, in The *Wall Street Journal* (September 23, 2011): "The notion that a small-market team could replicate what the A's did is silly. Any notion that you can have some sort of balance because of Sabermetrics is very misleading."

2. Analytics provide post hoc information, assessing performance data and looking for patterns retrospectively. That's useful, to a certain degree, in human capital decision making. Compiling track records of talent on paper, though, is not leadership. Getting that talent to win is a very different beast. Case in point: Beantown baseball in 2011. Despite exclusive access to Bill James, the "father of sabermetrics," despite arguably the most sabermetric-stacked lineup on the diamond (with postulated "greatest of all time" comparisons drawn to the '27 Yankees), despite a nine-game lead with less than a month left to go in the regular season, despite a majority of their remaining games against the weakest clubs—and a 99.6 percent probability of winning at least the Wild Card—the Red Sox failed.

We're sorry to disappoint all of you calculus majors; an inverse payroll-to-box-score relationship isn't the real story. The Rays-Blazers achievements—about-face turnarounds of languishing cultures in a relatively short period of time—weren't a product of new data discovery or crafty capture of undervalued assets. We didn't do anything in the economics or math departments that our direct competitors weren't doing. In fact, we knowingly performed "worse" on occasion, intentionally violating a few *Moneyball* rules here and there. When KP was in San Antonio, for example, the Spurs' mastermind executive team made an on-the-surface backward move to pay millions for the deemed "well below average" forward Bruce Bowen.

On paper, you'd never pay him two to three mil. But he can defend Kobe. He has the alacrity—a rare alacrity—to be limited to doing selfless tasks, even if there is a high possibility of failure. He happily takes on the hardest job on the court.

Players like Bowen should be pushing Bill James and company to dig deeper than individual assessment. Players like Bowen carry teams from good to great because they have a zeal for Helping the Helper, a zeal for putting teammates before themselves, a zeal that is not yet measured by sabermetrics.

Alas, the current holy grail of analytics is calculating the relative load of group success attributable to any given person. James published the book *Win Shares* in 2002, entirely devoted to this subject. Nearly one hundred pages are devoted just to writing out a formula self-anointed as the first measure to allow functional comparison of athletes' values across eras. With it, James proposes a system for teasing out questions of the ilk, "Who was worth more, Babe Ruth or Hank Aaron . . . or Barry Bonds?"

James's answers materialize in the form of Offensive Win Shares, OWS.

Michael Jordan led the NBA in OWS for eight straight seasons (not counting his hiatus for a cup of coffee in minor league baseball). His average with the Bulls was 11.2 OWS per year. In 2008, LeBron James topped the league in OWS at 13.7. Juwan Howard had -0.3. You read correctly; Howard's OWS was a negative number. Statistically, his performance caused his team to *lose*. KP immediately signed him when he became available as a free agent!

Over the first five years of Howard's career, he was a numerical standout. He was among division leaders in points per game (PPG) and player efficiency ratio (PER). His win shares were as high as 7.0. Then he went on a steady decline, bouncing from city to city, wearing seven different uniforms in eight years. General managers juggled salary cap shenanigans to handle the annualized $9.68 million salary he harvested through that period. Spanning the two seasons prior to the Blazers' picking him up, in addition to his negative win shares, he had 2.6 PPG and a 7.5 PER, ranking in the bottom ten of all NBA players who had league average playing time or more. Was Kevin out of his gourd!?

"Best work ethic and character in the game," says Jordan of Juwan.

"He's the Rock of Gibraltar," says Steve Fisher, Juwan's coach from his college days at the University of Michigan.

We qualify MJ's and Fisher's sentiments, however, by adding that we don't believe in the notion that a guy can just be a leader in the locker room. You've got to do it on the floor—basketball floor, trading floor, office floor—to gain respect. Perhaps that makes our assessment of Howard's potential ROIP (return on investment in a performer) all the stranger.

WINSTON CHURCHILL

True genius resides in the capacity for evaluation of uncertain and conflicting information.

At least, we hope, until you read this book.

The Blazers had a roster of young talent in Brandon Roy and La-Marcus Aldridge and Greg Oden. And Juwan still had some juice. The right kind of juice. His leadership platform is amazing—on the court, off the court, *and in between*. What stats don't tell you is how much, of whatever a player has left in his tank, he's able to bring to bear under pressure. Stats don't estimate the future dollar figure of what other teammates learn from how a player handles failure or a subpar performance.

Take Tampa's ROIP from Josh Hamilton. Was Eliot out of his mind shepherding so much time to a process that would end up in an MVP for *a different team*?

In 1999 the then Devil Rays selected Josh number one overall in the amateur draft. Seven years later he was out of baseball, never having made it out of the minor leagues, addicted to crack cocaine and alcohol, a record of injuries suggesting his body might be unable to handle the rigors of a long season, banned indefinitely by the commissioner. Letting him go in the Rule 5 draft to the Cincinnati Reds prior to the 2007 season, what had the Rays gained for the many multiples of millions they'd shelled out? Zero between the foul lines.

Unless you take Evan Longoria into account. During the Rays' 2006 Instructional League season, Longoria was a wet-behind-the-ears draftee—the third overall pick that year, skipping out on finishing his college degree at Long Beach State to put three million bucks of signing bonus in his pocket, becoming old enough to drink legally just as he hit professional baseball. A habit emerged of staying out late, showing up for training hung over, all the signs of disaster to come. Except there at Instructs was Hamilton, embarking on his now famous, life-saving comeback. Completely on his own initiative, he took Evan under his wing. They began taking extra BP together, after which they'd stay in the clubhouse, all other players having left for home, talking about everything from money to drugs to relationships. Josh started bringing Evan with him to church.

The transformation Longoria made in professionalism and focus was night and day.

Having seen thousands of supremely talented prospects come and go, we can confidently say that Josh helped make Evan's career that October. The Rays' opting to give Josh a second chance—and making the strategic decision to bunk him up with a bunch of rookies despite his age and tumultuous situation—there's an assessment of a player's impact potential that you can't tease out with win shares.

Twenty-four months later, among the fastest ascensions in MLB history, Longoria was producing runs in the World Series. He's now on a Hall of Fame trajectory. And he's arguably the fan favorite in Tampa. Erase Hamilton from the equation and how many wins would you have to forfeit? What percentage of Longoria's current contractual value—what percentage of ticket and merchandise sales—can we assign to Josh?

That's the kind of management thinking we strive to consistently put into practice, and that's the kind of thinking this book will show you how to implement in your organization. Identifying and then providing opportunity to an industry's leaders in helping—the Hamiltons and Howards—won't happen if you stick to sabermetrics, nor will the bottom-line gains that result from the punches they take for the team.

On Sunday, February 21, 2010, the Utah Jazz came into the Trail Blazers' backyard and embarrassed them. Limiting the Blazer offense to a pitiful 10 points in the fourth quarter, the Jazz pushed the game into OT. They then snatched away a critical Portland home W. In the locker room postgame, Juwan Howard was furious. He threw water bottles. He spit out a diatribe of expletives. He pointed the finger at . . . *himself.*

"This was *my* fault," he fumed, with passion and honesty.

The club had a redeye flight cross-country to catch that night. Howard wouldn't let his mates shower up and go about their business packing. Wide eyed, all the players listened as Juwan launched into an emotional soliloquy regarding the importance of preparation and the details of the commitment that was required of him in order to contribute.

"You can be *damn* sure I'm going to be ready when we lace 'em up again. I'm not going to sit around or go through the motions. I'm going to be *so* prepared. I'm BRINGIN' IT tomorrow night. You can count on that!"

The New Jersey Nets awaited.

There are of course a lot of times in basketball, as with a product launch, when you come out hot in the first quarter; you know it's not going to last. Sometimes you think, *Oh, no.* But in the first two minutes against the Nets that night, the Blazers were so dialed in that they put up an early lead and, no exaggeration, the game was over. The entire state of Jersey knew it. They could feel it, too.

Portland ripped off a .750 victory clip for the remainder of the season, earning them a playoff berth. Was there a correlation between Howard's play and the team's climbing up the standings, despite there being no reflection of it in specific win-share statistics?

Unequivocally!

Sometimes, actually, an employee's production numbers *get in the way.* Sometimes high individual yields come at the price of less development of team "intangibles"—variables that propel leading companies like toughness, confidence, energy, and combined creativity.

At his scoring prime, Howard's squads combined to compete in a grand total of three playoff games. In his last four campaigns—when his numbers were at career lows—he contributed to postseason runs every single year. Twenty-seven playoff games and an NBA Finals, in every one of which coaches, GMs, and broadcasters have commented that there is an essential ingredient in chasing championships:

Juwan Howardness. Helping the Helper.

In truth, performance engineering is only part engineering. And if we're to get the most out of ourselves and those around us, sometimes the engineering part must be exorcised altogether. Which is why we've written *Help the Helper.* Josh Hamilton and Juwan Howard tell us it's time. We live in a world where the principles of *Moneyball* so dominate Corporate America's fascination with sports metaphors that a dry, academic subject like statistical modeling can be converted into a feel-good dramatic movie—a box office smash, no less, surpassing the gate haul of every classic baseball work of art, from *The Natural* to *Field of Dreams.* Good grief. It *is* time. Time to peel back the spreadsheet façade.

We're going to show you what's behind the curtain. Or rather, what's *missing* behind the majority of curtains. It's not that performance metrics are the enemy; as we mentioned, we use 'em. You should as well. But output and accountability data can only take you as an individual or your organization so far (as it turns out the Oakland A's are realizing, notching a post-fad five straight seasons at or below .500). Human analytics describe results, they don't elucidate them. That's the shortcoming of relying on the "geek out" method. To advance in your career, or to get better as a unit or division or company, you need to understand the *source* of performance that, in turn, *generates* the statistics. You need to fuel that source.

That's what we did in Portland and Tampa. We took the common denominator across thirty years of studying the most successful teams—Helping the Helper—and made it the backbone of our culture. In the pages that follow, we'll teach you how to do the same.

Now, come with us on the journey to generating extreme teamwork. . . .

1.

Help the Helper

A Help the Helper (H2H) Culture: Starts Two Steps
Away from the Center of the Action

T he sun shone brilliantly across a cloudless blue sky on April 26,
2008, in the tiny 18,000-person town of Ellensburg, home of
Central Washington University. It was Senior Day for the
women's softball team—the last collegiate game the ladies would play
at home. It was a particularly special Senior Day because the Wildcats
had never reached the NCAA tournament before and they were trailing
the lead in their conference standings by only one game. The team
ahead of them was their opponent that very afternoon, Western
Oregon. A win could propel the Wildcats into their first postseason
appearance, breathing extended life into the careers of senior all-stars
Mallory Holtman and Liz Wallace.

With the score knotted in blanks, 0–0, two runners aboard, and
two outs, Western Oregon's smallest player, Sara Tucholsky, stepped
into the box. At five feet two inches and barely one hundred pounds,
Tucholsky was anything but an intimidating hitter. It was her senior
campaign, too, her last hurrah, just as it was for Central Washington's
captain, first basewoman Holtman. Unlike Holtman's school record
productivity, though, Sara had tallied just three hits in 34 at bats, none
for extra bases. In the home run department, 0-for-college. None in
high school or youth softball either. She was an easy target for hecklers

in the stands. Until . . . an 0-1 fastball shot off her bat like a missile, a no-doubter over the centerfield fence.

Coach Pam Knox high-fived the first runner as she rounded third. Then the second runner. And then, wait, where's Sara? Knox looked out to the diamond to see Tucholsky crumpled on the ground off first base. She'd missed the bag and, in doubling back to tag it, twisted her knee, tearing her ACL! Elation instantly turned to tragedy. Knox raced across the field to her injured player. But, by rule, if a coach or trainer provides assistance to an active runner, she's out. The runs would be erased. So would Sara's momentous achievement.

Recalls Pam, "It went through my mind, if I touch her, she's going to kill me. It's her only home run in four years. I didn't want to take that from her, but at the same time, I was worried about her."

She asked the umpires about putting in a pinch runner. They conferred and arbitrated that if Sara could crawl back to the sack on her own accord, a substitute could enter the game and the hit would be recorded as a single. The home run would still be forfeited. Coach Knox knew what she had to do but needed a minute to gather herself before making the change that would take away Sara's run—and the memory.

"Excuse me," interrupted Holtman. "Would it be okay if we carried her around and she touched each bag?"

The umpiring crew flipped out their rulebooks. In no section does it state that *opposing fielders* can't assist a runner. Wallace ran over from shortstop to help her teammate lift Tucholsky. The two—knowing full well that they might be losing an opportunity to advance to the playoffs—proceeded to make what is arguably the most unusual home run trot in history. At each base Mallory and Liz paused, lowering Sara gingerly so she could touch a toe from her uninjured leg. When they crossed the plate they were met with an unparalleled roar of applause from the crowd—which was watching their home team go down 3 runs to 0.

The Wildcats rallied for a pair of runs in the bottom half of the inning. They came up shy. Tucholsky's run was the game winner.

Speaking to the press after the loss, Holtman recapped, "Granted I thought of it, but anyone on my team would have done it . . . it's kind of a nice way to go out because it shows what our program is about and the kind of people we have here."

If these girls are willing to help an opponent like that, imagine the lengths they go to for their own teammates. Imagine being part of a rare group like that. Imagine Mallory and Liz being your teammates or employees. What would they be willing to do to help you succeed? What would you be willing to do for them?

This spirit of assisting others is the backbone of cultures that generate impactfulness of the magnitude that made Central Washington softball an overnight tale of heroism, busting YouTube hit rate records. Advertisers dream of moving people to this degree. The best performers in every field aspire to work for companies with ingredients this inspiring. Customers experiencing such verve instantly become customers for life.

Truly special teams like this change lives. In the process they experience exponential gains to their bottom-line-driving reputations. We'd like to share a few more examples:

Imagine being a member of the varsity basketball squad at Greece Athena High School in Rochester, New York. The manager is an autistic young man named Jason McElwain. He adores the sport. To such an extent that he's pleased as pie carting sweaty towels and fetching water. Coach Jim Johnson noticed how the game provided an outlet for Jason to improve the social and focal skills that are a tremendous struggle for kids with autism. Coach Johnson allowed Jason to sit on the bench. There was an immediate increase in team spirit. Starters began dedicating their performances to Jason.

Jim ruminated, "How amazing might it be to get J-Mac into a game for a minute?"

He pulled the trigger on February 15, 2006. Not in a throwaway game but in a battle against rival Spencerport High School for a division title! With four minutes left on the clock, McElwain took the court. Teammates quickly got the ball to him and yelled for him to shoot. Air ball. An air ball of all air balls, to be honest. Teammates fed Jason the rock the very next trip down the floor, this time for a layup. Jason missed that shot, too. Coach Johnson later admitted he was praying something would go in. He nevertheless stuck with his guns. He received the reward of all rewards. Jason's third shot was a three-point attempt. *Swish!* Nothing but net. The gym erupted. On the very next possession he hit another three-pointer. And then another. And another. And another. McElwain caught fire. He drained *six* in a row, topping a couple off with free throws to boot. He stayed in for the duration, racking up 20 points, *and* pierced the hoop one more time as the buzzer sounded. Insanely wild is nowhere close to expressive enough to describe the crowd.

Jason's mother, Debbie, was beaming. "This is the first moment Jason has ever succeeded and could be proud of himself," she said. "I look at autism as the Berlin Wall, and he cracked it."

Imagine another scenario: wearing a DeKalb Barbs basketball jersey on February 7, 2009. Their opponent was Milwaukee Madison, whose captain, Johntel Franklin, had tragically lost his mother shortly before tip-off. Madison's coach, Aaron Womack, proposed using the emergency cancellation rule. Franklin wouldn't hear of it; no way would he let his teammates miss out on a game. Coming directly from the hospital, Franklin arrived at the arena during the second quarter. Coach Womack called a time-out. He entered Johntel into the game while his teammates swarmed to console him. Since Franklin had not been recorded into the scorekeeper's book prior to the game, his taking the court would elicit a technical foul. The *other* bench erupted in protest. DeKalb coach Dave Rohlman pleaded for the referees to overlook the rule. They did not; a technical was called. The Barbs' Darius McNeal stepped to the stripe to shoot the free throws. He feigned the attempts, the ball traveling less than two feet both times. The DeKalb bench stood in ovation. They then clapped their nemesis Franklin onto the floor.

Or imagine being a team of just two—Team Hoyt, the father and son duo from Holland, Massachusetts, who have completed 240 triathlons . . . and counting, including six Ironmans. Rick has cerebral palsy. He's bound to a wheelchair which his father, Dick, now seventy-two years young, must propel. Dick trains every day by running up hills behind a wheelchair full of cement blocks while Rick is in school. Inspired by his pops, he's working on a graduate degree from Boston University—fifty years after his birth, fifty years after physicians informed his parents he'd never be more than a vegetable. Hall of Fame athletes by the benchful have been lining up at their door, volunteering to speak at functions to help the Hoyt Foundation raise money for disabled youth.

All are incredibly inspiring stories, to be certain. They illustrate the "impossible" that's made possible when teams and performers come together in special ways. They're not the stuff of fantasy or Hollywood scripting. Accomplishments like these come from regular people being willing to do irregular things. Not irregularly arduous or out of the box. Irregularly *helpful*. Like the actions of Mallory Holtman, Jim Johnson, Darius McNeal, and Dick Holt, who seek greatness beyond just box scores (two steps beyond, as we reference in this chapter's title).

It's what drives us—your authors—personally. It's what we're all about. And we're happy to state it boldly:

The #1 Reason for Success: People Willing to Do One Thing—One Little Thing—Better Each Day to Help Their Team.

As our beloved friend Peter Schutz, the CEO who converted Porsche from a floundering company with acres of unsold cars to Le Mans champions, likes to pronounce it, it's "ordinary people doing extraordinary things." That's the performance boost that comes from organizations' striving to be trailblazers of helping.

When we began our turnaround charge in Portland and Tampa, what we had to work with was our own industry's equivalent of ordinary people—average as compared with our competitors, should you be inclined to heed commentators. We didn't have the resources to change that fact (nor did we want to). We had to figure out how to tap into the ingredients that make groups like the Central Washington softball team, or the DeKalb basketball team, or the Hoyt family so special. Those are the kinds of teams that attract the best, get the best out of themselves, and end up being the best. They're the ones who write history—history that counts.

We set out on a mission to understand where that kind of organizational guts comes from. We started at the top. We asked, Are truly special teams the product of leadership?

STEVE JOBS

Be a yardstick of quality. Some people aren't used to an environment where excellence is expected.

Coming Up Short of Special

Alexander the Great, George Washington, Abraham Lincoln, Margaret Thatcher, Winston Churchill, Martin Luther King, Jr., Eleanor Roosevelt, Vince Lombardi—dozens of this breed come to mind when we contemplate paramount leaders of the past. Children study famous leaders in school. HR directors hang *Successories* motivational posters on office walls featuring snippets of their wisdom. Pundits write volume upon volume about them. Boy do they write about them. If you find yourself with an idle weekend morning (okay, admittedly a rarity) and you'd like to see a demonstration of our culture's obsession with leaders and leadership, try out the following slice of anthropology. It got us—thanks to the intersection of pouring rain, nobody to rip up a racquetball court with, and too many spiced espressos—kicked out of a Barnes & Noble one day, so we promise it's a hoot.

STEP 1: Pack a pad of paper (or laptop for all you nouveau note takers), grab a tape measure, and head into any large-scale bookstore. No, you can't do this experiment online. The punch is in person.

STEP 2: Find the Business Books department. Should the aisles be segmented into subcategories such as Finance, Real Estate, Marketing, and so forth, start with the Management section. For a more thorough trial, you may also want to include headers such as Organizational Behavior, Business Life, Biographies, and Human Resources.

STEP 3: Take off the shelf every title that relates, even tangentially, to leaders or leading. As you do, chimney them in the middle of the floor, à la the Columbia University library opening scene in *Ghostbusters* to which Bill Murray's character quips, "You're right; no human being would stack books like this." Make three piles. In one, stack texts themed around people or personal qualities. In a second, stack texts themed around company systems or strategies. Designate anything else to the third pile. Roughly halfway to the ceiling is when we got tossed, right when we had to start standing on a table. To avoid the heave-ho, you can accomplish a similar accounting using your notepad. It's just not quite as fun.

STEP 4: If you make it this far, run the numbers. Create a chart comparing mountain height, to book counts, to volume of filled and empty shelf space. Super ambitious? Keep a tally of recurring topical subtitle adjectives.

We don't mean to spoil a good cliffhanger, but as you might guess, leadership books are popular—forest-chopping popular. Assuming you could fend off floor managers long enough to complete the challenge, few titles would remain perched on their display wall home. Markedly more edifying, few would wind up in heap three. It's a revelatory exercise regarding the American conceptualization of leading.

The way our population defines exceptional stewardship affects training programs in every industry, how authority figures are selected and compensated, how groups and teams operate, how bosses and employees relate and communicate, how policies are constructed. The *Ghostbusters* test illustrates a trend in the commercial emphasis and packaging of leadership, a reflection of the collective thinking that our populace, literally, buys into. Nonetheless, we all know: what sells isn't necessarily what's healthy. Heroin comes to mind.

We'll get back to addictions in a minute. First, let's explore why leadership material so easily fits into two categories with scant information in an "other" class. Via our consulting assignments and corporate speaking engagements and our thousands of hours of study over the past two decades, we've been compiling an informal poll spanning entry-level workers, MBA students, and veteran executives alike, asking: "What constitutes *great* leadership?"

Depictions of course vary, though not nearly as much as we originally hypothesized. Career accomplishment, diplomas, and socioeconomic status aren't the answer differentiators. Rather, we hear remarkably repetitive language:

> *Great leaders set a compelling vision . . . keep the ship on track . . . listen and empower, but hold a high standard . . . communicate objectives well . . . know what the group needs for people, products, and positioning . . . draw smart, empirically informed conclusions . . . build enthusiastic consensus . . . create political and public capital . . . drive the organization's reputation . . . have strong moral fiber . . . work hard. . . .*

Phrases like this are the common substance of book titles and chapter headers. Socialization and formal education at work combine to, essentially, brand leadership as a top-down concept. The branding turns out, as our playful little experiment demonstrates, to be generally bilateral: who a leader is (style, character, values) and what action a leader takes (tactics, policies, decisions). Hence the two stacks of books.

When companies fail or sports teams rack up losing records, is it any wonder that a breakdown or absence of one or more of the above listed elements is blamed? Certainly, sometimes that is the culprit. There are plenty of singular data points to fingerprint institutions

underperforming because the head honcho had an ineffective leadership style, created inefficient procedures, botched choices . . . or
worse, abused power.

Which brings up heroin again. From Enron to the mortgage crisis to
Ponzi schemes, cases of the dark, addictive side of leadership continue to
make headlines. Malicious manipulation of leadership position and skill,
unfortunately, isn't limited to grotesque egos of a General Custer or an
Adolf Hitler nature. As our good friend Irv Grousbeck, co-owner of the
Boston Celtics and one of the most highly regarded faculty members at
the Stanford Graduate School of Business, teaches, "Ethical code isn't
tested by parents or professors, it's tested when you get handed power."

MARGARET WHEATLEY

**Even though worker capacity and motivation are destroyed when
leaders choose power over productivity it appears that bosses would
rather be in control than have the organization work well.**

Raising discussion of miscarried organizations, however, isn't to rail
on authority misuse atrocities. It's to point out how synonymous are
deemed the constructs of "leader" and "leadership." When a group
breaks down, our culturally embedded instincts prompt probes of the
person in charge, regarding their personality or their performance. Pick
your favorite example of an NFL team not living up to expectations, or
a college football program for that matter. Onto the hot seat goes who-
ever is the most publicly recognized figure. The airwaves become flooded
with speculation about head coach or GM replacement (as we personally
know all too well). Talk show hosts and shock jocks rant relentlessly,
prognosticating who'll be ousted and who'll take their place.

So much focus is devoted to determining which individual is responsible when a team falters that it can blind us. Media portrays only
a narrow window, sensationalizing the drama of headline characters.
Business experts lean heavily on case analysis, fueling the intense attention given to high-profile CEO firings. The leader-leadership one-and-
the-same mentality becomes further ingrained—the idea that
organizational slumps or stagnation are a leader character issue, or a
leader résumé issue, or a leader execution issue, or a leader policy issue . . . sliced one way or another, a leader issue regardless.

Lost in the mix: the cause of subpar group performance that is far less frequently addressed but far more frequently occurring. Many companies and teams fall short of their potential due to *too much* attention paid to the person perched on the mountaintop. *Too* hefty a priority is devoted to what the books in stack one and stack two report. The reason for the dearth of books in stack three parallels a hidden reason for lackluster bottom-line results: continuing to think of leaders as the primary driver of an organization's culture.

1st Order Teamwork

Without clarification, we find that the phrase "leading at the source" is presumed to be a euphemism for getting to the heart of the matter, the real guts of leadership. The presumption, however, is still that the corner office is the ultimate location of said heart and guts.

How many for-instances can we highlight in which the hiring of an ambitious new executive brought a sense of renewal and that VP's division took off? How many illustrations are at our fingertips of a poor leader let go and the group subsequently thriving? Newspaper columnists and documentary filmmakers love these stories. A superstar at the helm, with smarts and savvy, with verve and vision, will attract and inspire superstar followers, the tide of teamwork will rise, and off to bigger profits everyone will go. Or so says the commonly accepted wisdom in the realm of culture building.

This wisdom seems to be anchored by an innate fascination with leaders. Human beings are drawn to celebrities, politicians, and people in power like bees to honey. Check out the circulation statistics for tabloids. Persons-of-influence gossip (and television programming and Web site hits and, yes, volumes of books) follows a rapid tipping point pattern.

"Did you hear? So and so did such and such?"

Phoom—everyone knows about it. What Warren Buffett said, what Ozzie Guillen did, what Hillary Clinton was wearing saturates water cooler conversation coast to coast.

Like it or not, our species is wired to pay close heed to alpha personalities—what alphas do, communicate, prefer, and snub. Research on neural processing shows that the areas of the brain that light up like Times Square on New Year's Eve in response to leader presentations are not housed in the evolved cerebral cortex. "Hot" are the sections that regulate basic functions (the hindbrain, also known as the reptilian brain, controlling primal motivations such as breathing, pumping blood, and dominance or reproductive urges) and basal emotions (the limbic system, also known as the old mammalian brain, controlling hunger, fear, desire, positive and negative feelings, and subconscious value judgments). In other words, attraction to those in power is rudimentary. It's a survival-grounded mechanism to make sure we know as much as we can about who rules the roost so we can make "moving up the food chain" decisions that serve our interests without risking the dissent of the majority, who, as a moblike force, can significantly affect our status or health.

In studies exploring how this wiring affects preferences and decision making at work, subjects are given potentially career-affecting scenarios to contemplate, such as being up against a stressful deadline or having to write a critical white paper. Participants are shown a series of images in pairs, one picture illustrating a tool useful for successful completion of the task, the other picture of either a neutral landscape or a famous person who has no relationship to the scenario. Left-right placement of the photos is entirely random. As pairs are posted on a screen, subjects are asked to select which one would be most helpful in their predicament. The catch: images are flashed for only a millisecond, too quickly to consciously discern what the pictures are. Findings are

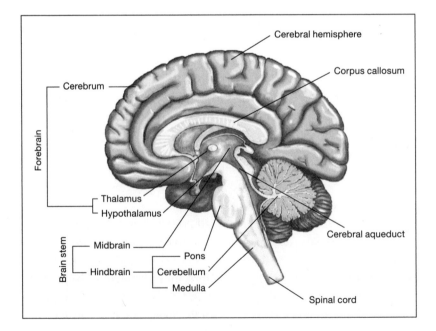

striking. Despite test takers' being unable to "see" the choices, selections don't turn out to be haphazard guesses. When it's tool versus landscape, subjects pick the tool at a rate much greater than chance. When the alternative is an individual of fame, subjects opt for the person at a rate much greater than chance. And when a control sequence of landscape versus celebrity flashcards is displayed, participants tap the celebrity at a near 100 percent perfect, savantesque clip.

From a sociodevelopmental perspective, the data demonstrates humans to be hyperattentive to leader characteristics. From a business management perspective, the data indicates that humans are geared to equate success with the profile of the person in charge. Neurologically, it explains an intoxication of sorts with what we label 1st Order Teamwork—predominant emphasis placed on one individual to guide, motivate, and run a group, be that a CEO, head coach, GM, captain, chairperson, managing partner, quarterback, president, general, or otherwise.

At the very moment we were penning this chapter, ESPN was awash with talk of the Indianapolis Colts. They were 0-13. Peyton Manning stood on the sidelines, knocked out for the season. He'd had three neck surgeries. Concern that his career might be finished percolated. Could he come back? When might he try ramping up a throwing regimen? If he could retake the field, would he be as good as he used to be? Everyone from bloggers to analysts to front office personnel to dear ole dad, Archie, weighed in on the subject.

With Manning under center, the Colts went to nine straight postseasons and made the playoffs in eleven of Manning's twelve seasons—138 wins, a gaudy .719 winning percentage, a season-record averaging clip of 12-4, and a Super Bowl conquest. Prior to that, the franchise had been to the playoffs a total of three times in twenty-two years! Jekyll and Hyde. Peyton in pads, the Colts won. Peyton in street clothes, the Colts lost. Often. And big. That's even with a veteran, two-time Pro Bowl signal caller signed to serve in his stead, Kerry Collins. Collins was talented enough to have won 80 games in his career as a twelve-season NFL starter. He might not be of Joe Montana/Dan Marino fiber, but *zero* W's?

The reversal of fortune occurred with an unchanged coaching staff, with the same Super-Bowl-ring-wearing offensive coordinator. It was with all eleven "wily" vets (players with ten or more NFL seasons of experience) retained from the year before, and nineteen of the twenty-two players with five or more seasons under their belt. It was with the addition of five *more* five-year vets to bolster the roster. It was with the team's leading playmakers on offense, Joseph Addai (RB) and Reggie Wayne (WR) and Dallas Clark (TE), in tiptop shape. It was with Manning at every practice and every game, holding a clipboard, talking situations and strategy with Collins, tutoring the other young quarterbacks.

Blatantly, the difference between 2010 and 2011 was the ball in Peyton's hands versus anyone else's. Supplemented, of course, by a hefty dose of hullabaloo.

Meanwhile . . .

The reverberant buzz around campus in Palo Alto, California, was the regaining of football royalty. Stanford was headed to its second consecutive NCAA top-five finish and second BCS bowl, only a solitary loss preventing what no one would have believed possible a short four years earlier: a trip to play in the national championship title game. The last time the pigskin world witnessed Stanford ranked as high was 1940.

Rising phenom Andrew Luck paced the surge. The back-to-back Heisman Trophy runner-up was being painted as the most poised, polished quarterback in college history. Fanatics were already forecasting NFL Hall of Fame enshrinement. Comparisons to fellow famed Cardinal John Elway were flying. If it's not Elway who holds the moniker of most sure-bet QB selected with a No. 1 overall pick in the NFL draft, analysts were saying, it should be Luck.

And the team slated to have the 2012 draft's supreme slot? The Colts. Which raised even more broadcast-studio and coffee-room stir. Would the Colts nab Luck? Would he replace Manning? If Manning returns to form, could two rock stars coexist on the same squad? Would Manning tutor Luck en route to Canton? Would there be a historic blockbuster trade? Would Manning leave for greener pastures?

Comparisons stoked the chatter. Andrew attended Peyton's youth training camps growing up; he assisted as an instructor at them when he was a teenager. Luck's father, Oliver, was a standout pro quarterback himself—a one-two leadership punch, no less, as he and Archie Manning were Houston Oilers teammates in the early 1980s. The families are close friends. Oh, and Peyton was a Heisman runner-up, too. So was John Elway. The coup de grâce, as if the above wasn't enough to flood the airwaves? In two of the three years the Colts were Super Bowl contenders during the twenty-two-campaign stretch preceding the Manning era, the field general taking the snaps was Jim Harbaugh— the coach who launched Stanford's football turnaround by recruiting Luck to the Farm!

To say there was a lot of focus in Indy on Peyton Manning's role in the franchise's fortunes would be a gross understatement. But it was considerably more than just a large volume of talk. It's a reflection of the 1st Order Teamwork culture that permeates the sport in today's marketplace. On most teams, the whole shooting match, from draft-day dollars to chalkboard diagrams to press conferences, pivots around the quarterback. Most consider a good QB more vital than a good coach, as reflected in their relative salaries (and the number of coaches shown the door for getting into a spitting match with their quarter-back). The industry's state of the union, in effect, hinges on the small handful of guys wearing jersey numbers under 20.

Toward the end of Peyton's tenure, though, the Colts became an order of magnitude more tipped than their brethren to the 1st Order end of the teamwork scale. They got caught up in what is called a God Culture.

God Cultures

Forgive us for any unintended nonsecular analogies or connotations. The term God Culture, as it pertains to corporate and team leadership, refers to an organization that subscribes practically unvaryingly to the character of one individual. Where that individual goes, the organization goes. There may be many other pieces in place to create success, but those pieces are overwhelmingly influenced, shaped, and propelled by the big dog.

Affectionately speaking, #18 was a god in Indianapolis. Intention-ally, but more important, subconsciously as well, the organization from top to bottom—players, coaches, executives, staff, interns—took cues from Manning. Their level of confidence, and thus their focus, effort, and teamwork, was supremely dictated by the words and actions of Manning. His ability to lift the team was supreme when he was sling-ing touchdowns. When injury caused him to move the dozen or so yards from the field to the bench, the consequence was exponentially more negative than the loss of his individual OWS. His physical pres-ence, calm country demeanor, authenticity, game knowledge, team-mate support, and locker room leadership were all still there. Psychologically he was the same. *Other* players were not, including the all-stars. The hit on their outcome beliefs, in many cases more placebo than real, took a toll on their own performance. Net result: a total pro-ductivity drop that was far steeper than statistics would predict.

That's why a team with plenty of talent to win games can suddenly win none. That's why a company with an exceptional b-plan and whip-smart sales reps can go bankrupt. Strip away their god, their idol, their icon, the one element so many look to for so much of their confidence and strength, and you get myriad mistakes and misfortune.

Another God Culture specimen: Apple. Straddling a smidgen under four decades, Apple was Steve Jobs. As an imaginative cofounder, he sprinkled funky, personal touches into the invention of the Macintosh, such as calligraphy he learned at Reed College (which fashioned a foundation for today's computers having font files). Apple took off. When he was ousted as chairman in 1984, the company went on a dive. Returning in 1996, Steve once again infused his sagacity of form-to-function organization-wide. The iMac followed. Then the iPod. Then iTunes. Then the iPhone and iPad. He finally ditched the "interim" qualifier on his business card in 2000, joking that from then on he would take the title "iCEO." When Jobs was up, the company was up, and vice versa. His sense of branding—no suit or tie in the C-suite; black turtlenecks and Levis—became the company's. Apple headquarters is a sea of black turtlenecks. Neither employee handbook nor operating bylaws detail a dress code. There is one anyway. Silicon Valley is now home to a scary number of technology guru wannabes walking around wearing black turtlenecks!

One massive positive of God Cultures is that when the leader is humming along, the organization is going to be successful, often hugely so. The business can get away with hiccups, off days, inefficiencies, and missteps because of an overriding confidence that "everything will turn out roses in the end." Thanks to the presence of an idol in control, team members experience less stress, fewer adverse pressures, less distraction by ordinary market fluctuations modulating the average worker's levels of optimism. In such an environment, good people can do more good work, unencumbered by many typical workplace worries.

RICHARD FEYNMAN

The first principle is that you must not fool yourself... and you are the easiest person to fool.

Sounds like a nifty recipe for extreme teams. Except, God Cultures do 1st Order Teamwork *so well* that they are teed up for disaster when their god departs. Peyton Manning went down and a virtual, principally subliminal, doubt rippled through the ranks. That uncertainty robbed would-be clutch performers of optimal focus, bulletproof confidence, and immunity to adversity. Losses, even when ardent odds said they shouldn't have happened, happened. Kerry Collins had the aptitude to notch at least a .500 record, especially with Addai, Clark, and Wayne in peak form to carry the scoring load. Instead, the Colts' record with Collins under center was .000.

Clouds may loom over Apple's future. With the passing of the god of everything "i," will the culture fall apart? Are the days of millions of units piled into shopping carts the minute an iPhone or iPad update is released now gone? That possibility exists. Fortunately, Jobs didn't suffer a sudden, unexpected injury like Manning. His pancreatic cancer had been metastasizing slowly, spurring bouts of gauged medical leave. Knowing the progression his condition would track, Jobs took early and active steps to appoint a core of successors in advance, engaging them in planning. They studied Apple anew. They drilled down with Jobs on fundamentals, preparing strategy for guiding, protecting, and moving the culture forward. Hope at HQ is that ample enough foresight went into the transition to allow SteveNotes—the sobriquet of Jobs's guiding philosophies which routinely dazzled attendees at company and industry expositions—to endure into the distant future.

Still, upon Jobs's formal resignation in August 2011, precipitated by a seismic dip in his health, AAPL shares quickly plunged 5 percent in just an hour. The drop was a repeat of history. Ford Motor Company, Disney, Microsoft, Starbucks—all saw similar swift falloffs when their God Culture's figurehead departed. In each case, an epoch of significant stumbling followed an organizational icon's forfeiting the reins. After Walt Disney's death in 1966, for instance, his inheritors worked tirelessly to honor the namesake's entity. Decisions down to the very smallest were vetted against extensive debate of Disney's preferences and personality. What would Walt have done? The effort was positively heartfelt, representing a burning desire to honor the visionary founder and "do it right." But it hobbled the company. Executives and managers were so busy trying to make careful choices and preserve Disney's legacy that they didn't react promptly enough to market movements.

Too much 1st Order Teamwork might very well be the reason Colts owner Jim Irsay made the unpopular decision to release Manning. Though letting entrenched leaders go is not necessary to prevent or escape a God Culture, sometimes being unpopular is. To be a Help the Helper organization, you need to be willing to take it on the chin and to put the folks at the bottom of your org chart first.

The Coaching Carousel

God Cultures provide a fairly extreme sampling of 1st Order Teamwork. They reveal how momentously team performance resulting from stock put in a leader can elevate or crash. Of course, organizations needn't be entrenched in a God Culture to be adversely effected by an emphasis on acquiring or supporting a superstar or a celebrity CEO. Too copious an amount of the bottom line attributed to one position, too high a percentage of the payroll going to one person, too much of the culture being dictated from one office, and extreme teamwork will not be generated. You'll be going in the opposite direction from leading at the source.

The same is true of placing too much importance on the "right" résumé in hiring leaders. It's a common cause of the frequent appearance of retreads in coveted leadership posts. In the sports world it's known as the "coaching carousel." Repeatedly, veteran on-field and front-office managers who've been fired for poor performance, who've racked up a record of more losses than wins, are hired ahead of young, full-of-potential candidates brimming with brilliance. No head coach or GM title on their CV, no love. Very little of it, anyway. The usual explanation given is that a high-public-profile, high-pressure, high-expectation job demands experience, someone who has been through the battle, as it were. It's claimed to be too risky to put a team like the New York Yankees at the mercy of someone untested. A manager is too central a cog to ride intangibles as hiring criteria. What if he or she fails? Fans, not to mention the person writing monster-sized checks, will have the GM's head (*and job*) for selecting a so-called unproven.

"How could you!?"

If you hire a leader based on extensive, tangible, media-friendly résumé data, on the other hand, and that person fails, you have built-in justification for firing them—at least, the kind of excuses that *sound* plausible in sound bites—allowing you to escape out the press confer-

ence back door without getting lynched. Rationalization is such a per-
suasive tool. Especially on ourselves.

"He's a lifer; been in the game over thirty years, fifteen as a standout
catcher leading on the diamond. He went to six All-Star games as a
player, won two World Series, and was a World Series MVP. He spent
five years as an ambassador in Japan and throughout Latin America,
then ten years running big-league clubs. The men under his tutelage
lauded his managerial skills. Besides, he's a hometown hero; grew up
right here, two miles from the stadium. We had every reason to believe
he would take this organization to the promised land."

And when asked about never having a winning season in those ten
seasons of coaching?

Responses jump out like: "The previous two teams he was with
didn't provide adequate resources to be successful (a sneaky defense for
swallowing $100 million in remaining contract to get rid of him); he'd
never been given the kind of roster that could win; his abilities had always been hamstrung by meddling administrators. We were excited to
be the ones to provide him a fully loaded platform and the freedom to
use it (a backhanded ass-covering to cast blame away from the root of
the failure)."

Fascinating. Hard evidence is the supposed fulcrum. But hard evidence existed *contrary* to tapping the more "experienced" interviewee.
A *Moneyball* approach is touted to validate not hiring one person (the
contender with real qualities of leadership, except statless) but thrown
out the window when hiring the other (the incumbent with demon-
strated subpar W/L output). It's backward—not unlike flashcard
choices in the neural preference studies we described earlier. The difference is that owners have more than a couple milliseconds to consider
their options. And the decision involves shelling out seven, eight, nine
figures. Expanded research reveals that tossing riches into the equation
increases the likelihood of selecting the celebrity instead of the performance tool. The higher the perceived stakes, the more human nature
kicks in, the more entrenched 1st Order Teamwork becomes.

Maybe more wisely worded: the higher the perceived stakes, the
more 1st Order Teamwork is a liability. It's the predominant cause of
the ridiculous sums of dollars going down the drain across pro and collegiate sports, paying a small country's GNP to fire coaches and executives, paying them *not* to work. Or, as is currently the case, affording
them double incomes to nab television color commentator spots while
overlooked is the hungry upcoming journalist with truckloads of Ivy

League talent, having slaved through the most demanding graduate school, working fast food jobs on the side to make ends meet, doing every grunt job in the industry imaginable. Opportunities she deserves, and would knock out of the park, are handed to a flashcard!

Ridiculous sums wouldn't have gone down the drain in the recent rash of CEO cannings, either. Just a few examples: Yahoo!'s firing Carol Bartz to the tune of a $9.4 million severance (after holding the job for only thirty months, roughly $78,000 for each week she held office, having already earned $59.2 million in salary for that period), The Home Depot's dropping an estimated $120 million (in combined buy-outs, stocks, and other goodies) on Robert Nardelli in order to ax him, Pfizer's tossing in north of $200 million in deferred compensation and pensions to show Henry McKinnell the door, and Hewlett-Packard's shelling out $12.2 million to a CEO who stepped down for falsifying documents! In addition to the financial tax of dumping a lion's share of company resources into the C-suite, it's a significant cause of malfeasance. The more one individual dictates culture, the greater the risk of power run amok. Yet we keep upping the ante to recruit, retain, and reward the almighty. Some quick stats (courtesy of the Institute for Policy Studies in Washington, D.C.):

- Walmart CEO Michael Duke makes more in one hour than an employee in the bottom half of the behemoth's income distribution makes in a full year. The company is seeing a U.S. sales decline reported to be one of the worst in history. Concurrently, Walmart isn't on any "Best Companies to Work For" lists.
- The average American CEO salary, not counting bonuses, option shares, and other types of compensation, could cover the cost to furnish a city with five hundred new teachers. And while CEO earnings have been escalating, American education has been going in the opposite direction, our kids' homework commitment and test scores dropping decade after decade. Need we point out the correlation of this contrasting placement of dollars?
- Median CEO pay jumped 27 percent in 2010—while the bulk of our workforce struggled with layoffs, foreclosures, unaffordable college tuition, and McDonald's for their children's sustenance. A good deal of the stock value gain used to justify CEO raises came from balance-sheet-enhancing job cuts.

LAO-TZU

The wicked leader is he whom the people despise. The good leader is he whom the people revere. The great leader is he of whom the people say, "We did it ourselves."

Are these illustrations a tad astringent? We hope so. 1st Order Teamwork is sexy. Sometimes a good splash of cold water in the face is essential. Really special teams aren't about superstars. Some have them; some don't. What we've discovered is that the person at the helm is not the ultimate source that vaults an organization into extreme teamwork. Nor is an alternate looks-good-on-the-surface method. . . .

2nd Order Teamwork

You can get kicked out of Barnes & Noble as readily with the height of your second stack of books as with your first. As pervasively as leadership is defined according to who's in charge, it's also defined by what that person is doing—the kind of leadership taught in business school. Leadership via interactional models, org charts, and group structures is what we label 2nd Order Teamwork. Instead of pinning culture on a person, per se, it's pinned on policy. Instead of the spine of leadership being the corner office, the spine is hierarchical design, and the VP core tasked with overseeing and carrying out directives.

Continuing with the NFL as a sample, 2nd Order Teamwork is all about the franchise handbook—the plays, the philosophy on offense, the philosophy on defense, and the regulations (from haircuts to curfew to no fraternizing with the cheerleaders). Typically, handbooks are titled boldly:

"THE DALLAS COWBOY WAY"

Teams that do 2nd Order Teamwork particularly well generally have diehard O and D coordinators who, night after night, stay at the practice facility watching game tape, grading performance, and scouting opponents into the wee hours. With extraordinary regularity, bed for them is a locker-room sofa.

"I'll see you in January," they joke with their wives as they head off to work on July 31, the first day of preseason.

Their wives joke back, "Not if you make the playoffs."

Such vast obligation is twofold in purpose: (1) It sets a tone at team headquarters. Players come to practice in the morning seeing their coaches wearing yesterday's clothes; they know tireless is the standard expected (it's no doubt a chapter header in the handbook). (2) All that film study is poured into practicing the "right system" over and over. Preparation breeds confidence. Confidence breeds toughness. A team with plays they trust is a team that will be more focused and will work harder, giving more of themselves to those plays in the book. More wins will be earned on that intangible alone.

Rice University basketball between 2002 and 2005 provides an excellent case study.

Being an academic powerhouse, Rice struggles to recruit blue-chip athletes. The school's ethos is that book smarts trump all. Stated another way: the overwhelming value at Rice is test scores and most decisions, practices, policies, and teaching are based on a "grades beat all" mentality. Genius is promoted on campus in countless procedures as well as in countless unwritten reinforcements, as starkly univariate (to substantial eye rolling of the theory of multiple intelligences pioneer Howard Gardner, no doubt). Perfect SAT scores will get you into Rice without a review otherwise; being captain of a three-time high school state championship volleyball team is of scant interest to the admissions office. Types of genius other than intellectual aren't applauded by those in power. They're often scoffed. Needless to say, it's not an environment terribly attractive to young men and women who have potential for greatness in arenas outside the classroom.

Coaches at Rice, like our dear amigo Willis Wilson, are forced to patch together make-do lineups, trying to jigger a way to squeeze something extra out of whatever talent they can persuade to come to West University Place, Texas. Put someone of Wilson's wisdom (wisdom distinguishing him as the only coach in Rice history to be decorated a National Association of Basketball Coaches coach of the year) at the helm of a top-twenty-five program and the return would be a stands-filling cash machine with year upon year of national championship runs.

But Willis is a dedicated teacher, and loyal as a jaunt to Mars is long. He could make a fortune and fill his trophy case by jumping to the NBA. He chooses to work with the underprivileged, in an athletic opportunity sense. For sixteen faithful seasons, he chose to turn down easier paths so he could stay at Rice.

One morning leading up to the tip-off of the 2002–03 season, the doc got a jingle from Coach Wilson. His boys were projected to wallow at the bottom of the Western Athletic Conference standings. He had a tandem of gifted sophomores in Michael Harris and Jason McKrieth, but they were not yet living up to their potential. Preseason practices were sloppy, mistake ridden, anything but championship-caliber intensity. Team confidence was missing.

"This is a talented group," Willis relayed. "They have the goods to run the table. They're not using them. They can execute plays other teams can't. But I don't think they realize why. If I could just get them to believe in what we're trying to do . . . if they'd just trust themselves, we'd take off!"

He was working to get the players to be the wellspring of one another's confidence, a feeling that they had an advantage, a secret weapon, in the person standing to the left and to the right of them every time they hit the hardwood. He wanted this group of young men to look inside, instead of to him as commander-in-chief.

Like all exceptional leaders who are skilled at skirting leadership pitfalls, Coach Wilson is not too proud to request assistance. He instills and fosters diverse support systems as family-felt components of his teams.

"Doc, can you help us out here? Can you talk to the guys?"

Saying yes to someone like Willis is a no-brainer. A roundtable lunch was scheduled with the lads ASAP. No coaches attended in order to free the players from any hesitancy at being evaluated. The doc put it to them.

"Gents, what's standing in the way of your shattering the limits everyone says buckle this program? What's it going to take to stand on the WAC's championship podium?"

The initial response wasn't exactly positive; it wasn't the substance of high-achievement strategizing. It sounded like a cacophony of complaining. Comments ran the gamut from the playbook being too complicated to practice being too structured to players feeling constrained. The venting died down. Then usually reserved senior guard Omar-Seli Mance spoke up.

"It's like we're tripping over our brains. We're memorizing all these intricate set pieces which are probably superfluous or too much icing on the cake. Yeah, we're Rice kids; we can outthink anyone in the country.

But I think we, as players, have forgotten that we are really good athletes, too."

He nailed it. So much effort and concern was going into mounting
unstoppable game plans that they were stuck at 2nd Order Teamwork.
The funny thing was, without knowing it, the players were grappling with
exactly the same performance impediment Willis was. The two sides of
the house were just coming at it from different angles. We tendered a deal.

"Will you trade? If Coach focuses on plays in the playbook that you
guys think kick ass, will you commit to going all out at the drills in
practice that Coach gives you? Are you willing to turn your brains off
and get after it with all-out belief, in yourselves, in each other, like
you're the Houston Rockets gunning for an NBA ring?"

The proposal was barely on the table when an orchestra of unified
enthusiasm roused:

"HELL YEAH!"

Doc jetted across campus to Coach Wilson's office, enthusiasm
flowing.

"Coach, will you trade? If we can get the players to give you everything they've got in practice, to put their heads down and go all out to
help each other conquer challenges, would you be willing to rip a collection of pages the players aren't feelin' out of the playbook?"

"HELL YEAH!"

His ever-so-subtle grin was that of a man who felt he'd just negotiated
the most favorable billion-dollar merger terms in his industry's history.
Practice that afternoon was one of the most spirited we've ever witnessed.
And it wasn't the only one. Save for the natural fluctuations of being human, the training atmosphere stayed like that for the entire season.

With a newfound locus of confidence—relying on themselves rather
than on their system—the team gelled. Predicted to require a Thanksgiving helping of luck to dodge dead last place, Rice led the WAC in
shooting and three-point percentage, lighting up the W column for the
school's highest win tally since 1946. The Owls dropped 106 points on
the other side of Main Street, besting a storied University of Houston
basketball program which Rice had never beaten before. And on the
closing day of the regular season, under pressure of the hunt for conference honors to earn Big Dance tickets, Rice blew out Fresno State by 21.

A similar mentality demarcated the 2003–04 season, sparking a BP
Top of the World Classic preseason tournament title, followed by a
school-record 22 wins. In 2004–05, continuing to notch postseason
appearances, Harris and McKrieth burst the conception that you can't

gather premier hoops recruits at Rice. The duo earned back-to-back dual All-Conference honors and a feature spread in *ESPN The Magazine*, which shared the touching made-for-Disney tale of two unlikely heroes finding their métier in kinship. The tandem's triumphs were underscored by the mentoring along the way they provided for rookie forward Morris Almond, who went on in 2006 to become the nation's third highest scorer and an NBA first-round draft pick.

Continued success, however, wasn't the result of a formulaic process. There were personnel changes. The playbook was modified significantly each season. None of the ensuing groups were copycats of that squad in October 2002 who found a rhythm for scorching the practice floor. It's tempting to try to find a blueprint that can be replicated. We urge you to note, however, that ceasing such a search was key to the Owls' breaking through. Extreme teamwork developed when they transitioned from depending on plays for confidence to depending on one another.

That's Not How We Do It Here

"That's not how we do it here" is an archetypal phrase drifting around organizations that prioritize 2nd Order Teamwork. Akin to assuming outstanding performance will follow an "outstanding" leader—the 1st Order Teamwork mirage—assuming top performance is happening because tons of time is being sunk into upholding policies (admirable as they may be) is the mirage of 2nd Order Teamwork.

We are reminded of an old parable about the family tradition of cooking a roast:

> One winter eve young Susie was watching her mother prepare a roast of beef. Her mom cut an inch off each end, seasoned it, and set it in a roasting dish. Tummy grumbling, Susie asked, "Mum, why do you cut the ends off the roast?"
>
> Her mother thought for a second and then replied, "I learned how to cook from my mother. That's the way she always did it."
>
> About a month later, Susie was visiting Grandma's for dinner. They were having pot roast. Susie watched the process and, sure enough, Grandma followed the same procedure, cutting the ends off before seasoning.
>
> Her little eyes popped wide with wonder. "Gram, why do you cut the ends off?"

"Well, my dear, I prepare meat just as my mother did. She was the most fabulous gourmet. You should visit with her, darling."

Now Susie was even more curious. Her great-grandmother was in her nineties, living in a residential convalescent center. Susie asked her parents if they could make the trip. Her folks happily scheduled arrangements for that weekend.

Upon arrival at the nursing home, Susie couldn't wait. She hugged her great-grandmother and immediately burst out, "Nana, when you are making a roast, do you first cut the ends off?"

"Yes, of course."

"Why do you do that?" Susie asked.

Her great-grandma chuckled. "So it will fit in the dish, of course!"

The punch line pokes fun at what we refer to as "backed into" customs—behaviors and routines arising absent thoughtfulness, a function of rote repetition, a wee excessive in "yes, sir," "no, sir" implementation. Such customs may once have had a purpose, born out of a certain commercial or operational utility. The trouble is in the transfer. Like a game of telephone in which core messages are lost or bastardized as they are iterated away from their origin, rituals can easily lose their functionality between generations or across team units or silos.

2nd Order Teamwork, when treated as the mecca of management, is susceptible to this syndrome. Policies, procedures, and formulas are contrived by a few. They are initiated in a manner that facilitates use and encourages follow-through. Alas, this often translates into "idiot-proofing" efforts. The behavior is passed along; mindfulness is not. Neither is trust. Practices are taught from one branch of the organizational chart to the next in this fashion. Employees copy them; they want to be perceived as conscientious, responsible, dependable. X and O enactment, over time, is fortified while the purpose of the X's and O's fades, becomes diluted, or falls off completely. People start scrapping two inches of perfectly good meat for no reason at all.

In today's globally evolving marketplace, it doesn't take but a singular tick of oil prices, a Google PR announcement, or a flap of a butterfly's wings for corporate policies to become outdated or dip in effectiveness or become counterproductive. A 2nd Order Teamwork organization tends to hold on to procedures past their prime, frequently because the procedures have become habitual. Sometimes policies become tantamount to the identity of the organization itself, or the identity of certain employees or divisions. In these instances, fear of change rears its ugly head, preventing opportune, nimble responses to competitor moves or consumer sentiment. If _____ is who we are, and _____ is altered or supplanted . . . Yikes!

Emphasis on structures and strategies as the main fountain of leadership squelches both innovation and initiative taking. In 2nd Order Teamwork organizations, it's less likely for employees, noticing a tactic or regulation no longer serving the best interests of the company or its clients, to take action on their own accord. When they do, when they attempt to tweak a team tradition in a positive fashion, they are hit with a lot of pushback.

"That's not the Widgets R Us way. That's not how we do it here."

It's an all too common expression. Used to deter negative attitudes, the expression can be a kind of beneficial self-policing. But if it's merely a product of socialization, couched as the drive to adhere to a precise path, it becomes telltale 2nd Order Teamwork.

How many times have you called the customer service line of a large company—your cell provider or a credit card company, for instance—in an attempt to correct a billing error? You explain the situation thoroughly. You offer a clever resolution.

"I'm sorry, we can't do that" is the response.

Upon inquiring why, you are halted with a cursory explanation of the company's standard rule. No matter how politely, clearly, reasonably, motivationally, or win-win you explain the extenuating circumstances, you get the same reply, in robotic manner:

"That's not our policy, ma'am."

Prior to 1920, it wasn't our policy in the United States to allow women to vote.

Oy vey. Using "policy" as cover to not problem-solve screams of a lack of teamwork. Incorporated policy is a cannibal of great thinking, creativity, progress, and the ingredients of market breakthroughs. When you tell your team that there are strict codes, you are implying that you don't trust them to resolve gray areas or design new and better methods. Absenteeism in taking initiative —extraordinary people producing *ordinary* outcomes—is the killer downside of 2nd Order Teamwork.

3rd Order Teamwork

Please don't get us wrong; bold leadership and bold practices aren't negatives. A dynamite team is good at both. You need individuals with high-quality leadership traits and training: role models, coaches. You need a carefully devised, empirically driven playbook: efficient systems that impart confidence. And you need to examine the two closely to assess your organization's effectiveness.

Surviving companies do one or the other decently well. Companies that approach the front of the pack do both well. No news there. Which is why we're writing this book. Companies that jump from profitable to one of the few really special places to work go a step further. They pursue, as their management priority, a third order of teamwork. It's "the source" of performance we highlighted in our introduction. It's where resounding, impactful, championship-driving, Moneyball-whupping teamwork lives.

Leveraging baseball to explore the sources of leadership, we must point out that Billy Beane is correct. Runs are the bottom-line commodity of World Series banners. Accumulate more, give away fewer, and you win. The 1st Order solution for this is to go buy the biggest, strongest, fastest, bomb-hitting, flame-throwing athletes on the block. Beane's revelations: (1) Large market franchises do this; they have purses allowing them to box out everyone else in competition for signing veteran All-Stars. (2) It's a high-risk proposition to sequester such sums in a small number of employees—the leaders, the superstars, the VIPs. So the Oakland A's empty their purse into a 2nd Order solution. Instead of building the organization around key people, an Alex Rodriguez or Josh Beckett, they build around a key strategy, sabermetrics—particularly OBP (on-base percentage) and DIPS (defense-independent pitching statistics).

The revelations we had in Portland and Tampa paralleled Beane's in a way: (1) Most franchises are jumping on the analytics bandwagon; the market giants are already there. (2) It's still a high-risk proposition, putting big dollars behind statistics. OBP, for instance, tabulates how consistently a hitter gets on the sacks. But hitters go nowhere without teammates to sequentially, as tobacco spitters say, "move 'em over; drive 'em in." OBP, DIPS, and the rest tell you nothing insightful about *how* a player goes about reaching base—their pregame routine, their approach at the plate, their gathering of intel on opposing pitchers, their extra reps in the cage, their body language.

That *how* has a tremendous influence on the performance of teammates and, thereby, creates a reflective influence from teammates in return. Compare fan favorites Prince Fielder and Lance Berkman in 2011. They hit in the same #4 and #5 holes in lineups of teams in the same division of the same league in the same pennant contention; they went head-to-head in the National League Championship Series. Clocked identical in foot speed, they walked the same number of times and stole the same number of bases. Fielder and Berkman were both in MLB's top five in OBP (.415 and .412). But Fielder, with one hundred more plate appearances than Berkman, had a 20 percent more frequent opportunity to score. Analytics would tell you that Prince is the better bet. Milwaukee invested in him proportionally, to the tune of $15 million (while Berkman accepted a $6 million pay *cut* in joining the Cardinals).

Despite Berkman's significantly fewer chances, the two scored the same number of runs. St. Louis won the World Series.

A 1st Order Teamwork company would opt for Fielder. He's younger, stronger, hits more home runs, and has merchandise-selling charisma. A 2nd Order Teamwork company would opt for Fielder. His OBP is a sniff higher, his opportunities to score are more numerous. We'd take Berkman every time out of the gate. Simply put, he helps his fellow redbirds, and they help him, in a way that converts individual performance into team success more efficiently—and more prolifically under pressure, when teamwork counts more than résumés or X's and O's.

The Cardinals aren't world champions because Albert Pujols occupied a clubhouse throne. They aren't world champions because of Tony La Russa's squeeze bunt calls or pitching double switches. By all means those items contributed. But they're world champions because of "Happy Flights"—the team's spirited internal slogan for pulling together, for grabbing wins by putting the team's morale and spiritedness before their own individual success.* "Happy Flights" were generated by guys like Berkman, for example, going out of his way to selflessly help role players David Freese and Yadier Molina and Jon Jay in pregame, contributions that resulted in those three guys knocking him home at a more bountiful clip than Fielder's mates knocked the Prince home.

That's leading at the source. That's the 3rd Order—Helping the Helper.

One of the most heavily used practice tools in basketball is the Shell Drill. In its basic form, it's a four-on-four exercise in which everyone is spread out on the floor. One person drives hard to the bucket. The next closest player helps. Simple. All good teams can do that.

---

*The name "Happy Flights" arose as a euphemism for how much more fun red-eyes were after a win—specifically how much fun it was to carry team bonding activity from the field onto the plane, making long, late-night rides a thing of enjoyment.

What the best do is Help the Helper.

Using the Shell Drill as an analogy for other professions, the ball handler represents a group's CEO, product manager, chief of staff, director, or senior partner—the person calling the shots. He or she barks out the play, sets the tone and tempo, and is the focal hub of everyone watching, fans and defenders, customers and competitors alike. A second team member—the helper—sets a pick or a screen, or gets open for a pass. The helper is akin to an assistant manager or junior associate or intern executing the tasks necessary for systems, procedures, and policies to follow design, the game plans necessary for their company's products and services to sing.

That is Help the Helper. X_2 recognized that the helper needed help. True Teamwork!

Despite what you read in box scores or hear sports analysts prattling on about, this one-two punch—great leaders with great plays (tasked to great, workhorse assistants)—isn't why the cream of the crop consistently win basketball games. Sustainable, ongoing success is not ultimately in the grasp of a ball handler. Nor is it an artifact of continually setting up a team's Kevin Garnetts, Kobe Bryants, and LeBron Jameses to shine. The ability to win, time and again, regardless of personnel strengths and weaknesses, regardless of external obstacles, is a third order factor—in other words, it's determined *two steps away* from the center of attention. Who is filling the gap left by the player leaving to go support the dribbler? What initiative is taken, likely to go unrewarded or unnoticed, away from the ball or basket, away from the pick, screen, or shot? Is such initiative instructed, or taken spontaneously? Is it taken only by role players, or equally by team captains and superstars?

At its essence: How is the *helper* being *helped*?

Help the Helper in Business

As we touched upon in the introduction, restaurants providing the most exquisite experience share with us a delectable, tangible understanding of Helping the Helper.

Ponder the success of Danny Meyer.* At age twenty-seven, without a dime in his pocket, Danny ventured into the restaurant business, an industry everyone knows is high overhead, low margin, with a track record for start-up failures. Friends, family, nearly every investor he approached said the same thing: too risky. He didn't let go of a revelation he'd had. That revelation, which he named "enlightened hospitality," was to invert the traditional business model of putting investors' needs first. Put the people who work for you first, he thought. Treat *them* with hospitality before wining and dining those at the top of the food chain (literally, in this business).

Danny scoured and scrambled and sacrificed to get his idea off the ground. He opened Union Square Café and got work providing hospitality in this order: employees, then guests, then the community, then suppliers, then investors. Twenty years later he's the CEO of one of the most dynamic dining organizations in the world—each of his restaurants a model of Help the Helper in action. There's a reason his book *Setting the Table*, which tells the story of his philosophy and his journey, is a *New York Times* bestseller!

One of the chief difference makers in Danny's fortunes is a burning desire he has and his staffs have for assisting fellow staff members—to the point of wanting to see *colleagues* cash in on the most handsome tips attainable.

Most highly regarded restaurants don't pool gratuities. Pooling is considered too proletarian, too demotivating; waiters are apt to resort to going through the motions. Psychologists call it "social loafing." In restaurants packed with discerning diners, loafing doesn't cut it. Waiters should be hopping to keep their customers happy. The best don't stop at happy patrons, though. When any one waiter, cruising by a table assigned to another waiter, spots a task begging to be tended to or notices a subtlety that could enhance the meal of the people at that table, the

---

*Danny's story came to our attention thanks to our publisher, Adrian Zackheim. Adrian deserves more credit than we could possibly put into words for making this book a reality. In addition to being a connoisseur of exquisite New York City eateries, he is one of the finest examples of a Help the Helper thinker we know!

waiter simply does it. No questions asked. Even if it means the initiative-taking waiter's own duties must wait (sorry for the pun). The priority at the mind's forefront is constantly, "What can be done, right now, with this pass through the dining room, to make this an environment of gratification?" One staff member pauses to help a second, momentarily leaving aside his own obligations. A third staff member stops to help the first, and so on in an ever cycling system of implied teamwork.

Owners of eateries reverberating like this certainly encourage and applaud the behavior. But they don't mandate it. It's unwritten principle. It's pride. In the high-stress environment of fast-paced five-star restaurants, waiters who "get it" know their success is a factor of their frame of mind. Their job is helping diners, so they'd better be in a helping mood. Quid pro quo, helping colleagues helps oneself. Award-winning waitstaff teams know it's a multifaceted advantage: (1) For their reputation; clientele rave. (2) For their income; the collective performance gains increased tips. (3) For their esteem; you have to take a personal hit to get the culture started so most do not—most bistros don't achieve this level of performance, leaving the door open for the few that do to know they're special. (4) For the love of their jobs; teamwork like this is just flat out fun!

What arises is an atmosphere of helping. The bounce in the step of the waiters and the je ne sais quoi of respect and appreciation when they interact with you seeps into your own mood and, as you depart, into the bounce in your own step. Though you may not have put your finger on it like this before, you remember those evenings. You want to go back for more.

Any industry can implement this. Help the Helper teamwork emerges when companies go beyond the 1st Order of teamwork and beyond the 2nd Order of teamwork—when they elevate beyond titles, division of labor, and org charts, when "helping" eclipses to-do lists or job descriptions as the predominant driving force of day-to-day work choices (for *everyone*, but especially for those in traditional leadership positions). That's not to say it's easy. Since companies tagged as having excellent leadership generally have a first-rate point guard and first-rate plays, those loci of teamwork become so socially reinforced, prioritized, and resource consuming that rarely is an alternative contemplated.

We're rather fond of this practice. It gives us an opportunity to distinguish ourselves from our competitors. When we take it to the extreme teamwork source, Helping the Helper—two steps away from the action everyone else is focused on—we take it to the house. Now it's your turn. We're passing you the ball.

YOUR TURN!

Prioritize Performance Two Steps Away from the Main Leaders and Action

Welcome to go-time. At the conclusion of each chapter we'll shift from explaining what we've learned makes the truly special teams so special to offering you a summary in the format of actions—steps you can take right away, today even, to make your team better. Whether the group you'd like to inspire is a thirty-thousand-employee company, a 2.5-child family, a dozen-person business unit, a community volunteer corps, a golf foursome gunning for a club championship, or a multinational marketing division, what would happen if you moved the teamwork needle just a tiny bit? What if your team was just 10 percent more invigorated or 10 percent more helpful? How many more sales would result? How many new clients would you gain? What kind of impact would you be able to make in your industry? *Help the Helper* is not about giant organizational shifts, cultural overhauls, or reinventing the wheel. Special teams become special by the little things they do. We can't give you a specific, like taking out the trash or making a client house call or updating a database, because the tasks that are the biggest help are different in every business. But we can tell you that if you take one, small, seemingly unnoticeable extra Help the Helper step every day, by the end of the quarter, you'll have a substantial gain. Imagine what would add up by the end of the year!

So, do *one* little thing, right now, to Help the Helper. Here are three examples to get you started:

1. Be like John Wooden's teams, which won with big players and small, fast break players and clock drainers, man defenders and zone defenders—teams not defined by a specific personnel profile or a specific playbook. His teams had something more radical in common; they made it a priority to be league leaders *away* from the ball. So do as they did. Identify one task, two or three steps removed from the outcomes your company cares most about, that goes largely unnoticed or unrecognized or is taken for granted. Bring it to the front of everyone's consciousness. Make a big deal of it. Pat your teammates on the back for it in a manner that is memorable. *Commit to doing this regularly!*

Write it down here. What is the task you're going to recognize *today*?

_____

Who are you going to recognize, *today*, for doing that task?

_____

2. Just as teams come up short of greatness from too much reliance on the person in charge for leadership (the point guard), they come up short from too much reliance on particular procedures. Be like Willis Wilson; help your teammates look *inside* for confidence instead of to the playbook. Pick one corporate, unit, or division policy and ax it!

Write it down! What is the policy or procedure or rule you'll ax *today*?

_____

3. Be like Lance Berkman or Danny Meyer; take the initiative to make someone *else* more successful. Make a lineup of the teammates whom you count on, metaphorically, to get on base in front of you or bring you in to score. For each, list the things they do that make you proud of them. For each, also list the things we call "traffic jam tasks"—duties your teammates don't have naturally flowing enthusiasm for, that get in their way or slow them down. Then list one priority of your own that you're willing to put aside. Use the time you'd normally put into that priority to instead do a few traffic jam tasks for your teammates.

Teammate 1

_____

Tasks of Pride

_____

Traffic Jam Task you're going to do for them this week

_____

Teammate 2

_____

Tasks of Pride

_____

Traffic Jam Task you're going to do for them this week

_____

Teammate 3

_____

Tasks of Pride

_____

Traffic Jam Task you're going to do for them this week

_____

Teammate 4

_____

Tasks of Pride

_____

Traffic Jam Task you're going to do for them this week

_____

Teammate 5

_____

Tasks of Pride

_____

Traffic Jam Task you're going to do for them this week

_____

What is one priority of your own that you are going to set aside today in order to be a Help the Helper champion, using that time to take the initiative to do traffic jam tasks for your teammates?

_____

Create a Dynasty of Unselfishness

An H2H Culture: Is Being Part of Something Bigger Than Yourself

W e're selfish creatures; it's as much a part of our survival DNA as is the attention we pay to alphas, celebrities, and CEOs. It's also where a separation factor resides for the truly special teams. Organizations that are enviable places to work (like Peter Schutz's Porsche, Greece Athena High School, and the Hoyt Foundation, all highlighted in chapter 1) realize that there is tremendous advantage to be gained by being leaders in overcoming human nature— by being leaders in unselfishness. Doing so is how companies vault from surviving to thriving. It's the teamwork version of *Good to Great*.

The question is, are you willing to be as unselfish as they are? As unselfish as the best?

To understand why only a few organizations reply with a resounding *"Yes!"* while so many do not, we find it's very enlightening to explore cultural entrenchments via this question: Why don't placekickers win full season or Super Bowl MVP awards?

Case in point: Adam Vinatieri, whose nickname is "Automatic." His accolades are many—two collegiate Division II national titles at South Dakota State, his alma mater's all-time leading scorer, the New England Patriots' all-time leading scorer, the NFL postseason all-time leading scorer, owner of eight NFL records (a couple of which he's broken *twice*), the only kicker to win four Super Bowl rings, and more. But no Heisman or MVP prize sits collecting dust in his trophy case. How is it, especially in such a media-blanketed industry, that one can add the most to the bottom line while a teammate gets the public credit for it?

Granted, there are scores of outstanding field generals who all deserve most valuable player honors. Adam's Patriot compadre, Tom Brady, for example, marched their team downfield on one against-odds occasion after another during the 2000–01 season, rising from obscurity (having thrown only three prior passes in the NFL) to lead a championship-starved city (and region) to glory. There are scores of workhorse running backs who deserve "The Man" recognition, too. Sprinkle in an occasional pass-catching machine of a receiver, highlight-film-dazzling cornerback, or a guy with L.T. on his license plates and you start to sketch the football award hierarchy. Kickers are usually at the bottom.

Heck, it's historically been a league pastime to *poke fun* at kickers!

For a moment, entertain a relatively drawn-out tangent with us (presented here as a three-act play; please bear with us to get to the end for the ah-ha moment). Contemplate Vinatieri's collective contribution to the Pats' run in winning three out of four straight Lombardi Trophies:

Act 1. Super Bowl XXXVI (2002)

Without Vinatieri, the Patriots wouldn't have survived even the divisional playoffs. Fans in Boston affectionately call it the Snow Bowl—Foxboro Stadium ensconced in a National Weather Service officially pronounced blizzard. The rest of the world refers to it as the "Tuck Rule Game." The Oakland Raiders had been in control all day, up 13–10 with a defense stifling nearly every Tom Brady attack. One minute forty-seven was all that stood between them and a ticket to the AFC Championship. Brady dropped back to pass. Incomplete. Brady dropped back again, Charles Woodson in pursuit. Woodson got to him hard . . . FUMBLE! The Black and Silver dove on the ball, seemingly clinching victory. Dejection washed over a packed house. Brady walked off the field, head down, Raiders jumping and hugging around him.

When past the two-minute warning in the NFL, a referee monitoring the game in the press box can signal for instant replay review of a ruling on the field via specialized electronic pager. The pager vibrated.

Oakland's merriment turned into a stir of confusion and demonstrative signaling along the sideline. Tension returned to the stadium.

NFL Rule 3, Section 22, Article 2, Note 2: "When a Team A player is holding the ball to pass it forward, any intentional forward movement of his hand starts a forward pass, even if the player loses possession of the ball as he is attempting to tuck it back toward his body."

The call was overturned. Despite frantic, vein-popping screaming from Raider coach Jon Gruden, it was an incomplete pass, not a fumble. New life for New England.

Brady, after dodging two more near-miss interceptions, was able to center the ball between the hash marks for Vinatieri—little aid though it was with the ground blanketed by the whiteout, only a couple yard lines visible thanks to sideline officials rushing across the field in between plays with handheld snow blowers. Forty-five-yard field goals are tough enough in sunny, zero-wind conditions; this one was into a swirl of flakes making neon yellow goalposts difficult to see. No time-outs remained. The clock ticked down 0:41, 0:40, 0:39 as Vinatieri and his holder, Ken Walter, tried to pick out a snowy spot to receive the snap. 0:29, 0:28, 0:27 . . . the kick was up, drifting right, wobbling in the wind, wobbling, dying, dying . . . GOOD! "Automatic" squeaked it just over the crossbar to save the game.

If this was in an infomercial, we'd cry "But wait, there's more!" Overtime. Once again off a snowy, windswept surface, the Patriots' Super Bowl hopes were placed on Vinatieri's foot. His twenty-three-yarder split the uprights perfectly, inspiring long snapper Lonie Paxton to dive to the ground, making snow angels in the end zone as the mass of weather-worn fans in Foxboro cheered on in jubilant disbelief.

But wait, there's more.

Two weeks later in New Orleans, the Patriots squared off against a St. Louis Rams team ranked third in fewest yards allowed and dubbed "The Greatest Show on Turf" for their NFL record three consecutive five-hundred-point seasons. Mustering a couple touchdowns in the first half was not enough; St. Louis's defense shut down Brady for the remainder of the duel. Meanwhile Kurt Warner got hot, stringing together passes for a pair of fourth-quarter TDs, including a twenty-six-yard gem to Ricky Proehl, off the bench, tying the game at 17 all. Now there was 1:21 left, the Pats pinned inside their own 20 and with no TOs. Legendarily animated commentator John Madden weighed in, the sage Pat Summerall nodding in agreement beside him:

"With this field position you have to just run the clock out. You have to play for overtime now. I don't think you wanna force anything here. You don't wanna do anything stupid. Because you have no time-outs and you're backed up."

Patriots coach Bill Belichick wasn't listening. The Patriots went for it.

Two plays later they'd moved the sticks all of ten yards; 0:41 left. Stuck inside their own 30. A first down punched it another ten yards, but still leaving at least one third of the field to chew before a field goal could be contemplated. With 0:29 left, Fox television operators panned down the New England bench, catching a cool-as-can-be Vinatieri taking a single, relaxed kick into his warm-up net. Madden's tune flipped.

"Now I kinda like what the Patriots are doing!"

A pass to Troy Brown took them over midfield with 0:21 left. Another dump up the middle snuck them within the outskirts of #4's range. The clock continued to wind down, under ten seconds. Brady hustled up to the line to spike the ball. Now there was 0:07 left.

"This is something that I'll admit as a coach and as an analyst, I don't think they should've done. But they have the guts," Madden intoned. Guts, as he continued to explain, because ". . . this has been a year about Vinatieri and making some great kicks, some of the greatest kicks that I've even seen in my life."

Forty-eight yards for all the marbles as time expired . . . right down Broadway. The southern, indoor, artificial-turf venue didn't keep Patriots players from feigning now signature snow angels in celebration of New England's first Super Bowl triumph—and the first Super Bowl in history to be won on a score in the final play.

Tom Brady was named Most Valuable Player.

Act 2. Super Bowl XXXVIII (2004)

It's as if the football gods tried to give MVP balloters a do-over. Once again it would require the craftsmanship of "Automatic" Vinatieri to propel the Patriots to the promised land.

First up: the Titans. New England scored on the opening series, just one handful of plays after kickoff. That would be it for Brady, however. Stingy on defense, Tennessee denied New England's offense a sniff at the end zone for the remainder of the day. They didn't even have the opportunity to take a deep shot for touchdown, barely making it into Titan territory the entire second half. No matter. One time past the 50, late in the fourth quarter, was the only chance they had to break the tie. So what if it was a forty-six-yarder and only the second boot that long that Vinatieri had attempted all season? So what if it was into the wind? So what if footballs don't fly well in arctic air and it was below zero degrees Fahrenheit, one of the coldest days in recorded NFL history? Adam's nickname was true to form. He pierced the uprights with plenty of room to spare for the three points that determined the game.

On to a matchup with the Indianapolis Colts. The Patriots repeated their prior week, punching in a touchdown on the game-opening drive only to see Brady's staff go silent for the remainder of the contest. Automatic to the rescue. With his teammates looking to him to counter Peyton Manning's second-half touchdowns, Vinatieri broke the league's playoff record with *five* field goals. An AFC title and a return to the Super Bowl were theirs.

But wait, there's more.

The do-over Lombardi Trophy run was capped by an eerily similar ending to Super Bowl XXXVIII. This time it was the Carolina Panthers who'd picked up free-agent Ricky Proehl to be a backup receiver. At a minute and change on the clock, Proehl came into the game, mirroring what he'd done two years earlier. He snared the tying toss . . . running an identical pattern! New England fans did a scoreboard double take to shake the déjà vu—knotted at 29 this time instead of 17. The ensuing kickoff was deep. The Pats again stared at almost the full length of the field in front of them, with 1:08 to play. But another element was different this go-round: John Madden didn't recommend kneeling on the ball.

"You've got Vinatieri here, Pat; you go for it."

They did. Brady slid his helmet on and came out firing. A couple of completions burned up some distance, and the timer. Now there was 0:15 on the clock, third down and three. But the first-down marker was beyond Vinatieri's career long. Vinatieri was on the sideline—throwing warm-up *passes* in preparation for a possible fake field goal.

Brady connected once more. Inside #4's sweet spot. The ticker stopped with 0:08 left.

No Super Bowl had ever gone into overtime. Adam had only missed four indoor kicks in his career; they were all on that very field, Reliant Stadium in Houston. Automatic assured that neither oddity would be the case this time. He and Walter walked off the spot for a forty-one-yarder. The snap, perfect. The hold, perfect. The kick . . . *perfect.* New England grabbed another crown. Vinatieri became the first player to be *the* deciding factor in two Super Bowls.

Tom Brady was named Most Valuable Player.

Act 3. Super Bowl XXXIX (2005)

For an encore, Vinatieri led the NFL in scoring the next season with 141 points. And though the Patriots' playoff path was considerably less dramatic, #4's services not needed to extend their hopes, survive snow, counter a future Hall of Fame QB, or simply give his coworkers confidence, he would be called upon yet again to set the margin of victory on the ultimate stage: a third Super Bowl victory, 24–21, after starting the final quarter tied with the Philadelphia Eagles.

Deion Branch was named Most Valuable Player. He didn't make a tackle or score a single point.

Not that points should have anything to do with who is most valuable. Branch is a great example of an MVP award gone right, as are the once-in-a-blue-moon MVPs given to a defensive specialist, and the salaries now coughed up to left tackles. Blind-side blockers never win public accolades. They do one of the most important jobs on the field, getting clobbered play after play, happy to be unsung heroes (save Michael Lewis's seminal work and the ensuing Sandra Bullock blockbuster). They're ultimate Help the Helpers.

Scoring statistics, on the other hand, are a major distraction from developing an extreme teamwork culture. Scoring statistics are selfish. Whether we're willing to admit it or not, they hold up individuals as reasons for team success. They draw our attention to what the superstars are doing, which is attention taken away from the little jobs behind the scenes, away from the action, going on without the spotlight, that significantly impact the way an organization operates—and the collective morale, which is a compelling factor of hard work.

HARRY S. TRUMAN

It's amazing how much you can accomplish when it doesn't matter who gets the credit.

Hall of Fame NFL wide receiver Jerry Rice put an exclamation to this point on ESPN's talk show *Audibles* in December 2011. *Audibles*, a discussion-format broadcast, features a panel of notable NFL guest personalities responding to viewer questions streamed in via Twitter. During one airing, when Tim Tebow's improvement progression as the quarterback of the Denver Broncos was a scorching-hot media topic, a fan asked:

"Which is more responsible for the Broncos' success, Tebow or their defense?"

Jerry's reaction says it all. Owner of a litany of touchdown and pass-catching recordbook entries, to go along with three Super Bowl rings, Rice is the statistical archetype of MVP. But he's an even greater model of Help the Helper. He absolutely blasted the Twitter inquiry.*

"*When* are we going to get past the idea that one person or one thing is the reason for a group's success? Get over it all ready. It's killin' us. I think it's a big reason why our economy is struggling and why we don't have nonpartisan teamwork in Washington. The Broncos aren't winning because of Tebow or because of the D. They're winning because all fifty-three players and the coaches and front office and maintenance guys and ticket takers are pulling together, doing their jobs well. *That question's awful.*"

The message was strong. Even stronger was the verve behind Jerry's words. That the superstar is so genuinely passionate about getting discussion off individual performances tells us volumes about how he approached his work—not the things he did, not all the receptions and yards, not the famous offseason training sprinting up Bay Area hills 'til he'd puke. *How* he did them—that's what matters. The statistic that should be brazenly displayed in Canton is Rice's all-time ranking among NFL players in: unselfishness.

There'd be a lot of his 49er teammates on that all-time unselfishness list as well: Tom Rathman, Wes Chandler, Brent Jones, Roger Craig,

---

*The *Audibles* fan would've gained far more by inquiring how to replicate Tebow's commitment to helping people who are suffering. Before every game, when the vast majority of athletes are consumed with getting themselves ready to perform—their minds absorbed in themselves—Tim selects a stranger in need to be his guest. He flies the guest and family into town, takes them to dinner, provides them with field passes, visits with them before kickoff, and after games personally walks them (or pushes their wheelchair) to the parking lot! We're pretty confident in claiming that Tim might be the most unselfish athlete in history. We're also confident in predicting he will enjoy a long and successful career—in large part due to the amazing leadership he'll develop as a result of his unselfishness.

Charles Haley, Ronnie Lott, Randy Cross, Keena Turner. A couple guys named Montana and Young took home most of the hardware. But credit isn't something they desired or even coveted. San Francisco's clubhouse in those years, winning ten of twelve straight division championships, was as unconcerned with statistics as an NFL franchise has been in two decades. The title of head coach Bill Walsh's autobiography: *The Score Takes Care of Itself.*

Wait. TDs don't matter? Tom Brady wasn't a force majeure in the Patriots' Super Bowl victories? Yeah, right. KP and Doc, whatcha smokin'?

Please understand, the above Vinatieri diatribe in no way is meant to criticize Brady. He earned every bit of his honors. So did all the other members of that squad who were sweating their ninnies off in 100-degree August three-a-days. But what if—and we're spitballing here—when brought up to the dais to be decorated for a second time as Super Bowl MVP, amid the rain of confetti and applause, Tom had turned and handed the trophy to Automatic with some kind of statement along the lines of "I want to give this to Adam. It's because of him that I can play free of worry. I know he's always got my back. He represents what is special about the contributions of every single player on our team"?

What if!? We are well aware of how much that would be asking of Brady. It's extraordinarily tough for any human being to think straight in moments like that, with all the swirling jubilation and chaos of celebration. Even if you could rationally deliberate in that spotlight, with mere seconds to process it all, you'd have to then risk snubbing the writers and broadcasters who voted for you. But that's exactly the character that separates the longest sustained dynasties. That type of unusually forward-thinking unselfishness distinguishes extraordinary organizations from organizations that just have success from time to time.

New England couldn't keep Vinatieri. He bolted for Indianapolis after Super Bowl XXXIX. Because they offered him a windfall? Nope. Because the Patriots were starting to fall victim to 1st Order Teamwork; they were losing a touch of the unselfishness that had made them so great. They let a few veterans go for financial reasons instead of making team chemistry the priority; they didn't fight like the dickens to keep their completely unselfish-minded offensive and defensive coordinators. And they didn't honor Automatic's giving to the team by bestowing on him in return a franchise tag as they had the previous season. When the Colts (on the rise in unselfishness at that point) buzzed to take the temperature of his willingness to leave New England, Adam told his agent:

"Let's not screw around. If Indy is interested, let's get this done."

They didn't even give the Pats an opportunity to counteroffer. And the Patriots haven't won a Super Bowl since. Their next appearance in the title match was running a perfect 18-0 record into being heavy favorites versus the New York Giants in 2008. The Giants, implementing a Help the Helper strategy themselves (as we'll revisit in chapter 7), snagged the upset, winning by a margin of, you guessed it, three points. Now that the Red Sox have finally kicked the ghost of the Bambino out of Fenway, was a new curse conjured in Foxboro? If New England doesn't capture another Lombardi Trophy for a couple decades, you can be sure the *Globe* and *Herald* will splash a few headlines referencing the Babe of field goals.

Don't make the same mistake in your business. Divert coveted awards to your Vinatieris and your teammates away from the limelight, especially when it's the hardest to remember to do. When it takes a magnanimous effort of unselfishness to hand over credit to someone else . . . that's when the biggest returns on H2H investment are available, such as retaining yeomen who are the fabric of your culture.

Billy goats, Bambinos, and other such nonsense aside, an equally informative question to ponder: what Help the Helper things did the Patriots do to vault into dynasty eminence in the first place that they've gotten slightly away from and as a result slightly declined in their industry dominance?

Prior to Super Bowl XXXVI, head coach Bill Belichick was given a choice by league officials regarding the customary pregame introduction. One team would come running out of the locker room to the public address announcement of their offense; the other to announcement of defensive players. As designated home team, the Patriots got to pick. Which did Belichick want? Neither. He asked that no one be singled out. He asked for the team to be introduced as one. The NFL rejected his request. Belichick didn't acquiesce. Helping his players maintain their unified spirit was worth any commissioner reprimand or fine. Game time rolled around, and the hoopla and cheering in the post-9/11 Louisiana Superdome was as raucous as ever. The St. Louis Rams' entry was broadcast first, Pat Summerall calling out the starters on offense. TV cameras shifted to the tunnel where the Patriots were huddled, ensconced in a dry ice machine cloud.

Summerall boomed out: "Ladies and gentlemen . . ."

A long pause.

"The New England PATRIOTS!"

In a moment that still elicits butterflies to revisit, the Patriots came charging out of the smoke together, all holding hands. Out in front was not Tom Brady, not Adam Vinatieri, not Bill Belichick. They were in the middle of the pack.

Unselfish Action #1: grabbing and raising a coworker's hand on the precipice of critical events—*before* challenges, not after acing them. For most people, holding hands with coworkers might be awkward, uncomfortable, outlandish. Thus this variety of unite-for-big-moments activity is shied away from, missed, or frowned upon (ridiculously) as a sexual harassment suit in the making. Yet another reason why Help the Helper cultures are so successful—they put aside personal discomfort, and fear of the extreme, in the interest of a level of teamwork realized by so few companies.

Unselfish Action #2: deep-sixing reward hierarchy. The biggest stat producers on extreme teams, aka "bottom-line" leaders, don't hustle for corner offices, wear flashy suits (Belichick wears old sweatshirts on the sidelines on national TV), or stand in front of the line. That's why Tom Brady didn't emerge from the tunnel first. The thought likely didn't even cross his mind. You can't control whose name the press sticks in the newspapers any more than Tom Brady can control whom MVP voters elect. But you can influence what sort of prize, within your organization, is most recognized, most discussed, and thereby most cherished—the prize of seeing a *colleague* happy, thriving, and gaining success.

Schadenfreude and *Mudita*

Schadenfreude is the modern-day derivative of second-century Old German terms *Schaden*, meaning adversity or harm, and *Freude*, meaning joy. Combined, they form a label for the experience of delighting in the misfortune of others. As much as we'd prefer to believe such an indulgence is limited to evildoers, for as long as language has existed there have been words for enjoying another's tumble. Neurological research confirms the relatively ubiquitous nature of the emotion. In functional magnetic resonance imaging (fMRIs)—scans of cortical activity during conscious, wakeful processing—when study subjects are shown photographs depicting people suffering in a range of fashions, pleasure centers of the brain light up in most cases. The findings explain, for example, the rubbernecking that clogs traffic on a should-be-free-flowing side of a divided highway resulting from drivers' straining to catch a glimpse of an automobile accident off the far lane in the opposite direction. A wreck southbound has no impact on the commute of northbound drivers. There's no purpose served by slowing down to examine the situation. Except the satisfaction of morbid curiosity. Schadenfreude. It's why graphic and violent news sells so well.

Enthusiasm for others' failures is linked to social comparison theory. In the 1950s, psychologist Leon Festinger postulated that humans don't evaluate themselves by objective standards nearly as much as by relational standards—that is, self-judgment based on how one stacks up relative to other people, especially people in close proximity such as officemates and neighbors. The idea is that, evolutionarily, our comparative status in our community affected our survival. The higher we rank, the better our success in attracting a mate, gaining protection from the group, having work done for us, and so on. When those ahead of us fall, we rise. The primitive foundation of our brain became programmed to perceive this as positive. Correspondingly, the degree of schadenfreude one experiences has been found to positively correlate with the level of success of the subject viewed as faltering. The more opportunity for one to personally gain from another's demise, the stronger the schadenfreude.

And so it goes with workplace competitiveness. Some is healthy—the open, lighthearted bit of trash talking, "Want to put five bucks on it?" form. That form is *fun*. It increases dialogue and strengthens relationships. A little bit of tongue-in-cheek razzing (not insults) is good for interpersonal chemistry and promotes a mentally tough, push-each-other-to-excel environment. On the flip side, *unspoken* office competition increases instances of schadenfreude, and often the sort of schadenfreude we call silent sabotage—subconscious emotion, eroding teamwork without our knowing it's happening. Who asks the chap in the chair next to them to cool it because your job security is better when he doesn't do as well? Who asks their boss for a promotion because Dick and Mary are missing deadlines? Correct, no one with good intentions. Our "trained" superegos try to live up to a higher standard than contemplating how colleagues' missteps may open doors.

Which is why exceptional companies go an extra mile to make sure competition occurs at the superego level, not the ego level!

Minor League Baseball is brimming with egos. And replete with schadenfreude. Teams post weekly, often daily, depth charts throughout their system—150 or so freakishly talented, growing men generally ranging from eighteen to twenty-eight years old (or younger if they're from Latin America with no birth certificates), full of testosterone (hopefully naturally), ranked in the advancement toward fulfilling boyhood dreams of becoming a major leaguer. The lot has to be funneled down to twenty-five, the number on a big-league roster. When a player at your position is called up, your hopes become a bit dimmer. When a player at your position gets injured, your chances brighten.

Most MLB executives tend to view this as a good thing. The general concept: throw all that talent in a pressure-filled cauldron and find out who has "what it takes" to make it.

"It weeds out the weak," say so many old-school scouts and GMs, oblivious to the opportunity to give their organization a big boost. Many of the new age, twenty-something GMs, meanwhile, are too busy running spreadsheets to see the problem. Or they didn't compete as an athlete at a high enough level. So they look at performance grading through the same lens they used to look at grading on physics exams—as an objective measure of skill rather than the social comparison phenomenon that it really is.

Just because on-field, physical competition is highly visible in sports doesn't mean the psychological component of competition is going to be overt. Athletes are as reluctant to acknowledge schadenfreude as are workers in any other industry. Tough-guy cultures actually make it harder for athletes to address and get a handle on performance-influencing emotions (which we'll drill into in chapter 7). A player "making it" doesn't mean he's transcended schadenfreude. It usually means he's better at hiding it. The traditional farm system of most baseball franchises enflames, not reduces, schadenfreude—a fact we took advantage of in Tampa.

Tradition is that franchises spread hot prospects throughout their farm system according to predetermined criteria. Commonly, newly drafted players go to rookie ball; returning talent on the younger end of the continuum is placed in A-ball; guys rapidly advancing, who might make big jumps, head to AA; veteran minor leaguers and journeymen anchor Triple-A. The profiling is a bit analogous to cutting ends off a roast. That's how it's been done for decades. Press for an explanation and you get some mottled, sounds-good wisdom along the lines of:

"Players need to be assembled according to similar stages along the development curve . . . so there's continuity . . . so coaches skilled at addressing particular learning-stage goals can be appropriately matched."

Hogwash. Lazy. The mark of a great coach is an ability to effectively handle diversity, an ability to communicate on many levels about many different issues. And putting players most directly in battle for the same job assures greater schadenfreude potential. That's not to say that you should always avoid pairings of same-career-point workers. Rather, that using career point as a decision-making variable in assembling teams is generally not the most effective scheme. Far better for attenuating the subconscious, internally conflicting, focus-mitigating effects of schadenfreude is to assemble groups based on who is most apt to help one another in that group enjoy a spirited, playfully ribbing, psychologically transparent version of competition. In other words, put people together based on similarity of competition and communication style.

Durham, North Carolina, the home of the Rays' top farm club, was where the front office stocked players in 2007 with more of a quiet, regimented approach to work, the players in the system who more actively observed their religious faith, players who relished spending free time in the clubhouse versus in bars.

This was AAA. Technically one step away from the big leagues. Outsiders assumed we were making the statement that those particular qualities were what the organization valued the most, what we thought were personality traits most linked to success. That wasn't it at all. Oodles of different personalities can be tremendously successful.* Instead, it was that those guys meshed well competitively. They held Bible study together. They made smoothies together. They played hour upon hour of Connect Four in the locker room (which saddled the doc with a fine share of tallies in the loss column); they had an ongoing Ping-Pong tournament complete with bracket, odds, and made-up Ping-Pong scouting reports! They came to work earlier than usual; they stayed later. For a group of otherwise introverted fellas, they were constantly chatting it up. They *loved* competing with one another.

---

*Contrast Dennis Rodman and David Robinson, for instance. Both are cream of the world-class crop. Rodman is the pinnacle of extroverted. Need we describe his colorful presentation? Robinson keeps to himself, is quiet, and falls on the introverted end of the continuum. They are as opposite as you get in terms of personality. Personality isn't what drives extreme teamwork (a variable we'll go into in more depth in chapter 8). As NBA veterans will be quick to tell you, Dennis and David both rank among the sport's most legendary in the lengths they went to help their teammates.

Barely 7 percent of minor league players become major leaguers. A Triple-A squad is lucky to produce one or two future stars. Twenty-one of the core twenty-five teammates from Durham in 2007 played at the next level; eleven went on to play together as teammates in Tampa!

Not only did the way those guys communicate and compete with one another virtually eliminate schadenfreude, their Bible study provided a source of performance-enhancing meditation. Independently of religion type—all religions can offer this; the Durham Bulls weren't of a single faith—spending time every day actively practicing positive values reduces the instance of emotions associated with schadenfreude. Buddhists call it cultivating "the four immeasurables": benevolent kindness, compassion, vicarious joy, and equanimity. Vicarious joy—feeling success yourself when you see a colleague getting the glory, doing well, or being promoted—is referred to as *mudita*. It is the polar opposite of schadenfreude.

The baseball program at Rice is an example of an organization that works hard to recognize and applaud *mudita*. During the doc's tenure there, he taught an advanced seminar in which students analyzed the components of *mudita*, gathered data on case studies, and designed application strategies. Head baseball coach Wayne Graham, a devoted scholar himself, requested that all his players take the course. His coaching staff then hammered home the principles on the diamond, relentlessly reinforcing that exercising *mudita* was of greater worth than individual accomplishment.

On one occasion, during a close contest with state rival Texas A&M, now perennial MLB All-Star Lance Berkman hit for the cycle (the exceptionally uncommon batting feat, which most baseball players never achieve in a lifetime, of tabulating a single, double, triple, and home run all in the same game). After diving into the third-base bag with a triple in his fourth at bat, Berkman jumped up exultantly to high-five Graham, who was in the adjacent coach's box.

"That's the *cycle*, Coach!" It was the first time in his career he had posted the rare achievement.

Wayne fired back in vigorous disgust, "Whupty doo, you hit for the cycle. Your teammates are playing like shit. We're losing a ballgame but *you* hit for the cycle. Where's your leadership? Get off the field!"

Graham pulled him out of the game right then and there. He put in a pinch runner for the one player that was carrying the team's scoring production up until that point. Sacrifice the outcome to make a point? Nope. The Owls won. And Lance gained a valuable lesson that's stood him well since. A quick learner, he righted his perspective and proceeded to enjoy every minute watching from the bench as his teammates pulled out the W.

Two take-home points: (1) How many project managers or division chiefs or regional VPs do you know who would tell one of their staff members to stop, to turn over their successful account to someone else, when that staff member celebrated a record production accumulation? Companies get so caught up in achievement that they can fail to see when it gets in the way of extreme teamwork. Wayne keeps the team first, at all costs. And as a result, the Owls have spent more days ranked No. 1 than any other program in the country over the past fifteen years. (2) How many employees do you know who would cheerfully, with a genuinely positive attitude, stay and support fellow employees after getting chewed out and demoted by the boss? That's the kind of extreme, putting your own feelings aside to do what's best for your coworkers, mentality that has fueled Lance's reputation—he has a long history of helping teams make it into the postseason—and championships!

David Aardsma is another great example. Ranking among MLB's winningest closers the past ten years, he was equally an all-star in the classroom. In 2003 Rice ran the NCAA baseball postseason table to reach the school's first national championship contest . . . in any sport . . . ever. The Owls knocked off perennial powerhouses LSU, Cal State Fullerton, and Texas en route to a best-of-three date with Stanford University to determine who would hoist the national crown. Rice grabbed game one. Stanford grabbed game two. It was winner-take-all in the concluding game of the season.

From spring start to end, Aardsma had dazzled as the squad's closer. There were a lot of close ballgames that year, a lot of one-run decisions. Dave would trot in from the bullpen in the ninth inning, and on many occasions in extra innings, to shut the door on would-be rallies. The '03 Owls had dominant pitching, with future big leaguers Jeff Niemann, Philip Humber, and others. While everyone contributed aplenty to the historic season, Dave was a cornerstone reason the Owls were still standing at the finale in mid-June.

Humber was the starter that night. Confirmation that his first-round draft position was well advised quickly became apparent as he aced the mighty Stanford hitters one, two, three in the opening frame. Scouting reports boasted that the Cardinal bats were the best one-through-nine lineup in two decades of college baseball. Humber shut them down the following inning, and the inning after that. He didn't relinquish a hit until the sixth. He didn't give up a run until the seventh. The Rice offense, carefree knowing that Philip was in total command, went on a plate-padding spree. Heading into the eighth inning the score was 14–2 Rice.

There were just two innings to go to cap off the near impossible—a national championship for a tiny little academic school known for Nobel Prize winners, not professional athletes.

Aardsma hadn't yet pitched in the College World Series. He had carried the team much of the year, but had yet to be called upon on the grand stage. The players on the bench were restless. The last outs took F-O-R-E-V-E-R. The game was well in hand. A couple guys in the dugout raised the idea that Dave should come in to ceremoniously throw the ninth inning.

"He's gotta see a turn on the mound."

"He's one of the top pitchers in the country; he deserves to be part of this."

"Should we go ask Coach to put Dave in?"

A group of fans in the Rice section of Rosenblatt Stadium started chanting his name. Aards-ma. Aards-ma. Aards-ma. While Humber polished the Stanford eighth and strode off the field, ESPN commentators noted that he had gone the duration and, with a high strikeout total, was getting up in pitch count. He was about out of gas.

As Rice took its final plate appearances, the ninth inning looming, it was Aardsma who walked the length of the dugout to have a word with Coach Graham.

"Coach," Dave said matter-of-factly. "I don't need to get in. Give it to Humber. It's his moment."

We urge you to ask yourself again, are you willing to be that unselfish?

MAHATMA GANDHI

Man becomes great exactly in the degree in which he works for the welfare of his fellow-men.

It was a defining goal for us at Rice. We'd set out to make *mudita* a recognized, practiced, rewarded skill, much as the Patriots had. The effort led to Dave Aardsma's approach to teamwork and, in turn, Humber's huge performance. It led to QB Drew Bledsoe, the No. 1 overall draft pick who ended up taking a backseat in Boston, to jump around like a little kid on Christmas morning, helmet bumping in excitement *with the guy who took his job*, right before Tom Brady ran onto the field to start Super Bowl XXXVI. Imagine being Tom Brady in that instant, knowing that the colleague you replaced is so positively happy for you. *Mudita* at its finest.

The results speak for themselves, especially Bledsoe's performance in the AFC Championship against the Steelers that year. Drew had to sub in for a hobbled Brady early in the match. Though having seen action in only one game all season, he didn't miss a beat. Most human beings in that pressure cooker of a situation would be adversely effected, to some degree, by a desire to prove they belonged, to re-earn their previous role, to impress coaches. Not Bledsoe; not that day. He knew how excited Brady was for him in return; he knew his back was covered. He could just go play. He came in throwing touchdowns, steadily, confidently leading the Pats to victory.

The Twitter Conflict

It's one thing to enjoy the success of another clan member's hunt. It's a whole new ballgame in the world of 140-character communication, YouTube hit rates, Google AdWords, and, in sports, $100-million-dollar endorsement deals. Technology today can provide people overnight fame and fortune—without having to produce substance or perform at a particularly high level (à la Paris Hilton). With the rampant popularity of Twitter, Facebook, and their brethren—and the corresponding explosion, if you will, of social comparison theory pressures—self-promotion seems to be a must to get ahead in most companies and careers. Possess tons of talent, but don't (effectively) e-blast it, and you may be passed over for a raise or job interview. The publishing industry attests to this with the flood of recent bestsellers devoted to social media marketing. Barack Obama forever changed the way presidential campaigns are run with the success of the crack team of tweeters he hired.

It's not that human beings haven't always been driven to gain respect and recognition as means of advancement; it's that the Internet Age makes it so easy, so much farther reaching, and at the speed of Wi-Fi. Add to the recipe a collective shift in the eighties and nineties to make sure every child goes home with a trophy or blue ribbon. Then pour on the responsibility-shirking shield computers allow for in interpersonal interaction—just like the shield automobiles provide, allowing people to act more aggressively toward others while driving than when in face-to-face situations. What you get is the "Me Generation." Substantially what Gen-Y has become.

A large-scale meta-survey of college students from 1979 to 2000 conducted by the Institute for Social Research, in conjunction with the American Psychiatric Association, reveals that twenty-somethings in the United States today are 40 percent lower in empathy assessments than young folks in the previous generation. Concludes the study: "Young adults today comprise one of the most self-concerned, competitive, and individualistic cohorts in recent history."

We hop on this as a tremendous opportunity. The more individual employee focused and the more electronic communication focused any industry becomes, the more of an outlier *mudita* expressions become. Therefore, the more powerful the tool becomes. We devote copious time to scanning the landscape of our organizations, looking for unselfish acts to cheer, looking for places we can implement or stimulate unselfish activities. We don't trash technology. We turn it around. LinkedIn, Facebook, and Twitter can be excellent utensils for giving credit *away*, for garnering pleasure by posting things that help teammates and coworkers gain more success.

Our stance is this: if we're going to boast, let's boast about someone else. We *want* expressive, passionate emotion flowing around the office. But we want it pointed out, not pointed in. Getting totally jazzed about the good work someone else is doing accomplishes four key performance enhancements that, in return, give you more success yourself:

1. It keeps your head up. In order to notice others' successes you have to be watching for them, which means you can't be looking down. Physiology research teaches us that body posture (as simple as raised shoulders versus lowered, eyes up versus drooped) has a massive influence over our mood, energy level, and attitude. So we tell our teammates and clients all the time, "Go searching for examples of other people doing great."

2. It keeps you from getting caught up in your own little world. When you think about your job duties, your deadlines, and your production scores, it's easy to get blinders on or lose perspective;

it's easy for your challenges and hurdles to magnify into larger issues than they really are. Flip the script.

3. It infuses more energy into your game. Taking pride and pleasure when other people excel allows you to experience success more often. Success breeds success; you are more apt to thrive personally when you're in the practice of having success-packed emotions.

4. It strengthens relationships . . . immeasurably! When you outwardly, viscerally communicate happiness to someone else regarding their success, you communicate to them that you've got their back, that you're there in the trenches for them. That extends confidence. They perform better. They are thankful. They do the same for you in thanks and appreciation. You perform better. They whole system improves. *Mudita* becomes ingrained as part of the culture.

It's really an age-old therapeutic tactic. Feeling a little blue? Struggling or stuck in some fashion? Don't pour more energy and resources into trying to fix it, banging your head into the wall, tying yourself up in knots. Put it aside and go help someone else. You'll feel so much better so much faster. It's completely renewing. And that renewal of energy, spirit, and attitude allows you to see through your own problems more clearly, find solutions that were escaping you before, and make new breakthroughs.

Kaleb Canales is this tactic's poster boy. He put these strategies to work in Portland—all the way from lowest man on the totem pole (borrowing a Northwest Coast tribal reference), an unpaid intern with the Blazers, to ascension to the head coaching throne. Kaleb is one of those workers you have to tell to go home. Otherwise he'd sleep at the Blazers' facility half the time, showering there in the morning as everyone else arrived for the workday.

Sometimes Kevin would even have to tell him, "Kaleb, quit working; go out on a date!"

Kaleb's dedication, however, is not at all that of a grinder or a workaholic. He is pursuing his passion—passion for his colleagues being an extension of his family. He begins every single morning, no exception, by asking somebody (a boss, a coworker, a secretary or custodian, all in equal amounts):

What can I do for you?

It's not a passing question, either. He means it. Just as you would mean it if you were posing the offer to your mother or sibling.

If we told him, "Kaleb, this building needs a new roof," before you know it he'd be up there with a hammer and nails. He's totally engaged in a desire to help. Even if he personally can't help, he'll find you someone who can.

www.CartoonStock.com

How do we get people into this mentality? How did Kaleb? When we say he means it like he's helping his family, we really mean just *that*—the Blazers are his family. He was given the time, and he took the time (the combination is important), to get to know something special about each of his coworkers. It's unselfish of an organization to allow interns and new hires this kind of time leeway, especially at the pace of business today and the stream of seemingly must-do-immediately tasks. Kaleb seized the opportunity when he was provided with it, bringing him personally closer to his office relatives. His payback thank-you is embedded in the enthusiasm of his "What can I do for you?" It's a team-enhancing enthusiasm as it sets a tone in Portland to communicate to colleagues:

I'm here . . . I'm present . . . I want to help my family be great . . .

The Blazers were quick to secure Canales with a long-term contract. The brass has gone out of their way to find ways to promote him—a marvelous illustration of how extreme teams structure the top of their food chain. Not because he's basketball royalty. He didn't come from a long line of coaches or pro athletes. Not because he is a celebrity, millionaire coach. He isn't (yet). He's at the top of the pyramid because of the value placed on Help the Helpers. He's also at the top of the pyramid because he understands there's a fundamental human need fulfilled by being part of something special.

Being Part of Something Bigger Than Yourself

Hall of Fame psychologist Abraham Maslow would have enjoyed living in Oregon. He was a trailblazer. He ignited the charge to focus psychological research on exemplary people rather than on the mentally ill. As he said: "The study of crippled, stunted, immature, and unhealthy specimens can only yield a crippled psychology and a crippled philosophy."

His work led to the seminal 1943 paper "A Theory of Human Motivation," which laid out stages of growth human beings progress through to become optimal versions of themselves. Along the way, Maslow posited, fulfillment of a hierarchy of needs is sought. First, physiological homeostasis must be attained. People must be able to feed, clothe, and shelter themselves (stage one). Humans then move to seeking security (maintaining employment and good health—stage two), love and belonging (achieving friendship, sexual intimacy, and a family—stage three), esteem (personal and career advancement, and the respect of others—stage four), and finally to self-actualization (discovering a purpose and meaning—stage five). In building teams, we call the top of the pyramid "being part of something bigger than yourself." We then add a sixth stage: helping someone *else* achieve self-actualization.

Many organizations fail to provide opportunities for people to achieve self-actualization. Or they get in the way of it. It's easy to *think* the opportunity is there. Close more sales, design great new products, help the company make more money. Contribute to the greater good, right? Nice in theory, but most of our working population vacillates between stages two and four—trying to establish or advance a steady career, buying a house, getting married, having kids. Companies tend to wrap those need fulfillment desires into motivations for advancing the corporate bottom line via promotion, bonuses, and vacation time. Messages that sound as if they are serving a larger purpose—"Our shareholders are counting on you [to work your buns off]"—ultimately just feed individual effort and satisfy individual job descriptions. The result is employees stuck short of stage five.

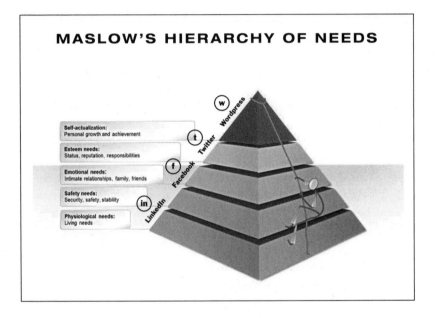

Stage five (and six) happens when you put your job description aside, when the question transforms from "How can I do my job better?" to "How can I help a teammate do his or her job better?" That's what Kaleb is all about. The drive is to be a member of a group of people functioning at the highest level of evolution, doing incredible things, and sharing the experience with one another. The product is the kind of extreme teamwork office environment that made Portland as trailblazing as Maslow.

Surprisingly, promoting such a mentality doesn't require a complete company staffing reconstruction or a massive refurbishment of compensation structures. It doesn't depend on finding diamond-in-the-rough Kalebs who already think this way. But it also can't be achieved with lip service. You can't walk around and command people to operate at stage six; it's not a matter of coaching. Self-actualization is a feeling. The sense of belonging to something bigger than oneself must be kinesthetic, not verbal—and certainly can't be conveyed in a staff memo!

Step one: Feel it yourself. Pick a teammate and ask the Canales question, "What can I do for you?" Then make the practice a regular habit!

Step two: Create traditions of unselfishness. We don't mean extraneous traditions along the lines of Secret Santas or Casual Fridays. We mean traditions in work itself. Traditions akin to the one Roy Williams initiated with the Kansas University Jayhawks in 1988. He called it the Gut Check. Just once a year, during preseason, he would walk into the gym and inform everyone, "We're scrapping the practice plan today." They didn't have a chalk talk or execute a single basketball drill. They ran. And ran. And ran. The purpose was to experience the outermost limit of human capability. Some of the guys got to a point of exhaustion at which they could only crawl. They had to keep going until every player puked. KP calls it one of the most unifying exercises he's ever felt.

The significance is not a toughness that any one player learns, though that can be a nice by-product. It's A) the experience of having to find a way to pull your teammates through extreme adversity and having them find a way to pull you through. It's B) an unparalleled *feeling* of being part of the history of the program—a gutsy (literally) accomplishment shared with players from years past, to be shared with players long after graduation.

"To this day," recalls Kevin, "the mere mention of a Gut Check makes me react physically."

Coach Williams didn't have to tell guys the importance of self-actualization or instruct them to pursue it. They ran in self-actualization's basketball shoes. It didn't take long before recruits were coming to Kansas knowing they'd have to do a Gut Check. They signed letters of intent anyway; they wanted to be part of a tradition that strong. To opt for that brutal of an undertaking when you don't have to, when there are other equally good programs and coaches pleading with you to play for them, is ultimate unselfishness—sacrificing your body and pain threshold in the name of prioritizing tradition over yourself.

A startling thing happened when Roy changed schools. In his first team meeting at the helm of the University of North Carolina, one of his players raised a hand.

"Coach," he asked. "Are we going to do a Gut Check?"

The athletes at UNC knew all about the experience before Williams could even bring up the concept. They, too, wanted to be part of something bigger than themselves, bigger than even one school or one program—a member of that special clan of basketball warriors.*

The End of the Bench

Step three: Watch what Duke basketball does. In specific, watch the end of Duke's bench . . . all game long. Preseason, early season, midseason, it doesn't matter; you'd think they were playing in a world championship. They're on the edge of their seats. They're high-fiving and hollering. And they look exactly like the players at the starters' end of the bench. There's no difference between #1 and #12 on the depth chart. When a player comes off the court, every single guy stands up, claps the player off, and pats him on the back. They're all totally engaged; they're all prepared to go in the game. The best way to describe it: they *love* being there.

   BENJAMIN FRANKLIN

We must all hang together, or assuredly, we shall all hang separately.

The year-upon-year excellence of Duke's program isn't defined by the number of blue-chip signees, All-American banners, or player of the week awards. The team's reputation is defined by the very last player on the bench—how that person acts and reacts in all manner of settings and situations. And everyone on the squad knows that is how Coach K is going to measure their culture. Is it any wonder starters go endless extra miles to help walk-ons?

Rhetorical question, eh? It's better if we ask it this way:

"Are you watching what the end of *your* bench does?"

After you get into a Kaleb Canales habit, after you identify and initiate some core work traditions, you need a metric for the execution and impact

---

*Fascinatingly, most fans don't know that a significant cause of the drawn-out length of the 2011 NBA lockout was a desire to correct branding gone awry. The old Celtics-Lakers rivalry–type spirit has been replaced, in recent years, by the LeBron versus Kobe–type rivalry. League marketing has shifted from a team concept to an individual superstar focus. The *players* wanted less selfishness in their image and were willing to extend negotiations as long as it took to work with the owners to get it right.

of these two Help the Helper strategies. That's where the end of the bench comes in. To know whether or not your team is improving in the performance domains of *mudita*, unselfishness, and self-actualization, keep an eye on what the people at the bottom of your org chart are doing. Look for trickle *up*. In other words, a sign that your leaders and superstars aren't practicing Help the Helper actions is that those beneath aren't giving Help the Helper back; they're remaining concerned with their own stage two through four development; they're not practicing stage six need fulfillment.

The same holds true for customers. Customers, it would be wise to think, are teammates in the execution of commerce. Alas, how many times have you seen a company offer a promotion such as this:

REFER A FRIEND!
For every five of your friends who sign up, we'll give you $250!

That's not a Help the Helper policy. That's giving to people only after they've given to you first. Definitely not unselfish. Definitely not creating opportunities for customers to feel that they are part of something bigger than themselves. Companies with the highest referral rates don't offer promotions of this nature. They find ways to help their customers with nothing asked in return. They want their customers to be successful. They assess how well the organization is doing by the degree of unsolicited recommendations and rave reviews customers give back.

Compare that with the service centers at a chain of automobile dealerships in Houston (which we'll keep anonymous). When you drop off your car for maintenance, the service department gives you a handout explaining that you'll receive a third-party call to rate the quality of their work, how well you were treated, and so forth. The handout goes on to explain their 1–5 rating scale, with 5 being the highest accolade. In bold and underlined text, it asks you to please give scores of 5 when you are called! Often, the service manager will ask you personally, "Please remember to give me fives when you get your feedback inquiry!"

Doc responded by selling the vehicle he'd bought from this dealership. How are customers supposed to feel sincerely valued, feel like listened-to members of the commerce partnership, when they are *told* what feedback to give? That's not teamwork. That's customer service dictatorship. And although this is a severe case of it, subtle customer service dictatorship occurs all too frequently, in every sales fine print and call hold time and automated interaction that nonverbally says to people, "We have priorities greater than you." Doc promptly switched his business—gladly taking a financial loss in the transaction—to a competing German automaker with a go-out-of-their-way-to-listen maintenance department. He found it appropriate that the car would be spinning up miles on the odometer for commutes to College Station, Texas, to help Texas A&M Aggie athletic teams in pursuit of national championships. A&M, home since 1876 of the Whoop, Reveille, Midnight Yell, and so, so many more rich traditions, knows a thing or two about being part of something bigger than oneself.

Aggie women's basketball head coach Gary Blair, for instance, has seen a share of adversity that could make any mortal cantankerous. He could easily have become bitter. He witnessed, live, when he was in high school, the assassination of President Kennedy. He served in combat conditions in the marines. He began his coaching career during an era when women played six-on-six hoops with game rules as restricted as women's rights at the time. He's coped with the ups and downs and handcuffing of the NCAA for three decades. Yet he remains the finest of southern gentlemen. He's remained a positive man through the wars. In 2011, he decided to hold himself to an even higher standard of positivity. He started drawing a + symbol on the back of his hand in bold black marker before each match. Not as a simple pregame routine, however. He vowed to continually glance at his hand each minute to

remember that his job as a leader wasn't to demand a good attitude *from* his players; it was to give a good attitude *to* them. His demeanor was his duty to serve.

Three heartwarming escalations followed. A couple of weeks into conference play as he was scanning his bench to plan substitutions, he saw the girls all had + marks on their hands. Less than a week after that, walking onto the court at Reed Arena in College Station, he gazed up into the crowd. A full house of supporters wearing twelfth-man T-shirts . . . and + symbols on their hands! What Gary was giving to the community, they were giving back to him. Six months later, the Aggies found themselves making gallant come-from-behinds against the nation's three biggest powerhouse programs, Baylor, Stanford, and UConn. The girls and coaches could easily have gotten down on themselves when, at game start, they were being beaten up by favored opponents. They instead kept looking at their hands—all the way to the net-cutting ceremony of the 2011 National Championship crown.

Are your clients acting and reacting like Aggie twelfth-man alums? Are employees at all levels of your organization acting and reacting like the end of Duke's bench? Would your superstars act like Drew Bledsoe or David Aardsma? Do you get fiery about extreme teamwork the way Jerry Rice does?

If so, you're succeeding in this chapter's mission. If not, or not to the magnitude of big performance gains à la the Blazers and Rays, try modeling one of the stories on the previous pages. Or try this . . .

YOUR TURN!

"What You're All About" Posters

We've found that a simple, powerfully effective way to become more unselfish is to tell teammates what you're going to do to be better. It says you're engaged. It says you're about doing what it takes to help the team. It gets people excited.

1. Announce this kind of unselfish commitment in the form of a big poster. Use giant easel paper, poster board, foam core, or whatever arts and crafts medium you feel suits your personality. Start at the top of the blank slate by writing a Help the Helper–natured title.

What will the title be? In other words, what succinct phrase best answers the question, "What are you all about?"

_____

Next, make the centerpiece of the poster a list of three things (perhaps with illustrations or other highlighting decoration) you are promising to your teammates that you will do better.

What are they? What do you vow to unselfishly do better?

_____

_____

_____

Finish by tacking up the poster outside your cubicle or office. Then enjoy the Help the Helper discussions, motivations, and inspirations that ensue as your colleagues read it—and as your boss reads it!

2. Role modeling is a fantastic strategy for enhancing extreme teamwork—both your serving as a role model and your studying role models to assist you with your own quest to be the best version of yourself you can be.

Who are the three most unselfish people you know?

_____

_____

_____

What is one action, each, that they do to be unselfish—that you will copy *this* week?

_____

_____

_____

Hire the *Front* of the Jersey

An H2H Culture: Defines the Right Ingredients
Differently from Most Companies

"**H**ire the front of the jersey" is an expression we borrow
from sports to communicate to executives and human
resources managers the emphasis we place on employees
who value the identity of the company over their own. At the USOC,
we call it the "power of the rings"—the performance-altering pride
athletes feel when they don a jacket displaying the Olympic logo or the
words TEAM USA. When Portland's reputation in basketball was being
the "Jail Blazers," Kevin used to wear a golf shirt with the team logo
everywhere he went in public. Many scratched their heads:

"Aren't you embarrassed by the organization's rap? Aren't you worried about what people will think of you?"

Pondering how a corporation's reputation will influence your own
is backward in terms of Help the Helper thinking. We want people
around us who ponder how their reputation can contribute to the
team's. Whenever such a topic came up in conversation about the
Blazers (frequently on airplanes), KP would unswervingly reply, with
fervent passion:

"We're changing that. I'm proud to be part of the process."

We want people on our end of the tug-of-war rope who get more
jazzed about the team name on the front of their uniform than they do

seeing their name sewn on the back. This chapter will tell you why, and even more important, how to get there. It's devoted to what we refer to as Front of the Jersey folks, what we've learned from them, and how to get your team brimming with them.

HERB BROOKS

When you pull on that jersey, you represent yourself and your team-mates. And the name on the front is a hell of a lot more important than the one on the back! Get that through your head!

We commence with a true tale about a fellow we consider to be a Front of the Jersey Hall of Famer.

Grinning All the Way to the Bank

Hanging over the railing at the top of the home dugout steps at Al Lang Stadium in St. Petersburg, Florida, on a sunny late February morning in 2007, the doc stood watching the action, spitting out a steady rhythm of sunflower seed hulls in tune to the din of cracks of wood and pops of leather. Baseball fever was in the air, dashing the doldrums of winter. Spring training games had just commenced. Lockers were double-booked with extra minor league prospects and nonroster invitees.

Any major league camp is an invigorating place to be; the optimism a fresh new season brings combines with the hopes of a host of new faces. The Rays' camp was particularly invigorating. Stuart Sternberg, entering his sophomore campaign as Rays' principal owner, after spending a season studying, listening, gathering information, and conducting due diligence, was ready to make changes. Sweeping changes. An overhaul of Tropicana Field (fresh with a tank of live manta rays for kids to enjoy). Dropping "Devil" from the team name. And putting a performance enhancement specialist in uniform.

Journeyman Carlos Peña sidled up next to Eliot. Peña, an unlikely professional baseball product of Northeastern University (home to six months of snow per annum, New England colleges aren't exactly breeding grounds for the boys of summer), had bounced around the big leagues without enough sustained output to call one city home. Four different teams in six years carried his 100-plus strikeouts, struggles to hit over .220 in batting average, and bottom third of the league on-base percentage. Tampa Bay tendered him a minor league contract in the offseason when nobody else was willing to give him another chance. He was considered an impossible-odds long shot to earn an MLB job.

"Doc, whatcha got for me?" he inquired as he leaned over the post. "I want your help; teach me everything you know."

From that day forward the two would hang over the dugout railing each afternoon talking baseball, first about the mental game, then about success in general and where it comes from. They kept returning to the same three subjects:

1. Great hitters aren't happy, positive people because they're getting on base. It's the reverse.

2. Great performers don't do everything well. They don't try to. They do one or two things *exceptionally* well, love doing so, and don't let limitations in other areas distract or diminish that love.

3. From #1 and #2, they help their teams—without *grinding* to try to help.

"You know what," Peña announced two weeks into the conversation. "This stuff reminds me of Little League. I used to love coming to the ballpark, putting on a uniform, horsing around with my buddies. No worries in the world. I had that feeling briefly with the Tigers a couple years ago; I led the American League in home runs for the month of August. But I wasn't trying to hit home runs. I was just having fun getting in the box, swinging hard. I didn't complicate it or think any more than that."

A distinctive talent of Peña's is his ability to clear his mind, and keep it clear, under pressure. At tense moments, such as 0-2 or full count or trailing in the ninth inning with the tying run on second and two outs, he can relax his hands better than anyone in the business. Another talent is his smile. His ear-to-ear grins, as demonstrative as the shots he puts into the bleachers, instantly put you in a good mood when you see him.

He'd gotten away from using either talent. His career, like that of many conscientious people who strive to do their best, had hit a snag of trying to live up to every expectation of paycheck signers. He had been trying to perfect every well-intentioned piece of mechanics instruction, trying to cut down on strikeouts, trying to garner and hold on to playing time, trying to be the complete "five-tool" player scouts hype.

"Starting today," Peña said, "I'm going back to being that kid who totally loved competing. If I strike out, I strike out. As long as I'm having fun, I'm going to be happy. I'm going to be the happiest man in pro ball."

His demeanor did a 180. He hit two bombs that day. He also struck out; the grin didn't leave his mug even for a second. It was a permanent fixture in the clubhouse and on the field for the remainder of spring training. When camp broke on April 1, the Rays extended Carlos a spot on the major league roster.

At this juncture in the story, most people assume the promotion must be a result of an impressive number of round-trippers or some similar gaudy statistic to make the front office giddy. Peña launched zero more balls out of the park. He hit .214. One of the team's *pitchers* had a higher batting average! Moneyball proponents weigh in: Peña must have had attention-grabbing OWS figures, right? Negligible. As a point of reference regarding Peña's Moneyball worth, the A's had him when he was a hot farm prospect and the baseball world judged him the frontrunner for AL Rookie of the Year. Billy Beane jettisoned him less than two months into that season. Utterly overvalued, Beane explained.

A word of encouragement manager Joe Maddon offered says it all. As the squad entered Yankee Stadium for batting practice on Opening Day, he pulled Carlos aside walking up to the cage. Holding Carlos firmly by the arm, looking him squarely in the eye, Joe paused—a pregnant pause, interrupting thoughts that might be rattling away, creating a significance to the exchange. In the sincerest of voices, he coached:

"You can hit a buck fifty and I won't take you out of the lineup. Don't stop doing what you've been doing."

Over the years, Maddon's squirreled away a few pearls for making teams tick. As a roving hitting coordinator for the (then California) Angels, he observed that players would tighten up when he'd come to town. They wanted to impress the boss. They'd listen too intently to coaching minutiae; they'd get too mechanical. When it comes to execution, a busy brain, thinking technically or analytically, is tracking the wrong objective. It's keyed in on perfectionism rather than playing hard. Joe responded by crafting motivational T-shirts. On the front was a baseball, vividly animated, with wide eyes and a torqued mouth, scorching through the air, screaming. In bold print, the shirts read:

I GOT LOUD!

If you hit a liner absolutely "on the screws," as the baseball expression goes, and make an out, you have nothing to show for your handiwork. Your stats drop. Joe would counter human nature and statistical thinking habits by telling you, "You got loud!" And he'd give you a T-shirt. The guys dug it. They liked wearing the tops during BP and rating which balls were loud coming off the bat. It increased communication during pregame, which is a time when it's easy for athletes to get quiet, too caught up in their own thoughts. It also reinforced focusing on productive *Approach QUALITY* (good swings and good contact) instead of counterproductive *Outcome QUANTITY* (hit tallies and batting averages).

Two decades later Maddon was still sticking to his guns. If the Rays were going to become a playoff contender, they had to believe they could beat the wallet-thick, All-Star-laden, division-powerhouse Red Sox and Yankees. If they were going to believe that, coming from the we-can't-win cellar the franchise had been languishing in since inception, they had to have the kind of psychological talent that wouldn't be deterred by a loss, bad outing, or getting lunch handed to you in an at bat. As Joe astutely recognized, what they needed was what Carlos Peña did best. Which meant maintaining his spring training dedication to an analysis-free mind, relaxed hands, and shining Chiclets. Especially the shining Chiclets—being the happiest man in baseball, Peña's favorite topic of banter. The getting-on-base part hadn't yet materialized as a consequence. Maddon knew it would if Carlos held faith in banter topics number two and three—prioritizing his core differentiating skills, letting that define him, and not trying to carry the team. That's why he made the message of backing Carlos, no matter what, so emphatic.

Peña came out of the chute cold, dipping below the .200 Mendoza line by the end of April, a measly four home runs in the power column. His beam never faded. If you didn't know the box score, you'd assume from his body language that he was leading the league in the full gamut of offensive specialties. Maddon stayed true to his word: 0 for 4 nights, grounding into multiple double plays, the golden sombrero of three Ks in a game—none relegated Peña to the bench. Poor performances meant Carlos had to be all the more steadfast in his process.

He was. So was Maddon. In May, fruit finally started blossoming for their seed-planting efforts. Peña ripped off a .365 BA tear, rocketing six HRs and fifteen RBI in a three-week span. His sabermetric-swooning .414

OBP rolled right through into August and September, .402 and .443 clips, respectively, to come to rest ranked in MLB's top five on-base percentages. He notched career highs in eleven capacities.

The beauty was that Carlos didn't know!

Packing up in the wake of the season finale in Toronto, after a win over the Blue Jays, a teammate walked over to Peña's stall to shake his hand. "Hey, man, congrats. Fifth best in baseball getting on the sacks; solid."

No signature smile in response. Carlos merely raised his eyebrows. "I was!?"

CP was too intent on being successful in exercising the traits he'd committed to back in March. Not noticing individual achievement was a marker of how extraordinary his talents really were, as well as his adeptness at concentrating on what matters most.

There was an additional marker, more subtle—more important. In the waning months of the season, when the Rays were already mathematically eliminated from the postseason, twenty-plus games behind in the Wild Card race, fan attendance at the Trop *rose*. Earlier in the year, Tampa hosted the Red Sox and barely seventeen thousand people showed up. In September when the BoSox came to town, more than thirty-four thousand turned the stiles. Ticket interest had *doubled*. Twice as many fans wanted to watch an out-of-contention team for the duration of the final month (822,007) as wanted to watch in May (410,659), when the Rays were in the hunt.

What kindled the flame? The answer is crucial to our understanding of organizational turnarounds and the rooting of extreme teamwork cultures. Three very important elements were given priority attention.

ELEMENT ONE: Peña's imperviousness to negatives, from striking out to losing a ballgame, affected his mates. When you regularly go to work alongside someone who is in a good mood, your own mood lifts. It's called "emotional contagion" in the research literature. As discovered by social neuroscience pioneer John Cacioppo, a distinguished University of Chicago professor, humans have a hardwired, subconscious inclination to mimic pronounced facial expressions, postures, expressive jargon, and nonverbal gestures, and thereby the emotions tied to them. Specific cells are designated in the brain to trigger this; they're called mirror neurons. You've likely experienced them at work, "catching" a yawn when someone else yawns and then suddenly feeling tired yourself. That's emotional contagion in action. It explains the phenomenon of Rays employees' (and not solely those on the diamond) imitating #23's spirit.

Emotional contagion is an element of every sizable corporate leap we've studied. In each case, there are team members who infuse a definable performance-facilitating tone. But it's not bowl-you-over, in-your-grill, or mandated behavior. It's more of a personal commitment that seeps from person to person.

Wall Street thought Steve Jobs was crazy when he announced the launching of Apple Stores. Apple had only four products; how would they fill the shelves of a retail outlet? They didn't. The plan wasn't to provide a buying center. It was to provide an ownership experience. Senior vice president Ron Johnson headed the initiative by exhaustively studying constructs like emotional contagion. He put unprecedented dollars into a novel concept: a mock store in a warehouse, operating as a kind of flight simulator, testing influences of the store's design and personnel. They learned that employees' own fondness for using Apple products was one of the strongest predictors of success. As a result, they now only hire frontline workers who are avid Apple users—to such a degree that the percentage of hires from applicant pools is as low as Ivy League admission rates! The enthusiasm these young men and women communicate, without intentionally trying to do so, has considerable impact on customers' enthusiasm for buying and using Apple products. Apple Stores now account for more than $10 billion in annual revenue for the company. Emotional contagion, in fact, is *the* beating heart of the success of the iPhone.

Nutty lines at Apple Stores in reaction to the launch of each new iPhone seem like instantaneous emotional capitalization. But remember, the first iPhone was predicated on over a year of ramp-up teasers, user testing, and an internal love affair courting process. It takes a while for emotional contagion to proliferate organically. Just as it took a while for the majority of the folks in Tampa to realize that nothing was going to make Carlos quit grinning. It eventually caught on. By September, a clubhouse previously characterized by players as a black hole for optimism—"the place winners go to die," commented one—was a place of growing enthusiasm. Guys on the bench began standing up at the entrance to the dugout instead of sitting down in the shadows. Strides onto and off the field were getting discernibly springier.

ELEMENT TWO: Building a Help the Helper culture requires systematic, performance-facilitating trait development. For a trait (such as unselfishness or toughness) to become a success-driving tool, it must be strengthened, honed, and polished. It must be practiced deliberately.

That means strategically small, targeted areas for implementation and stepwise evaluation of progress.

Had the Rays gunned from the get-go for everyone to follow Peña's and Maddon's lead in optimism and process-mindedness, had the goal been to triumph in all facets of the game, they would have failed. That was the pattern of the previous regime under GM Chuck LaMar. Sign a bunch of proven veterans who'd won a World Series (Wade Boggs, Fred McGriff, and the like), plop in a vociferous manager (Lou Piniella), and voilà, instant winning culture. It doesn't work that way. You need to identify a specific, focused list of traits—not traditional measures of talent—to cultivate. Then you need to select precise, incremental areas where you aim for those traits to generate initial returns.

For the reinvented Rays, that initial building block was late-in-game, pressure-induced character checks. Save pennant chase atmosphere, nothing is more thrilling than winning in dramatic, extra-inning fashion, or the nail biting of a one-run, all-the-marbles-on-the-line ninth. In our studies, we've learned that data surrounding single-run-margin matches tells us more about team psychology than any alternative quantitative metric. In 2007, up to mid-August, Tampa Bay had the lowest incidence of one-run games in the American League, 16 total (out of 162 possible). Conversely, they battled to the ninth inning, final out on 17 occasions in the 40 remaining contests. That's an edge-of-your-seat cliffhanger nearly every alternating night—in which they notched a winning record, 10-7! They also won every extra-inning game in the concluding two months of the season. Fans took notice. Though their hometown boys wouldn't be suiting up that October, they were exciting to watch.

ELEMENT THREE: Sternberg and the executive suite stepped up to the plate. Rather than leverage the fresh bolus of gate revenue to acquire the hottest free agents on the market, they used the offseason to *release* talented-on-paper players. A number of the cuts and trades were not sound financial moves. Fixating on the balance sheet doesn't engender teamwork; often it's just the opposite.

It was vital, heading into 2008, to stoke the momentum instigated by Peña's attitude and bolstered by Maddon's coaching. Leadership was not about the front office providing answers. It was about asking a question organization-wide: "Who's on the bus?" Who is making an approach like Peña's a priority? Who is putting the traits defining the team's one-run and extra-inning wins in front of statistics, records, and individual kudos? Who is proud to wear the TB logo even though the franchise isn't winning yet? Who is having as much fun as Carlos in the process? The front office axed the players who weren't, no matter how productive, popular, or full of potential those players were. They went scouring for players who'd love to be on the new type of bus. Fernando Perez, Cliff Floyd, J. P. Howell, David Price, and Grant Balfour are a few examples—guys who'd jump right in when Peña commenced a tradition of dancing in the dugout before games.

The tipping point was hit. Tampa went from dead last, to finding a source of Help the Helper leadership, to emotional contagion, to a targeted build an explicit domain, to asking who's on the bus, to more emotional contagion, to the World Series.

Today people think of Carlos Peña as one of the sport's most feared long-ball threats. A dazzling image comes to mind of flashbulbs exploding as his towering shots took to the sky in the Home Run Derby. But it's insightful to note that he didn't capture an individual Big Fly trophy or earn All-Star honors until 2009, a year *after* the team succeeded. In the epic 2008 campaign, #23's statistics were *lower* than in 2007 in *every* single category. So were a majority of the Rays starters'. The team as a unit put up diminished figures in every impact column:

	H	HR	RBI	BA	OBP	SLG
2007†	1500	187	750	.268	.340	.433
2008‡	1443	180	735	.260	.336	.422

† Worst in MLB   ‡ AL Champions

In 2008, the Rays were at or below league average in each of these classifications. The top five OBP teams were watching from their living rooms while Tampa played in the Fall Classic. So much for sabermetrics predicting who will rise to the challenge. *You* have to do that.

R. MEREDITH BELBIN

Do you want a collection of brilliant minds? Or a brilliant collection of minds?

Who's on the Bus?

Mathematics don't yet exist for calculating team cohesion, namely the sort of cohesion that produced the 1950 Miracle Match (when a bunch of no-body U.S. soccer players upset No. 1 England in the World Cup), the 1954 Milan Miracle (the tiny-town Indiana high school basketball story that inspired the movie *Hoosiers*), the 1969 Miracle Mets, and the 1980 Miracle on Ice. To be the next made-for-the-movies miracle, or to just stand out as your industry's leader in teamwork, you're going to have to put down your abacus to ask the question, "Who's on the bus?" You're going to have to take a cue from USA Hockey coaching legend Herb Brooks.

In assembling a team to pit against the indomitable Russians, Brooks held an exhaustive tryout. He watched; he calculated; he picked care-fully. When the final Olympic roster was posted, it wasn't stocked full of the country's best players. Administrators and assistants second-guessed Brooks furiously. He let them rant. And then pragmatically said:

"I'm not lookin' for the best players. I'm lookin' for the right players."

Therein lies an important lesson concerning the limits of analytics for building winning organizations. To channel Aristotle, the whole is greater than the sum of its parts. Referencing teams like the 1942 De-troit Red Wings, 1978 Washington Redskins, 2003 Minnesota Vi-kings, 2010 France World Cup footballers, and the 2011 Boston Red Sox (five of the biggest collapses in the chronicles of sport): the whole can also be substantially *less* than the sum of its parts.

The chief mediating variable, of course, is teamwork. The Yankees' compiling as many A-Rod superstars as possible and the A's compiling as many blistering on-base percentages as possible is actually the same fundamental strategy. It's "best" collection. It's hiring and promoting based on individual valuation . . . and hoping championship chemistry emerges. Spawning extreme teamwork as a by-product, *that* takes a miracle—far more of a miracle than hockey gold in Lake Placid. Not to take anything away from the history-shaping efforts of our boys in red, white, and blue, but the 1980 coup of coups was less "miraculous" than you might think. It was, in fact, craftily designed. Herb Brooks was a master at engendering Help the Helper leadership, commencing with how extraordinarily well thought out the roster was—how much time and effort went into, ahead of time, isolating the precise ingredients needed for that particular group, in that particular context, to jell, to lift each other's capacities and outputs.

Brooks was asking, in a highly proactive manner, "Who's going to get on the bus?" He was taking the critical step toward a Help the Helper culture of harvesting real talent: identifying a finite group of traits to define the makeup of the team, to place higher in priority than individual productivity.

Equally critical, his answer did not hinge on genetics. Real talent, when it comes to remarkable team feats, is not the stuff of callisthenic tests or SATs. If you subscribe to the school of thought that speed, strength, IQ, musical genius, photographic memory, height, reaction time, and their various ilk are responsible for distinguishing those who are world class from the rest, we adamantly suggest you snatch up a copy of our compadre Geoff Colvin's recent book, *Talent Is Overrated*. Colvin does a Pulitzer-worthy job of compiling and elucidating centuries of investigation into what really separates the Mozarts, Tiger Woodses, and Warren Buffetts of history. As he deftly pens:

> *"The gifts possessed by the best performers are not at all what we think they are [page 6]. . . . Whatever it is that makes these people special, it does not depend on superhuman general abilities [page 7]. . . . The chief constraint is mental, regardless of the field—even in sports, where we might think the physical demands are the hardest [page 8]."*

Geoff would enjoy getting to know Carlos Peña.

Had Peña been born twenty years earlier, Herb Brooks would surely have recruited Carlos to play ice hockey.

Consider how far from normal it is for a grown man, a tough-guy professional athlete no less, to do a rendition of *American Bandstand* on the field before competition. It's even farther from normal to engage in such silliness before the biggest games of the season, the biggest games of one's career. Such circumstances are replete with tension. Competitiveness, seriousness, testosterone are in order. So why was the muscle Carlos flexed in the dugout, prior to each pennant-chasing game in 2008, dance-floor muscle?

Simple. Staying cool when pressure spikes isn't normal. Welcoming and enjoying a cacophony of butterflies in your stomach isn't normal. Zippo self-consciousness when millions of eyeballs are on you, and zippo concern for the bottom line when millions of dollars are at stake, isn't normal. Performers use parameters like these to describe something else that isn't normal: an elusively rare state we call "The Zone" in which time slows down, physics seems to bend to your will, and world records are broken. The Zone is abnormal. Its characteristics are highly abnormal.

It's no secret; pursue normalcy and you won't get into The Zone.

Peña doesn't have an ounce of interest in being normal. He literally dances to a different tune. For six years he tried the tune most professional baseball players download; he tried the tune of Moneyball. He tried too hard to adopt common wisdom and fit into a model of what an elite hitter is supposed to look like and supposed to post for numbers. It was coming to grips with a functional, operational understanding of abnormality that created the opportunity for him—in other words, that separation-factor talents aren't box-score items; separation-factor talents are the *roots* of the performances of box-score items. When that clicked, opportunity turned into a vaulting platform for the Rays with Peña pinpointing his talents, perfecting them, and pursuing them relentlessly.

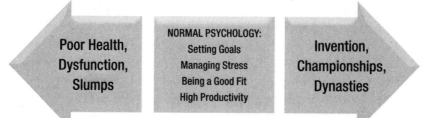

That's exactly what Brooks did as well: first pinpointing traits that would flourish by charging an iron curtain, then perfecting those traits, pursuing them relentlessly with no regard for Vegas odds, the scoreboard (including the Soviets' 6–0 rout of the NHL All-Star team), or the weeks of discouraging sparring results (including getting crushed 10–3 by the USSR at Madison Square Garden in a "home" hosted warm-up exhibition) leading up to the Games.*

If you want extreme teamwork, it's what you need to do, too. Identify two to four traits, the abnormal type with respect to what is tradi-

---

*We consider it imperative to draw attention here to Brooks's locker-room speeches. The fantasy of movies, à la the pre-period "you were meant to be here" scene in *Miracle*, is that rousing pep talks are the tool great leaders use to bring out the best in their people. In reality, great leaders like Brooks rely substantially more on talking to their employees and colleagues individually, asking them what they are about, personally discussing inner strength, inviting them to drive the bus long before critical pressure situations present themselves.

tionally labeled and lauded as talent—traits at the *source* of performance (not just variables that score performance). If you construct and maintain a roster of employees who are interested in being comfy, stress free, settled nicely into the pack—normal—then that's what you're going to get. Results will be normal; you'll build a purely average company. If you want something more special than that, go looking for Front of the Jersey people; don't wait for them to come to you!

Who's *Not* on the Bus?

Look for Help the Helpers whom you can bring into your organization anew. But look inside your organization to an equivalent extent. Engaging in the pursuit of employee excellence shouldn't be restricted to filling job vacancies. Companies that pride themselves upon truly special teamwork use the Front of the Jersey analogy with current staff as much as they do in seeking new hires. As referenced in the footnote about Coach Brooks, team unison stems largely from individual conversations, well in front of crucial deadlines or deliverables, regarding what causes people to get on your bus, what keeps people on your bus, what causes people to get off your bus. We find ourselves repeatedly borrowing from Stephen Covey: "Seek first to understand." We'll dig into that concept in greater depth in chapter 4, but we feel it's essential to bring up a brief aside here. We want to call attention to the fact that "who's on the bus" is just as much about listening as it is about looking.

Scan down the roster of your team. Push yourself hard: How much have you chatted with each person to really know where their heart is? Surely there are a handful of folks who are already, absolutely on the bus. They love wearing the company logo. They're your version of Kaleb Canales. Surely there are also a handful of folks who aren't on the bus. Maybe you can let a couple go. Maybe you can't. Either way, our challenge to you is to be the ultimate Help the Helper leader: take the initiative to go to them to see if you can understand; see if you can find a way to help them get on the bus. Go work for *them*. Be a bus-driving facilitator instead of merely handing out or revoking bus tickets.

Perhaps they won't get on the bus. Perhaps there's a different bus (in a different division, or with a different employer altogether) that would light them up and bring out their best. Help them get on that bus. Or perhaps they aren't as skilled as you'd like or want. It's important to reflect that the most successful companies we've studied are rarely a collection of valedictorians. They win because they have a greater percentage of people—along the full continuum of skills and abilities—on the bus than do their competitors. It's not that they have every hand in their unit pulling the tug-of-war rope; it's that they have a greater percentage pulling in the same direction than do their competitors. Remember, a Help the Helper culture is not about doing things perfectly. It's about doing things better. It's about a collective excitement, an emotional contagion that grows from piling up small steps taken in an extreme teamwork direction. And that includes doing a better job of understanding who's not on the bus, why, and what you can do to help them.

The Fallacy of Assessing "Good Fit"

When we explain, in lectures, the concept of asking who's on the bus, audiences tend to leap to an association with their current organizational practices:

"Oh, you're talking about assessing hires to see if they are a good fit. We do that."

Folks who mention the colloquial "good fit" are typically referring to job interviews' serving as a litmus test to gauge how well prospective employees will get along with existing staff. Sometimes candidates are paraded around the office, shaking hands, as if thirty-second meet-and-greets will provide revelations. Sometimes it's a day-slogging lineup of subinterviews (with VPs, HR directors, a veritable who's-who sampling of the company directory). By the time a potential hire is finished being "on," intense half hour after intense half hour, exhausted from the effort of trying to say all the right things, do we really think we've obtained an accurate window into his or her personality? Sometimes it's a stack of pencil-and-paper personality tests (which, as we'll explain in chapter 8, have near zero predictive validity). Sometimes it boils down to the CEO's taking a prospect out for a long lunch, scrutinizing table manners, posture, order style, food choice, and humor meter in reaction to the boss's lame jokes. And we believe this covers the performance intangibles that make people shine in their work? Honestly?

All nice-sounding lip service, making those involved in the process feel like they are taking action to promote teamwork. But a bunch of bunkum when it comes to excellence. A teamwork hallucination resulting from Front of the Jersey elements being brought into the equation at the *end* of the hiring process. At best, you propagate a fine little working environment. Everyone seems to get along well enough. Your team communicates okay. Project managers are reporting that their groups' deadlines are being met. Quality control indicators suggest that "good fit" methodology works fine. Those indices are exactly correct. Results are fine. You are effectively attaining the norm in your industry; you'll continue trading wins with your competitors.

For people like Herb Brooks and Carlos Peña, that's not satisfying. If your tactic for assembling teams is to check off the "good fit" box, they'll go hitch a ride on a better bus. Good fit procedures, as well intentioned as they are, come up short of the substance of 1980 USA Hockey and the 2008 AL Champion Rays for four reasons:

1. It's an ad hoc approach. You have a short-lister already selected, you've gathered the data (résumé, references, past performances), and *then* you ask the research question, "Is he or she a good fit?" Scientists will tell you, ad hoc assessment provides weak, often problematic, conclusions. The stronger, more reliable approach is a priori—coming up with the question and specific variables *before* selecting subjects.

2. It puts culture last. By the time you get to exploring "fit" at the interview stage, you've passed over the majority of candidates. Exceedingly, as unemployment rates climb, you have to pare hundreds (perhaps thousands) of cover letters down to one, two, maybe three choices. It's an uncommon organization that makes those cuts based on the traits and talents we're discussing in this chapter. Granted, a large number of applicants may not meet minimum standards. But out with the proverbial bathwater go performers like Mike Eruzione, the heart and soul of the '80 Olympic team, who didn't stand out on paper in any manner whatsoever and whose stat line prior to the Games was at, or even below, average in many areas.

3. It uses the wrong metrics. How a person carries him or herself when having lunch for the very first time with their hoped soon-to-be boss, for example, is considerably artificial. Speech is filtered. Posture is constrained. "Smart" entrées are ordered. Behavior in interviews is anything but a reflection of who a person *really* is, inside, where it counts. Carlos Peña would never dance during a formal, staged tryout; as conscientious human beings do in that situation, he'd be attending to appearances—doing the "right" things. Scouts' observations would therefore be inaccurately recording his leadership potential. To boot, there are scores of performers, truly remarkable at helping teammates, who don't do well when put in the spotlight. In other words, they are gifted at propelling their teams in part because they don't want the credit, because they are ultimate Help the Helpers. Ipso facto, interview conditions will have the reverse effect rather than bringing out their best.

4. It's overgeneralized. When we ask hiring executives what they mean by "good fit," we get a collage of feel-good sound bites, a haphazard hodgepodge of personality adjectives. We hear decision makers in the same division of the same company, who both interview prospects, flying from the seat of their pants and recognizing *opposite* characteristics! One says, "Good fit is a worker who appeases colleagues; we don't want a gang of contrarians around here." The other says, "Good fit is someone who challenges colleagues; we don't want a flock of yes-men." Extreme teamwork doesn't arise without a *defined* set of concrete, premeditated descriptors.

"Good fit" making intuitive sense, as well as being the language of many decently successful companies, creates selection bias. Coping with stress, for instance, is an aptitude included in many a hiring criterion profile. Sitting under the microscope of corporate bigwigs who are firing intentionally uncomfortable questions at you and evaluating your every word is stressful. Therefore, the thinking goes, "character interviews" (as they're dressed up) will expose who's "got it." This logic violates all four principles above. Yet, because a famous Fortune 500 company or the latest IPO success utilized it, the strategy is considered effectual. Not analyzed is data on hundreds of start-up flops, IPO failures, bankruptcies, and fall-from-grace Fortune 500s that tackled team chemistry the very same way (not to mention all the companies doing moderately well that have great products and services, but aren't leading their industry).

How many corporations can you think of that are profitable, humming along just fine, but not truly special? Often what's holding them back are assessment methodologies that impede identifying Front of the Jersey or Help the Helper mentalities—assessments that are also susceptible to being "gamed" almost as easily as a job candidate would change his or her behavior to say the right things or order the right meal at an interview lunch.

One major technology consulting firm that recruits across the Ivy League and top-tier schools was well known for its behavioral-based interview approach. The firm had Wall Street credit. But its interviews were poster children of "good fit fallacy" principles 2 and 3 as well as being highly subject to gaming. Our friend John Katen (who is legitimately brilliant and did *not* game his interview) was hired by this firm. He soon confirmed what we know to be true of these "stuck in the middle" companies. He witnessed a large contingent of high-skill people functioning below their talents. He witnessed a high attrition rate. Once an insider, Katen was exposed to the formulaic underpinnings of the firm's hiring approach. In his first few years, John learned of a number of new hires who had been coached by friends already employed there—coached on the right key words to drop and the right examples to give so interviewers would check the boxes necessary to extend lucrative job offers. What's worse? The interview approach was designed to give high marks to *back of the jersey* behavior and low marks to Front of the Jersey behavior.

This firm had invested, no exaggeration, millions of dollars into the "science" of interviewing. The return on that investment was (1) an approach no more effective than simply hiring based on college grade point average, (2) extensive mediocrity in productivity results compared with what their hires were capable of, and (3) lots of turnover!

"I said at the interview I was honest and hardworking - I never said I was competent."

Why didn't they alter their practices? They were falling prey to today's ever-so-common assumption that sabermetrics-style personality checkbox hiring devices equate to enviable teamwork. They *assumed* they were gathering the best employees and *assumed* those employees were giving their best, based on effort sunk into a test. In the hiring process, they weren't actually sinking effort into people. After the hiring process, they relied on positive numbers to convey information about teamwork. The company was profitable. People must be working together, right? Only they were doing just the minimum working together required by their job descriptions. The organization wasn't innovating, leading new developments in its industry, or setting any records.

Profitability can be accomplished by amassing a crew of "good fits" and salting them with human resources seminars. Innovation and record setting takes a concerted, pound-the-pavement personnel search.

Playing Pickup

So what do you do? You don't wait for job applications to fill your inbox, that's for sure. You don't put on a snappy suit and hit the job expo circuit, collecting résumés. You don't even posture your way into prime billing during Ivy League corporate recruiting season. You absolutely need to be farther out in front of your market opponents than that. And you need to be proactively gathering, testing, and double-checking the two to four traits you specifically nailed down as the right kind of talent for the culture you are building. Extreme teamwork doesn't abruptly show up one morning on divine inspiration; people who make up extreme teams don't wander through your door randomly. You've gotta go get 'em!

Creating a version of Olympic trials or spring training for your organization would knock your foes on their ass. You needn't go that big, though, to start getting the right people on the bus. You can do just what Herb Brooks did—by taking initiative as simple as playing hoops. Pickup sports contests reveal enormous amounts about character in a very short amount of time. Instead of months and months of trying to get your hands around key Help the Helper traits of potential hires, you can learn the same amount in just a couple hours on the court. Play some basketball!

This suggestion makes us recall KP's days playing pickup with Oral Roberts basketball assistant coach Tom Hankins.

To be honest, Tom wasn't tremendously athletic; he didn't shoot lights out. But the son of a gun won every game he played. Pickup against old farts, in the inner city where a busted nose isn't a foul, on eight-foot goals . . . even Wiffle Ball! He was the *best* at being a teammate.

He was a heck of a teammate for a number of reasons: (1) No matter what the circumstance, or what was riding on a game, he defended like it was Game 7 of the NBA Finals. Up by 30 points in a meaningless summer game, he'd put himself in harm's way to take a hard charge. (2) He figured out the uniqueness of every venue, such as YMCAs back then having no three-point line, but layups worth only one point. He did the calculations and would always be prepared; he'd provide his teammates with homework and show them how to take advantage of the information. (3) He has what we call the "Adapter Trait." (4) When he picked his teams, it was never about statistics; he always took the guys who would do the dirty work, like rebounding. (5) He was willing to do whatever it took to win. In particular, he'd watch to see what jobs his teammates weren't good at or didn't particularly want to do and, no matter how uninspiring or difficult those jobs were, he'd volunteer to do them.

KP was a 150-pound sophomore. One time he had to guard a beast, a physical specimen that would make Moses Malone look skinny.

Hankins came over and said, "Kev, I got 'im. You go score."

He was *always* like that.

Playing hoops like this brings character to the surface. It doesn't take long to discern who on the court has teamwork ingredients unlisted in box scores. When you play with guys like Tom, you know immediately that they're Help the Helpers you'd want to have with you if you were going into a brawl. Pickup, since rules aren't as constrained and the game is more wide open, emphasizes intangibles—the types of traits this chapter is dialing in on. For that reason, we urge you to explore opportunities to trade out traditional job candidate screening (at the least, a segment or one portion of screening procedures) and substitute some team sport competition.

 PLATO

You can discover more about a person in an hour of play than in a year of conversation.

Of course, as evident as it is that playing pickup reveals tremendous awareness regarding a person's *performance character*, one might be tempted to slough off the notion of actually putting prospective (and current) employees on a basketball court. Only a percentage may be athletes or in good enough fitness, few have played much basketball in their life, injury potential is too high, and so forth. We'll concede there are a handful of constraints. But we won't concede our recommendation to try it. The "it's not realistic" excuse is you communicating to us that you're not entirely willing to do what it takes to be the best. The good news is that few, few people are. If we can therefore get you over this hump, we can help you vault teamwork the way we did in Portland and Tampa. Getting away from the "winning is the measure of achievement" mentality is important. That's why the Rays seem to be more successful than the Blazers, but it's the cultural 180 of both franchises that is the real success story. That both organizations win more games now is a notable and desired by-product.

Hooping it up is still unfeasible? We bet there's at least one competitive sport that isn't. How about golf? Though not quite as telling in domains such as response to fatigue, clock-affected decision making, close-quarter teammate interaction, and Help the Helper efforts and tendencies, there is still plenty of margin on the links to learn how someone reacts to failure.

Failure, it turns out, is a key to solving the "Who's on the bus?" inquiry. Thanks to our work in pro sport, we've been able to survey a wide cross-section of scouts and scouting departments in the NBA, NFL, NHL, and MLB over the past twenty years. What we've learned might surprise you. Two distinctions are the envy of most franchises: (1) Finishing at the top of league standings with bottom-of-the-league payroll. (2) Repeat championships. Notable is that the organizations that achieve these conquests tend to outperform others in a unique dimension. They tend to be more successful at ferreting out athletes who have a knack for dealing with failure in positive and productive fashions. How do they do this? Upon closer inspection, we've found that these organizations, to a greater extent than their opponents, pay heed to athletes' worst performances. They *like* to watch prospects having an off day, missing shots, making mistakes.

It's a tad counterintuitive. To beachcomb for future all-stars, it follows that spotting all-star output would be a good thing. Scouts with the most impressive track records will be quick to tell you, though: anyone can look great when they are playing great. It's easy to have an excellent head on your shoulders when life is gravy. Life is seldom gravy (we type, knowing how much of an understatement it is).

No matter how freakishly focused or dexterous, everyone will drop the ball, numerous times in their careers at that. People who excel when there is a chance of falling flat on their face, severe penalties awaiting, are those who've A) had ample experience in similar pressure situations, and B) learned how to bounce back stronger if failure does come to pass. Those who are part of Help the Helper cultures want teammates around them who are adroit at handling the unpleasant side of competing at a high level. Talented scouts know this. So they go searching for it; they want to witness it. They want to watch how kids respond to the age-old prizefighting query:

You just got hit. Now what are you going to do?

Raptly competitive team sport settings make such responses outstandingly transparent, providing a clear picture of who's-on-the-bus characteristics.*

BILL RUSSELL

Concentration and mental toughness are the margins of victory.

If you prefer, you can apply the same core principle to construct non-sport routes to reach the same ends. You can follow the lead of Virginia Tech's Carilion School of Medicine, for example. Carilion is the nation's newest medical school; its inaugural class matriculated in August 2010. Founders were aware that, as a brand-new institution in a centuries-old trade, establishing a reputation for training world-class doctors would be an uphill battle. Going head-to-head with Harvard, Johns Hopkins, and their brethren to recruit top students would initially be a losing proposition. Spearheaded by Dean Cynda Ann Johnson, charter faculty probed research for current graduate education trends germane to health care outcomes. If they were going to climb this mountain of designing a school to produce leading physicians, they'd better have empirical knowledge of the steepest parts of the mountain.

---

*It's important to note: if you use a game like golf, you need to put something on it. A friendly match, strolling around a golf course, is no different from a traditional job interview. It needs to be fully competitive, as much like pickup basketball as you can make it.

Reading about a discovery by oncologist Harold Reiter, chair of M.D. admissions at McMaster University in Ontario, ignited a light bulb. Dr. Reiter's study of medical admission procedures found that professors interviewing students formulate evaluations within five minutes, irrespective of conversation content or duration. Revelations past the five-minute mark in a discussion rarely change interview scores. Reiter's conclusion: the component of the doctor identification process that reaches deeper than MCATs and biology grades has been amounting to a handshake and a first impression!

Virginia Tech administrators were alarmed. Aptly so. Being a smarty pants who can memorize every bone and tissue in the body, all in a single afternoon sitting, while munching on biscotti, is handy for smoking college exams. It's of meager bearing, though, on skill in caring for the sick. To offer a mere whisper of a list of imperative hospital duties: bedside manner, collegial cooperation, attentiveness, genuine empathy, coordinating chaos in the OR, negotiating with insurance carriers, and delivering bad news. Yet research shows, our finest ivory towers are weighting numbers that look good on paper as infinitely more valuable than interpersonal skills—for a profession that comes down to some of the most personal of all human interactions, such as having to tell someone they're dying of cancer.

The kicker: research is divulging that in the bulk of health disciplines, communication errors are the leading cause of malpractice, accounting for nearly 100,000 annual deaths!

Integrating the findings, in collaboration with Reiter and others, Virginia Tech devised a new system to vet future physicians. They tossed out reliance on standardized tests, swapping in a medical rendition of pickup basketball. In what they call a multiple mini interview (MMI), med school prospects spend a morning role-playing real dilemmas. Candidates for admission line up in a hallway of doors to intake rooms, not unlike runners lining up for a marathon start. Under the gun of limited time, a bell rings and each candidate heads to a separate door where brief scenario backgrounds are posted. They get a skimpy few seconds to read the sketch before entering the room, where waits an actor (usually a highly experienced nurse or health care worker) portraying a complicated case, a difficult patient, a diversity or language barrier, a diagnosis problem, an angry colleague, or an ethical conundrum. Students have less than ten minutes to greet the subject, gather information, discuss the presenting situation, and establish a rapport. The bell rings again and the aspiring physicians rotate to the next room.

Brrrng; switch. *Brrrng;* switch. And so forth, at bat after at bat, without time-outs. The "actors" keep score and take notes on students' performances, creating a live competition atmosphere.

There are no right and wrong answers in the MMI; it's not a test of trade information. As Carilion's administrators point out, the profoundly important part is how students respond when they hit an obstacle, when they have trouble relating, when someone disagrees with them or challenges them, or when exhaustion sets in. Sounds like what the shrewdest NBA and NFL scouts are hungriest to observe, eh? Indeed. Less than two years into the pilot program, MMIs are proving to be so proficient at snagging real talent that twenty-one medical schools are already copying the model, including ranking toppers Stanford, Berkeley, and UCLA. A Pac-12 medical unit extreme teamwork arms race is brewing. . . .

A Lesson from Pro Scouting

Is it hard to implement pickup basketball games or MMI role playing or some substitute form of competitive tryout to make Help the Helper traits more tangible? You bet. Is it time consuming to get your fanny out into the trenches, trekking far and wide to observe and evaluate performance "at the source" rather than relying on spreadsheet, ad hoc, outcome data? Absolutely!

Our survey of professional sports scouting departments disclosed another eye-opener that puts it in perspective. Contrary to what the media often claims, offering multimillion-dollar signing bonuses is not the differentiating vehicle in procuring the world-class talent that leads to extreme teamwork. Franchises with the largest player ROI pour the largest distribution of resources into *preparing* for the draft. They spend more money scouting than they do on No. 1 signings. As we like to phrase it:

Spend an inordinate amount of effort on the selection process.

Corporate America, by and large, doesn't think this way. As we discussed above, investment put into identifying, studying, and pursuing Help the Helper kinds of intangibles generally amounts to a few phone calls to references (who, on a list provided by the job applicant, shockingly say warm fuzzies), an interview conversation or two, and maybe consulting a headhunter (who doesn't get paid if you don't hire his or her recommendations). Validity issues aside, outlay is perhaps three or four hours devoted to what makes a person tick. In contrast, teams like the Trail Blazers allocate thousands of hours.

Have you ever wondered why your organization doesn't have a scouting department like an NBA franchise? The knee-jerk reaction is, "Well, NBA owners have tens of millions of dollars at risk in their players." Stop to calculate payrolls, though. Midcap companies and up shell out a *heck* of a lot more. The big boys pay their CEO a greater sum than all players on the Chicago Bulls roster combined. What if you're a start-up? You might only have a couple million at stake in personnel. You don't need a full NFL or MLB slate of scouts. But proportions still hold true. Tabulate scouting hours per employee. The difference between most businesses and professional sports teams is a factor of ten!

Are we suggesting that you dole out radar guns to your HR staff? Of course not. Radar guns measure the wrong kind of talent (in baseball, too). Are we suggesting that you create a scouting program? *Yes!* If you were the first on your block to have scouts akin to those of the Blazers and Rays (that is, not the tobacco chewers, but rather students of human performance), even just one or two, you'd be on your way to becoming the teamwork model of your market. At the very least, make sure your organization isn't underperforming by assuming that recruiters (both in-house and contracted) are doing the sort of diligence we're casing in this chapter. Recruiters who attend job fairs, visit college campuses, and spend twenty hours a week surfing LinkedIn are most commonly promoting their company and/or raking through performance indices in the realm of grades, degrees, sales track records, awards, and the like, as opposed to going on Coach Brooks–type safaris.

Transform your recruiters into scouts. Play pickup with potential hires or hold future employee golf tournaments. Design your industry's variety of MMIs. Hold Brooksian tryouts. Or simply get out of the office and watch people in action. Whatever you do, put an inordinate amount of time and money into defining who's on the bus *beyond* what statistics and résumés capture—based on "abnormal" performance qualities. Not only will you build teams that are greater than the sum of their parts, but you'll create a platform that brings out the best in your Carlos Peñas (whom you might not even realize you've got). In turn, you'll spur emotional contagion, which helps others be their best. Leading at the source. Helping the Helper.

People want to get on *that* bus. As we'll see in the next chapter, it's an incredible boon to sustainable motivation.

YOUR TURN!

Helping the Helper Ingredients

We'd like to remind you that hiring the Front of the Jersey is an analogy equally important in new employee acquisition—changing your team's personnel—*and* in fostering with your current staff a pride in your company's logo. *Do both!*

1. Be like Joe Maddon; identify two to four "intangible" traits that you will commit to as more important to your team's success than résumé entries—traits you will go out of your way to recognize, support, and foster.

Write them down! What are they?

_____

Just as Maddon did with Peña, who will you pull aside, *today*, to point out one of these traits that they are particularly adroit at—and to tell them you've got their back in sticking to that trait?

_____

2. The 1980 USA Hockey club was anchored by a kid no one would've selected based on his stat sheet—Mike Eruzione. Bring out your own Eruziones by engaging in the who's-on-the-bus conversation with your teammates and employees.

Who are three people in your organization who are totally onboard?

_____

_____

_____

Who are three people in your organization who are *not* yet onboard? For each (write it down here), what can you do to help them get onboard?

Teammate:

_____

Onboard Helping:

_____

Teammate:

_____

Onboard Helping:

_____

Teammate:

_____

Onboard Helping:

_____

3. Locate and recruit performers like Tom Hankins! What competitive situation, like pickup hoops or the Virginia Tech School of Medicine MMI, will you implement in your very next hiring effort?

_____

4.

Ditch the Stick *and* Ditch the Carrot

An H2H Culture: Is Motivated at the Source

There is a reason why the University of Virginia is a candidate every year for distinction as the number-one public university in the country, for both undergraduates *and* MBA students. Nestled in the shadow of the Blue Ridge and of our nation's capital, founded by Thomas Jefferson, the university is a place where leadership is a big deal, an educational priority. But not just as a classroom exercise—with research professors waxing on theoretically about leadership competencies, styles, and models while young folks frantically scribble down copies of chalkboard diagrams to be memorized and regurgitated a few weeks later on a final exam. No, leadership lessons at UVA are a distinctly community effort—far more dynamic, far more real. A constant flow of intimate interaction with influential thinkers makes the student experience feel quite a bit like channeling Washington, Jefferson, Adams, and Franklin.

One particularly salient example of this is a visit General Norman Schwarzkopf made to Virginia's Darden School of Business. The topic of discussion: motivating people. The eye-opener: he earned four stars on his shoulder thanks to insight considerably contrary to his conservative, eat-nails-for-a-snack reputation.

"It doesn't take a hero to order men into battle. It takes a hero to be one of those men who goes," Schwarzkopf quipped.

A roomful of future CEOs nodded in agreement. Such wise words. Schwarzkopf strutted through the audience, ruminating about eighteen-year-old boys under his charge dashing into combat during Vietnam, Grenada, and the Gulf War. All that was missing from this being a Sunday sermon was a spirited *Amen!* Until Schwarzkopf shifted abruptly—

"That's not courage. I can get *any* human being to run into the line of fire."

In a flash of West Point wrestling honors, the general yanked a student up by the arm, spun him around, and, simulating a pistol, jammed an index finger into the student's temple.

"There's a battlefield right here, in front of us. It's being lit up with explosions, chaos, men screaming as bullets rip through them, blood everywhere," Schwarzkopf barked out ferociously. "You've got a choice. Stay here and I'll shoot you. Or you can go out there and they'll shoot you."

The general paused for a brief eternity. Silence. A sea of shocked expression. Not the smallest twitch of motion in the crowd, not even a blink, everyone's attention pinned to their startled classmate.

Searching for the words, a reply finally crackled, "Ahh . . . I'll . . . I'll go out there."

At which point General Schwarzkopf pulled the young man in for a big hug, immediately metamorphosing from bear to teddy bear.

"Thata boy," he roared with the approval of a loving grandfather.

A stunned look still on his face, the student teetered back into his seat as his peers erupted in applause.

But Schwarzkopf turned serious again, snuffing the claps. "No, no, do you understand?"

With all of these brilliant MBAs enrapt, he proceeded to hammer home the point: there's a subtle, yet mammoth difference between rushing a vastly fortified enemy position and successfully sacking it. The former is an exercise of will. The latter, Schwarzkopf explained, is an exercise of love. Anyone can "motivate" others by appealing to willpower. You do so with combinations of pain and pleasure, the magnitude of which correlate to the urgency or magnitude of the task at hand. You get action as a result. We all know, though, that action and optimal performance are rarely one and the same. Optimal performance, such as an outnumbered band of soldiers overcoming the odds to find a path through a gauntlet of certain death, takes substantially more than flinging oneself into harm's way, gritting one's teeth, and praying not to be shot. An uncommon level of focus, purposeful commitment, and clarity of thought is required.

"You don't get that by sticking a gun to someone's head," Schwarzkopf said. "That'll get you anything *other* than clarity of thought, as our friend here showed us today."

Schwarzkopf turned to the (ahem) volunteer role-play participant, only partly in jest:

"Pretty clear in your thinking, were you?"

The military is generally depicted as a staunchly disciplined institution. Officers must manage platoons full of otherwise dropout-bound teenagers, the argument goes, so being expert in motivation is critical job number one. Make a mistake and you're cleaning latrines. Shine in obeying your duties and medals are pinned on your chest. Pain and pleasure. Punishment and reward. Balancing the stick and the carrot. It's a system our armed forces live and die by.

Sort of.

Hardnosed drill sergeants screaming at GIs to prepare them to survive warfare isn't exactly an informatively accurate metaphor. Which is why General Schwarzkopf remained huddled with business students in Charlottesville for three hours longer than his originally agreed-upon obligation, emphasizing that what it takes to compel ordinary people to do extraordinary things, to continually strive for excellence, particularly in times of uncertainty or conflict, is drastically misapproached. Brandishing a stick will get results, likely quite quickly. Doling out lots of delicious carrots will get results, too. Neither, however, is the fuel of the highest levels of performance or exceptional accomplishment because, as the general stated it, neither serves the ultimate purpose.

"The purpose of war is freedom. The purpose of charging into combat must therefore be freedom. The purpose of commanding troops to do so: likewise, freedom. It follows, then, that the purpose of motivation *itself* must be freedom. Having to select between a reward and a punishment is not really a free choice. Love is. Until you find a way to elicit love as the driving force—be that love of country, love of God, love of a code of ideals, or love for the person fighting next to you—you are a failure as a leader."

Perhaps an extreme position in some regards, but it begs reflection coming from a man nicknamed Stormin' Norman. When motivating troops on your own team, or simply working one-on-one with an assistant, do you think in terms of trying to achieve particular outputs? Do you look for motivational tools and strategies that will be effective means to an end? *Or,* is love and caring about how people are doing the order of the equation? Do you think in terms of making those around you better—helping others be the best people or performers they can be?

Let's answer that question via another question . . .

LEE IACOCCA

Motivation is everything. You can do the work of two people, but you can't be two people. Instead, you have to inspire the next guy down the line and get him to inspire his people.

Enlisting (aka Joining the Party)

What is one nearly universal truth of New Year's resolutions to lose weight?

The ensuing flurry of postholiday activity—joining a health club, downloading a calorie tracker app, getting up at 6:00 A.M. for spin class, stocking the shelves with Slim-Fast, you name it—usually vanishes by February 1 or so (sometimes in the blink of a week). Less than thirty days is all you need to deep-six a good goal. Of course there are the success stories, but by and large resolutions don't last. The reason: introspective pledges are almost always built on a foundation of suboptimal motivation. For an entrenched reason of some sort, you haven't been _____ ; it hasn't been part of your daily routines and priorities. You're now going to force yourself to fill in that blank, force yourself to change ingrained habits. You look forward to the accolades, or plan to treat yourself for reaching a certain number on the scale. Enter the carrot (or giant piece of chocolate cake). You vow not to be embarrassed when you slip on a skimpy bikini come winter vacation in Tahiti. Enter the stick, in this case fear that rolls of fat will flop over your drawstring, jiggling as you stroll down a crowded beach. Whatever the aim, fitness or otherwise, resolutions tend to hinge upon:

Reaction to momentary circumstances—a whirlwind of mashed potatoes and gravy just consumed.

www.CartoonStock.com

The spirit of the season; the sense of renewal that a new calendar block brings. Ever wonder why so many good intentions (or shall we say procrastinations) follow a pattern of "I'll start on Monday"?

Desire for specific outcomes—an "ideal" weight, a compliment, fitting into a favorite pair of jeans.

When outcomes don't fall into place immediately (contrary to a flood of Internet pop-up advertising, it takes a minimum of five months to lose twenty pounds in a healthy, sustainable way), initial engine revving is all you've got propping up the initiative. That burst of impetus is almost always of the nature of General Schwarzkopf's gun to the head. Not meaning life or death; meaning acted upon to avoid some kind of pain and/or gain some kind of pleasure. Those impulses are transitory. The stick and the carrot just don't cut it for powering the type of fortitude it takes to make sizable, enduring life changes.

Love isn't the only thing that *does*. We've witnessed Schwarzkopf's words (and especially lack thereof) play out in sports teams, universities, and corporations alike. What we've learned to put into practice is that the juice of "ultimate purpose"—the juice of the teachings from Jefferson to Schwarzkopf—is in the feel. Freedom isn't something you count, measure, hire, or fill your bank account with. Love isn't something you buy or sell. Freedom and love aren't held; they're *felt*. The pinnacle of motivation, therefore, is not doing or accomplishing. It's feeling.

To lose weight, throw out (literally, perhaps) the frozen yogurt indulgences, the skinny jeans, the tickets to Cancún. Throw out the focus on yourself. Replace all that material and internal concern with an intimate team of fitness strivers who will greet one another with smiles every day, who'll share sweat-spilling challenges, who'll push and encourage one another, who'll high-five through ups and downs. *Not* to create a reward system of pats on the back. To give a richness, daily, to the experience—a sense of pride, community, empathy, commitment, and yes, love (which needn't be the same for each member of the group). If you do that, you transform actions into feelings. Feelings are the substrate of sustainable effort, determination, willingness to take risks, willingness to fail, to keep going against the odds, to persevere in the absence of the light of noticeable progress. What you'll discover is that your personal trainer no longer has to whip you to charge a battlefield we call the gym (a battlefield complete with casualties—all the workout quitters and skippers). You'll win a sense of freedom in a fight that so few win.

You'll also remove one of the largest impediments to success: *you.* That's not intended to be a get-personal criticism. Anyone can become caught up in their own world without realizing it. Spending too much time gazing inward ties you up in knots. As we coach slumping athletes all the time: "Turn off your brain. Get out of your own way!" The fastest, easiest, most surefire way to do so is to focus on helping someone else. By steering your energy toward others, toward your team's prospering in feelings, you transform *wanting* an end point into *having* relationships, relationships that go far, far deeper than a few lost pounds.

Speaking of the process of developing bonds and winning wars, if you've never seen Stephen Hopkins's film *The Ghost and the Darkness*, now would be a superb time to put down this book in pursuit of multimedia learning. The movie is an astonishingly factual saga about an East African railway construction project in 1896. We'll spare giving away the dramatic climax, but suffice it to say: uniting myriad culture-clashing indigenous tribes, speaking dozens of incompatible dialects, to victoriously build a historic bridge, had nothing to do with setting up or managing effective reward systems. It's an excellent case study, on many different levels throughout the picture, of Help the Helper leadership. Ask yourself at the conclusion, if you were walking out of the brush alongside Colonel John Henry Patterson (portrayed by Val Kilmer), to what lengths would you be willing to go in your work?

It's Okay for Men to Hug

We hear a couple groans out there. "I'm not into all that touchy-feely 'group therapy' stuff." If that's the case, we submit that you should try experiencing, through a local amateur sports club or vicariously if by no other method, being on a championship squad like the 2011 Dallas Mavericks. The television-glamorized, packed-arena, roaring-crowd environment isn't the pudding. It's the triumph-creating chemistry. It's palpable. Fascinated by why the LeBron James, Dwyane Wade, Chris Bosh All-Star stacked Miami Heat couldn't close the door on the underdog Mavs despite repeatedly going ahead, *Wall Street Journal* (June 9, 2011) sportswriter Scott Cacciola noticed a significant difference in the way the players related to one another. He decided to tally every incidence of physical contact—from faint hand taps and fanny pats, to full embraces and demonstrative chest bumps. The stats were eye-opening: Dallas hugged its way to the franchise's first-ever NBA title, with Mavs players in touch a whopping 82 percent more of the time than Miami.

Empirical examination confirms it. A sociology team at the University of California, Berkeley, coded every game of the 2008–10 NBA seasons. Findings published in the journal *Emotion* revealed that teams with statistically more frequent instances of "tactile communication," as the investigation titled it, cooperated more and had better win-loss records. The league's top two touchy-feely teams, the Celtics and Lakers, accounted for five of the six Finals slots in the three years spanned by the study.

But don't worry; we won't roll out the couch. We will, however, enlist the relevance of therapeutic practices by introducing you to our friend and colleague Dr. Douglas Newburg.

Doug is a pioneer in medical education. He's venturing to turn modern surgery upside down, to scores of patient thank-yous, by suggesting that doctors *should* be emotionally attached to their patients. Old-school physicians scream, *"Transference!"* That's the clinical no-no of getting to know the sick with too much individual familiarity. It's been systematically beaten out of med students and residents for the past century, the establishment railing against the so-called dangers of losing "scientific objectivity" and the claimed potential for burnout. To which Dr. Newburg says, "Horse hockey!"

In the early 1990s, Doug inaugurated an interview-style study of the qualities of world-class performers that propel them through obstacles. His research sample (which he continues to add to, to this day) is made up of people with elite résumés from a broad spectrum of careers . . . with a catch. For inclusion in his database, subjects must have more than paper success; they must have achieved a covetable character to their life—joy, vibrancy, verve, peace, flow. Doug coins it "profound esthetic happiness." Dotting the list of thousands of interviewees: multiple Grammy winning pianist Bruce Hornsby, NFL Hall of Fame linebacker and broadcaster Howie Long, Olympic gold medal decorated swimmer Jeff Rouse, and *Time* cover featured Harvard Business School professor Tony Athos.

Fascinatingly, the more Newburg's subject pool diversified, the more similar they sounded. It wasn't that they spoke of similar achievement strategies or precise points of common wisdom. It was an overarching tone. Passionate, exceedingly personal, leaving old-fashioned professionalism in the dust—resonating with emotion.

Whether it's a coincidence or not can be debated, but at the same time as Doug was starting to catalogue data, renowned heart surgeon Dr. Curt Tribble joined the standing lunchtime game of pickup at the UVA basketball arena where Doug was a staple. Doug had played for the University of Virginia as a varsity walk-on when the Cavaliers were a preeminent college program. Except for a brief hiatus to sell computer software, he basically never left. A court full of other great athletes and coaches, Tribble included, made up the daily noon "hardwood run." Competition was always intense.

So was postgame conversation. Curt and Doug hit it off smartly. Curt was grappling with issues of lackluster output and burnout among his residents at the hospital. Needless to say, he was interested in Doug's academic exploration of those issues. He invited Doug to present his findings during Grand Rounds.

Doug agreed, with a caveat.

"Sure. But I won't be giving the kind of dry, academic lecture these kids are used to."

Newburg didn't bring overhead transparencies or stand behind a lectern. He shared his own poignant story, from being a benchwarmer in college, poked fun of by *Washington Post* sportswriters, to failing as a salesman, to returning to graduate school in a quest to understand it all. Slam dunk. Trained-to-be-stoic junior physicians poured out questions of serious emotional depth.

"Our conservative medical system just doesn't let doctors do that," Curt explains. "I knew we were onto something."

Curt drove the point home, on the spot, by appointing Doug to be the director of performance education at the department of surgery. The two then got to work testing the notion that emotional engagement kindles energy and, as a result, higher levels of performance, not the opposite, as transference-scaredy-cat traditionalists would lead us to believe. Doctors Tribble and Newburg encouraged their staff to outwardly share their hopes and dreams. They held conferences to discuss putting feelings back into the practice of medicine, akin to the era of house calls when physicians knew everyone in town by their first name. They allowed residents to listen—really listen—to patients, to connect with them instead of taking fact-only histories and physical examinations (H&Ps) and maximizing clinic churn speed.

A paradox, to outsiders, occurred: burnout decreased while time card hours increased. Employees started passing up their habitual Starbucks stop to arrive at work earlier. They *requested* overtime. As Curt and Doug refer to it, a "constant low buzz" developed around the ward. Patients thrived. The program rose in national stature. They eventually even rejiggered the admissions process to include a proactive search for potential applicants with "low buzz energy"–generating tendencies.

Are we surprised?

Healing, by its very substance, is a feeling-based business. Converse logic that practitioners shouldn't weep as if for a sibling when they lose someone is flat nuts. It has no doubt contributed to the escalation of malpractice suits. The public looks to doctors as leaders. When caring about people is eclipsed by insurance management, exam room turnover rate, and doling out prescriptions (jockeyed for by Big Pharma reps) as reigning hospital directives, we all know what results. Diminished health care—on *both* sides of the service delivery formula, in provider performance and in patient compliance.

Competitors adhering to the prevailing avoid-transference "wisdom" made it a snap for Dr. Tribble's unit to grab a market advantage. Such a gain isn't limited to the arena of surgery, though. In any field, the best in people is brought out when they are emotionally plugged in to their work and coworkers, and when they are chasing an emotional purpose, a purpose distinguished by feeling rather than reward.

Buying In: Brown Versus Williams

Musing on the topic of bringing out the best in others, we affectionately tap two coaches KP played for in college, Larry Brown and Roy Williams.

PAT RILEY

A champion needs a motivation above and beyond winning.

"I learned more in those three hours a day at Kansas than could be packed into any formal education program. We went way past X's and O's. A Harvard MBA couldn't touch it," Kevin proffers. "Still today, I don't make a major decision in life without consulting with one or both of them."

How did coaches Brown and Williams lift the performance level of their athletes so regularly? Why did KP and his teammates buy in?

On the surface, Larry Brown is the Webster's dictionary definition of the stick approach, seemingly motivating by fear. Practice is brutal. He gets on everyone; no one skates, ever. It doesn't matter how many things you're doing right, or how much effort you're giving, or the enormity of the contribution you are making—workouts will be punishing. He'll make you grind. You've got to take it or you're gone. He's basketball's Vince Lombardi.

He also has an amazing photographic memory of the court. He remembers the smallest details of possessions four plays ago, or more. "You needed to V-cut here . . . there was a backdoor there, when #11 slid out." And he lays it on you. He expects you to adjust better than anyone. He's *so* damn hard.

It's legendary that the Jayhawks just don't lose at home. The field house, named in honor of the late coaching legend Dr. F. C. "Phog" Allen, has showcased 650 Kansas victories in its time—the most winning seasons in college history, multiple perfect campaigns, a 62-game victory streak, and only 106 defeats (an average of fewer than two losses per season). Yet, in 1988, the preseason national #1 hometown heroes dropped three straight at Allen, to rivals Kansas State, Duke, and Oklahoma. They lost six straight games in total. Unheard of! Campus was stirring with negative vibes. Their hoopsters weren't going to make it to the Big Dance.

"Coach was *killing* us," Kevin recalls, with a tenor that hurts just to hear.

But every single guy in the locker room, starter and sub alike, was willing to take what Brown was dishing out. It crystallized them. There was a collective pull to demand positivity of one another. No matter what Coach made them do, no matter what the school newspaper printed, no matter what the playoff bubble projection, they used it as fuel to help one another, to unite in preventing any circumstances from beating them mentally.

The Jayhawks didn't just punch an invitation to the NCAA tournament; they ran the table. In sweet, poetic-justice fashion, they captured the national championship by consecutively knocking off: K State in the Elite Eight, Duke in the Final Four, and Oklahoma in the grand finale.

We would wager there aren't ten guys in the history of the game who could teach as well as Larry Brown. Observers misperceive his tough-nosed rigor as creating an atmosphere that would block the kind of emotional engagement Doctors Tribble and Newburg achieved. They're wrong. He's so damn hard. But he's so damn right.

Basketball is a complicated game; it's very difficult to play the right way. So knowing your coach will pick up on every little subtlety and important intricacy—what an amazing feeling. You can turn off the worry switch, let your mind be quiet, and just go play. You know your boss will have it covered if you happen to miss anything. *That's* freedom. (And in a system under Brown which onlookers mistakenly think is a dictatorship.)

Roy Williams, among numerous other convictions, lives by a high standard of language. He only allows himself six curse words . . . a year! To the best of our knowledge, and from what we've witnessed, he's never exceeded the limit; not once. That's as poles apart as they come from Coach Brown.

On the surface, Williams is the classic depiction of the carrot. There is no fear playing for him. He treats everyone with the utmost respect, recognizing good deeds and rewarding hard work. In Williams's camp, coaching is a constant stream of praise and back patting. He believes that people won't give you all they've got until they know how much you appreciate their effort. Once a member of his roster, you are a member of his family evermore.

"No matter what you're up to or where you are in the world you are, you know Coach Williams has your back," former players say.

He's probably the most organized man in the NCAA. To this day, every morning players get a comprehensive outline of that afternoon's practice, meticulous to the minute.

Highlighted at the top of the page:

Offensive Emphasis of the Day

Defensive Emphasis of the Day

Thought of the Day

Players have to memorize all three. At the start of practice Roy will quiz everyone, and freshmen to the nth degree. As a unit, they talk about each emphasis, what it means, how the group is going to execute them as a team, and why they are important. The thought of the day is about life in general; it's always personally impactful.

Coach Williams had hardly been at Kansas a year when the first defining moment presented itself. They'd plucked a transfer from the previous year's national champion. The bench was loaded. Yet pre-season polls had KU No. 7, a slap in the face in players' minds. Further stoking locker-room grumbling, their ranking robbed them of a pre-season NIT home stand. To open the year they had to go on the road to LSU, into the backyard of a Tiger squad featuring the tandem of Shaquille O'Neal and top first-rounder Chris Jackson (later to rename himself Mahmoud Abdul-Rauf). Needless to say, there were some pissed-off athletes.

Roy convened an LSU pregame meeting. He had one simple request.

"Guys, I've never had a hugger. I'd love a big-time hugger."

Confused brow furrowing washed over the team, prompting the query, "Coach, what's a hugger?"

Explained Roy, "It's one of those games that's so toughly fought, so hard earned, that you go around hugging everyone when it's all over."

His description, ensconced in his naturally invigorating tone of voice, created a visceral visual that lit a fire for warm-up.

"It hit us like a ton of bricks," KP fondly remembers.

The Jawhawks took down Shaq and company by eight. A ten-minute hugfest ensued.

Yes, indeed, from a thirty-thousand-foot perspective Larry Brown and Roy Williams appear to be contradictory. One gives the impression that punishment captures championships. The other reinforces rewards as the way to go. The stick and the carrot rearing their heads again, elbowing for their place in the leadership limelight. Who can argue with Coach Brown's and Coach Williams's track records?

This chapter won't. Which is exactly the reason we are including them. The distinction General Schwarzkopf makes between what it takes to rush into the line of fire and what it takes to capture an all-but-impenetrable bunker is the very same distinction between what a camera would portray of practices during that era at Kansas and what was really driving the players' hearts. There's a façade of punishments and rewards. It's there because those motivators are real elements in any organization. We say ditch the stick and ditch the carrot, but employees need paychecks; there are revenue and thus job consequences for making mistakes. The military has sticks and carrots, sports franchises and medical centers have them, every company does.

Therein lies the problem—and the teamwork opportunity.

From an 80/20 principle perspective, 80 percent of motivation is the visible, outcome-oriented variety: salaries, home mortgages, bills, promotions and demotions, deadlines, diplomas, awards, newspaper headlines, corner offices, vacation time, stock options, time-outs, strokes of praise, tongue lashings, running suicides up and down the court, and yes, championship rings. The remaining 20 percent of motivation, however, is the stuff that truly moves people, that changes life scripts, from slush pile into *Rudy*. It has zip to do with goals and what happens if you do or don't hit them.

Truly great teams get this. They have a thoughtful, well-planned system of sticks and carrots, just like the ones Coaches Brown and Williams use, but that's not the separation factor. They are happy to let opponents believe it is, let opponents try to copy their scheme or "outmanage" it. Meanwhile, they are attending to the pulse of their people. The real focus, in conversations and interactions and practices and group working sessions, is not how; it's *why*. And great teams don't accept "to make money" or "to win" as the why. There are more emotionally purposeful reasons to do what you do. The best teams foster an environment in which people help one another stay connected with, prioritize, and pursue those reasons—equally as individuals and as a unit. *That's* what fuels exceptional performance, the kind of commitment to clarity of thought Schwarzkopf was going to extremes to illustrate.

The *why* for the 1988 Jayhawks had to do with toughness and pride. The why for Roy Williams's Jayhawks had to do with love and sense of family. For both coaches, their personal why happened to be invested in teaching. For us, throughout our careers as athletes, the why was the thrill of competition—intense competitiveness, the "leave it all on the floor with your teammates and opponents" type.

JOHN QUINCY ADAMS

If your actions inspire others to dream more, learn more, do more and become more, you are a leader.

Excellence doesn't require absolute uniformity across everyone's why. But it does require understanding one another's motivation on this level, making purpose and love and feel be topics of conscious, ongoing dialogue, and most important, having team members take initiative to actively help their mates keep *why* front and center.

The Why Tool

Would you like to be part of an extreme team enough that you are willing to push your friends and office fellows out of their comfort zone? Or, at a bare minimum, stump them a wee bit?

We hope so! We've discovered that the apex of great teammateship does not come in the form of classic supportiveness, being there to lean on, an ear to bend when the going gets rough. Common, everyday support systems, you may be surprised to learn, tend to nurture remaining at current levels of performance and even staying stuck in current slumps. Consider the following exchange.

Employee A: "I'm totally slammed. I've got to work through the weekend or the marketing brochure won't be completed in time for our new product launch. But my kids have two soccer games *and* a school play on top of my youngest one's birthday party. I don't know how I'm going to fit it all in. I'm not going to get any sleep, that's for sure."

Employee B: "I hear ya. You just described my every weekend!"

Employee A: "You too, huh? Boy, what I wouldn't do to get off this hamster wheel. Heck, I'd take it if I could just get one more *hour* of vacation."

Employee B: "Tell me about it! All I do these days is fantasize about running away to a deserted island. Wouldn't it be sweet to get away from it all and have no boss and no clock and no bumper-to-bumper commute?"

Employee A: "Uncle Sam's killin' us on that prospect. I've lost forty percent in my house. My 401(k) is even worse. I couldn't afford a single day on an island."

And on it goes. The two proceed to trade woes for the entire sixty minutes of their lunch break. On the surface, they seem to be genuinely caring for each other, connecting, empathizing. Do they return to the office rested and rejuvenated, as lunch downtime should accomplish? No way. They're as "stuck" as they were prior, perhaps worse. They've just rehearsed, for a full hour, performance-tamping feelings. Their team contribution in the afternoon, we'd confidently predict, isn't going to be the stuff of inspiration.

Truly special support systems, contrarily, help colleagues rehearse performance-*driving* feelings. That often requires going against human nature. It's comfortable to commiserate. It's not so comfortable to head into a gale-force wind, metaphorically speaking, when life's gusting at you. But that's what extreme teams help one another do. That's what General Schwarzkopf helped his troops do—without a sidearm; *with love.*

Take a page from his playbook, and from Coach Brown's and Coach Williams's. Care about your teammates to this extent by not letting them off the hook easily when it comes to motivation. Don't settle for the stick or the carrot. Go to the next level. Use fancy "technology" we call the "why tool."

STEP ONE: Reserve time to visit with everyone on your team individually. Yup, you read right; we're asking you to get out of the comfort zone digital electronics are providing—that of quicker, more impersonal, sound-bite communication. We realize we'll get pushback in recommending an action that is time consuming.

"There's work to be done! How am I supposed to squeeze extensive personal chats into an already overtaxed day?"

Time savings is a sizable chunk of the reason so many organizations rely on sticks and carrots; they're highly efficient in the short run. Average teams grab whatever quick gains they can. Extreme teams are more interested in generating lengthy, positive ripple effects in their communities and markets. That's *the* key to long-term, continued growth.

STEP TWO: In individual conversations, ask your mates, "Why do you do what you do?" Likely, you'll hear something that has to do with outcomes. Outcomes are the 80 percent of motivation we brought up a few pages ago—paying bills, putting children through college, earning stock options, and so on.

STEP THREE: To whatever the answer, ask, "Why do you do that?" Or, "Why is that important?" Or, "Why are you pursuing that?" Chances are, you'll either get another outcome-related response or a significantly odd facial expression.

STEP FOUR (and five and six and seven . . .): At each iteration, ask a variation of "Why?" *again*! As long as you keep getting outcome-oriented thoughts, keep at it; keep exploring. Be a great teammate; don't settle.

To give you an idea of how it's apt to go, when we break out this tool with college students, our banter customarily goes something like this:

"Why do you do what you do [e.g., study for exams]?"

"Well, to get good grades."

"Why do you want good grades?"

"To get a good job, of course."

"Why do you need a good job?"

"Uh, duh, guys, to make a lot of money!"

"Why do you want to make a lot of money?" This is where we get monstrous eye rolling. But we refuse to quit. We press on, genuinely, for a serious answer.

"So I can buy a nice car and have a nice house for my family."

"Why do you want those things?" We anticipate an incredulous look or two.

"Ah, 'cause I like nice things. . . ."

"Why? Why a car and not a Winnebago?"

Chuckling. "I can't drive a Winnebago to work!"

"Why?"

"Come on, Doc and KP, that wouldn't be cool!"

"Why?"

We'll spare you the additional thirty pages it would take to get to the bottom of the why tool with eighteen-year-olds. We needn't delineate how their motivations diverge from those of forty-something corporate division managers. The aim is the same, nevertheless. Stick with it until your colleague has difficulty coming up with an answer. That's generally the juncture at which you transition from outcomes to spirit, from the motivation 80 percent to the motivation 20 percent. That's when you'll start getting to the "ultimate purpose" Schwarzkopf was talking about. You'll uncover where their professional loves reside. They might love, for instance, consensus building. They might love problem solving. They might love getting their hands dirty, or working with numbers, or taking risks. There are hundreds, nay thousands, of deep, heart-and-soul-focused, purposeful *feelings* that compel extreme teamwork motivation. That's where the gold resides—a fountain of extreme teamwork fuel.

Why is not a mythical fountain of the Ponce de León variety. But it does give life. Help the people around you drink from it!

YOUR TURN!

The *Real* Why

Take a page out of Schwarzkopf's or the Dallas Mavericks' playbook. Motivate at the source by hugging! And while you're at it, try at least one of these:

1. Start developing the passionate buzz Doctors Newburg and Tribble tapped to reduce burnout. Find a stick-natured practice and a carrot-natured practice that you can replace with a practice of getting to know colleagues, customers, and clients on a more personal level.

What is one stick that you can remove this week?

_____

What is one carrot that you can remove this week?

_____

2. Introspection is essential for leaders. Make a regular date with yourself. Commit to spending time each week examining specifically what makes you tick so you can use that knowledge to give to your teams.

Who are you more similar to, Coach Brown or Coach Williams? Or are you more similar to a different legendary Help the Helper coach?

_____

_____

What passion(s) do you have in common?

_____

3. Crank up the why tool! Commit to understanding the ultimate purpose of your teammates. Commit to helping them keep their ultimate purpose front and center.

Who will you take out to lunch or take out for a cup of coffee *today* and totally engage in a *why* discussion, to the genuine depth and willingness of possibly being stumped (momentarily, of course, since you'll help them get to the goods)?

5.

Manage Energy, Not People

An H2H Culture: Doesn't Take Invigoration,
It Gives Invigoration

Pause for a minute. Contemplate the folks you know who are talented but underperforming in their careers—or hitting a plateau, or stagnating, or entertaining some form of midlife crisis, or simply not excelling. Do they *want* to be that way? Are they *intentionally* underperforming? Of course not. With nary an exception, people inherently want to do their best. We've never known an athlete, worth but a modicum of his or her salt, who doesn't want to win. Unless a mental illness bites, people don't *choose* to have a slump. Something gets in the way of the ambition to do top-notch work. The environment tamps down their spirit. Market fluctuations take moods along for a yo-yoing. Demands and deadlines coax the skipping of healthy nourishment.

And people just plain get tired.

Physical fatigue is a visible performance-eroding culprit, showing up in degradation of dexterity, strength, alertness, reaction time, and the like. Getting quality rest is paramount. Without revitalizing our bodies, even rudimentary job assignments are compromised. Take driving an automobile, for instance, a task so thoroughly practiced that as an experienced adult one needs only minimal coordination to perform it adequately. Substantially replicated research reveals that losing a mere hour of sleep is enough to cause functional impairment. Stay awake for sixteen hours and the effect is equivalent to a blood alcohol level of .08—legally drunk!

Imagine this scenario: your four-year-old daughter wakes up vomiting at 2:00 A.M. She's flushed and sweating. Nothing you try seems to aid in making her more comfortable. You pull out a thermometer . . . a 103-degree fever. Off to the emergency room you dash, where the on-call pediatrician decides it's a situation in need of close monitoring. With the added hospital hubbub, your daughter is understandably frightened. You stay vigilant at her bedside through the night until finally the doctor says she's out of the woods; her temperature is down and she can go home. Unfortunately, today is big-pitch day at the office. A game-changing potential client has flown into town for final due diligence before they make a decision. You're the project director; you're the one this prospect trusts. You've got to be there. With thoughts drifting to your daughter all day, you suffer hour after hour of number crunching and question peppering. It doesn't go well. The client finds a discrepancy they can't accept and, scramble as you may, you aren't able to come up with a solution they deem satisfactory. At 6:30 P.M. they pull the plug on the deal. You're exhausted. You've been up for almost seventeen straight hours. You just want to go check on your little girl. As you roll out of the parking lot, your mind is clogged with should'ves, could'ves, and what-ifs. You don't recognize it but you're in the same condition as someone leaving a bar after hitting the bottle (with no designated driving pal to snatch away the keys).

Heaven forbid you get into a car wreck. If you did, though, an opposing insurance company would be quick to explore sleep deprivation in assigning fault. Medical facts and crash statistics would support their position empirically. It's not news that our litigious society relies on hard data to judge human error, performance dips, and undesirable outcomes. But physiology isn't the only contributing factor. There's an element at play we call "psychological fatigue." We need not be tired for it to drop a deuce on us.

Psychological fatigue, not to be confused with sleep-related brain deficiency (haziness or memory loss, for example) is a diminution in emotional, spiritual, or attitudinal components of our skills, our contributions, and our output. This condition is marked by a weakening of variables such as:

* Purposefulness of drive

* Dedication of focus

* Fine attention to detail

* Guts and gumption

* Willingness to go an extra inch, or an extra mile

* Enthusiasm for challenges and problem solving

* Competitive zeal and reveling in the competitive process

* Stick-to-itiveness

* Championing the cause

Continuing with our fictitious ill-child situation, traffic ticket likelihood would still be heightened without the seventeen-hour drag. Even working off full rest, had your daughter instead been rushed to the ER at 6:30 P.M., just as your prospective client deep-sixed your proposal, doubling a day-ending barrage of bad breaks, the weight on your mind would take a toll. Psychological concessions to your ability can be equally as potent as those resulting from sacrifice of a full night of slumber—for the same reason cell phone use while driving is dangerous. It's not the act of holding an instrument to your ear, or operating machinery one-handed, that creates risk. Tests by the Insurance Institute for Highway Safety (IIHS) have determined that hands-free devices do not reduce accident rates. The culprit is increased "cognitive load" from participating in a conversation, not increased physical or coordination load. "Participation" is meant loosely, too. A 2011 study at Carnegie Mellon University found that as little participation as listening in on someone else's dialogue triggered a 37 percent reduction of spatial management economy, critical for processing busy intersections (as well as busy desks and hectic workplaces).

Neurologists point to the operation of the frontal lobe, where a majority of the cerebral cortex's dopamine-sensitive cells are housed. Among other duties, dopamine helps effectuate emotional responses and is the chief executive in distinguishing motivational consequences of actions, that is, deciding which course will produce the most satisfying result. Scans show that when the brain is taxed by information volume, distractions, multitasking, conflicting requests, and so forth, frontal lobe operation deteriorates. Dopamine activity decreases; psychological fatigue increases.*

The insidious part of all this is a lack of accompanying perception. Biologically, research reveals that at low to moderate levels of fatigue (both physical and psychological), people tend to be unaware of the hits they're taking. ("I'm fine; I can make it to the next exit.") Even when conscious of their suboptimal faculties, people are conditioned to keep it to themselves. Socially and culturally, the prevalent ego atmosphere in sports and business dissuades admission of diminished capacity. It's a competitive sin to disclose weakness. Demonstrating we're in control, showing grit no matter what—those are the dominant behaviors most teams reinforce. To such a degree that people are widely reluctant to so much as suggest to a teammate that grinding it out might not always be the best way to go. Reflect on how long it took our society to finally accept it as a necessary practice to tell a friend he or she is too inebriated to drive. Do we do the same when someone is too tired or too distracted to drive? Hardly. That feels too much like treading into a territory of making accusations that they're not capable or not responsible.

This confluence of factors makes psychological fatigue a silent barrier to exceptional teamwork. When conditions arise along the lines of those in the scenario we sketched above, customary collegial "support" is a pat on the back, an admonition to hang in there, or a cap tipping of sympathy:

"Sorry to hear about your daughter . . . sounds like a rough night."
"Oh man, I've been there before. I know what you're going through."
"Keep your chin up."

Or even the rhetorical offering, "Is there anything I can do?" We all know how that question is answered ninety-nine times out of a hundred.

Interchanges of this variety sound good as a flyby. But they lack performance-transforming substance. They blow "you can do it" smoke, maintaining the cultural standard that everyone should be able to handle matters themselves. Or worse, they foster a manner of

---

*Interestingly, laboratory investigation of psychological fatigue shows no correlation between the relevant frontal lobe declines and prior night sleep duration. Robust sleep is not sufficient for staving off psychological dips.

social comparison. They imply, "I have to deal with it; you should too."

Suppose, however, as you grabbed the files to go meet with your prospective client, juggling a cup of coffee and a bottle of NoDoz, one of your teammates came to you with this statement:

"I'm out the door right now. I'm going to pick up my wife. You know she's a children's doc, right? She's cleared her decks at the clinic. We're going to go spend the day looking after your daughter for you. We've got your back. You go knock this pitch out of the park."

Your teammate doesn't pose this as a brainstorm or idle inquiry to communicate concern. Like the waiters we opened this book with and described in chapter 1, lifting great restaurants with their style of Helping the Helper, your teammate is taking proactive initiative. Employing a defining characteristic of extreme teamwork, he's taking helping one step further; he's also removing the burden from you of having to devise and process options for collaboration. He's done that work for you.

A hug and a high-five follow. You both head off to get after it.

Psychological fatigue can be eliminated in a snap of the fingers like this—if you're willing to do what it takes to be an extreme team. Imagine how reenergized or relieved you might feel. Imagine how it might alter your facility to dial in, maybe identifying subtleties in your meeting you'd otherwise miss, or buttressing you from drifting off target a tad less, or clarifying your mission. Big deals, like championship games, frequently hinge on nuisances. An inch here, an ounce there is usually what separates number one in an industry from number two. You needn't worry about wholly eliminating psychological fatigue; a touch less is often a bottom-line difference maker.

PAUL McCARTNEY

I love to hear a choir. I love the humanity . . . to see the faces of real people devoting themselves to a piece of music. I like the teamwork. It makes me feel optimistic about the human race when I see people cooperating like that.

The Silver Screen Con

To be better at leveraging the performance-enhancing relationship between extreme teamwork and fatigue reduction, it's useful to understand a common shift in aims that goes with group membership.

When folks with any smidgen of talent strive for a particular team
affiliation—a law student cramming for grades to warrant an offer from
a major international firm, a computer programmer trying to get a job
at Google, a pilot applying to NASA's astronaut program, a soldier training to become a Navy SEAL, a flight attendant networking in hopes of
hooking on with the Southwest Airlines crew—they are in pursuit of a
particular lifestyle, identity, caliber and quality of work, or value system.
The group they aspire to join represents connectivity between who they
are as a person and what they do or want to do. In short, they are seeking a certain experience. The team is a conduit of that experience.

Achieving membership changes the game in most cases. Motivation,
focus, and effort poured into the invigorating chase of desired experiences is switched. Switched to executing obligations, fitting into a hierarchy, keeping the boss happy, attending to rules, policies, and accepted
practices—maintaining membership. Using a physiology analogy:
people find new reserves of courage, pushing their bodies past barriers,
when exercising to join the ranks of, say, triathlon finishers. When the
race is over, however, their exercise regime converts into daily treadmill
spins, staring at a wall, maintaining fitness. It's a redirection of energy
that significantly influences effectiveness, efficiency, and total energy
altogether.

Take a young attorney, for example. The passion she has for human
rights propels remarkable library stamina, evening after evening in the
stacks, studying beyond the wee ticks of the clock. She is filled with
hopes of leading class-action suits, standing up for the oppressed and
the disadvantaged, and speaking for the little guy. She has her sights on
the ACLU's top legal house. It's the home of the platform, resources,
and colleagues she envisions pulling together to help her succeed in
defending the Constitution.

It's not an atypical story. Scores of Ivy League law grads have these
dreams. Scores of Ivy League law grads also drop out of high-profile
firms in their first couple years out of school.

The misassumption is that the hours nuked 'em. Preparing for the
bar exam, heaped on top of regular all-nighters doing case research for

senior partners, adds up to a heck of a lot of sleep deprivation. We don't deny that. But physical fatigue is rarely the source of burnout. These are kids who spent three years at über-competitive Harvard, Yale, or Stanford, routinely awake past midnight, essentially training their intellectual endurance to the degree Olympians train lactic acid thresholds. They're well conditioned. It's the psychological fatigue that zaps them. On campus, they're surrounded by other aspiring attorneys with incredible visions. At the office, they're surrounded by people punching the billable-hours clock. Professors wax on about famous cases and remarkable trial strategy. Managing partners harp on filings, deadlines, and schmoozing whales (their wealthiest clients). Moot court puts them at the center of the action. They don't see the inside of a courtroom as a firm associate. The vigor of engagement they brought to studying law is squashed by A) the slog of mundane tasks on the job, and B) the general manner in which labor is approached in most organizations.

Disenchantment is an apropos layman's term. From a sociological perspective, we euphemistically call it the Silver Screen Con. Not to indict brilliant writers and directors, but it can be argued that motion pictures do a disservice to a wide range of professions. It's not their fault. A film has, give or take, 120 minutes to render tales spanning a much longer time frame. Within that constraint, producers have to figure out how to put butts in seats . . . and keep them there. They can't accomplish that by depicting the workday thoroughly or entirely accurately. They don't use limited screen time portraying FBI agents filling out paperwork, surgeons reading dry scientific journal articles, jewel thieves doing data entry to catalogue inventory, or a heroine sitting in commuter traffic. Gripping, make-you-think legal flicks originating from our friend John Grisham's brilliance don't win awards by chewing up reels with attorneys writing briefs, tending to banking, or hundreds of other necessary business operations. BORING. That stuff doesn't capture the imaginations, emotions, and interest of ticket buyers or remote control clickers.

It doesn't capture the imaginations, emotions, and interest of employees, either. It's why we *metaphorically* call job portrayal in theater and on television a "con."

Consider the popularity of police dramas. There are too many on the air to list. In spite of the market flood, they get high ratings. CBS's six-Emmy smash *CSI: Crime Scene Investigation* itself spun into three separate shows (the original *CSI: Las Vegas*, *CSI: Miami*, and

CSI: New York). One reason for its success is how fascinatingly forensic science is presented. Jerry Bruckheimer's artistic wizardry gives
audiences a peek into the world of crime-fighting chemistry, physics,
and genetics in a way that makes basic lab equipment "cool" and
geeky scientists "sexy." It's hard to watch the jocklike, quick-witted
investigators, scoring convictions with their slick work (from crime to
solution in forty-five minutes) without the thought popping into your
head, "Man, that would be a pretty sweet job." What in actuality is a
fairly lonely occupation of microscopes and dank basement laboratory scenery is splashed on the tube as a rock-star team having a blast
nailing bad guys.

The following series of excerpts from the drama's pilot season (episode number eight), chronicling two hotshot Level 3 investigators putting down one particularly taxing case, illustrates how much fun it
appears you would have being on the *CSI: Las Vegas* team—and as a
result, how little fatigue would probably affect you.

First Assessing the Case

WARRICK: *This is a crime, not an accident.*
NICK: *You, ah, care to back that statement up? My phantom driver
against your criminal?*
WARRICK (raising his eyebrows): *How much?*
NICK*: Fifty.*
WARRICK: *I don't get out of bed for less than a bill.*

Then Receiving Dumbfounding Fingerprint Results

WARRICK: *So what do you say? You wanna up the stakes?*
NICK: *To what? A deuce?*
WARRICK (demonstratively slapping five with Nick): *It's a bet.*

Upon Yet Another Work-Inducing Evidence Twist

WARRICK: *You find his watch and ring?*
NICK: *. . . Um . . . No.*
WARRICK (pretending to jingle change in his trousers): *Whoa ho. My
pockets are getting fat.*
NICK: *You want to take it to three?*
WARRICK: *YOU wanna take it to three?*

Still Toiling Away

NICK: *You look tired, buddy. You want me to make you a bottle . . . go night-night?*
WARRICK: *You want me to clack that jaw? Make YOU go night-night?*
LAB TECH SANDERS: *So what's the pot up to?*
NICK: *We don't bet on cases.*
LAB TECH SANDERS: *Ah, of course you don't . . .* (pause) *So who's winning?*
NICK and **WARRICK** (simultaneously): *I am!*

Finally Solving the Case, Exhausted

NICK: *Shall we call it a push?*
WARRICK: *No winner?*
NICK: *No loser.*

Nick's pager beeps. It's a call to investigate a fresh new robbery crime scene.

NICK: *Double or nothing?*

The episode then faded to black as the two raced off, right back to work instead of calling it quits as they had intended. Their weariness instantly turned into a refreshed enthusiasm and a spring in their steps.

In reality, the CSI team working for CBS is an artistically licensed stretch from forensic teams working for most cities. CSIs don't go on bulletproof-vest-wearing raids, conduct interrogations, or do many of the activities we watch them engaging in on television. DNA assays take weeks to process; evidence examination is slow and methodical. In truth, they don't actually "solve" cases; they are data analysts who must adhere to neutral objectivity so as not to diminish their validity as state witnesses.*

If you're reading this while taking a break from filling out university applications to pursue a master's in criminology, we don't mean to

---

*Television programs like *CSI* have actually caused a bit of backlash from district attorneys around the country. The growing notoriety of forensics on the screen parallels a decline in conviction rates in cases pivoting on scientific evidence. Many DAs claim that juries are increasingly expecting to be wowed like they are when they watch TV. Proof in court is rarely that exciting. The letdown sways verdicts.

dampen your enthusiasm. Quite the opposite, we very much want you—and everyone chasing noble goals or meaningful work, be that in law, medicine, finance, engineering, architecture, agriculture, you name it—to hold on to ideals of career resonance. Rather than view movies as a con, we want you to see them as a slice of Help the Helper potential.

That film filters various professions down to a dramatic display of imagination-stirring highlights, exaggerated as they may be, doesn't mean those elements are lacking in the "true story" world of business. They're there. But they tend to be mightily overshadowed by the sheer volume and trudge of the details left *off* the silver screen—the details that contribute to psychological fatigue. When you're cozied up in your home theater, ensconced in the sixty-inch plasma magic of *Remember the Titans* or *A Few Good Men*, your mind follows the same big-picture (figuratively and literally) pattern as when you are outside a respected group looking in. You gladly suspend deliberation of a job's undesirables so as to allow inspiration to win the day. For most folks in most companies, gaining membership (or winning a new client) is like flipping off the TV. Back to earth. Back to the grind.

The requirements of real life don't have to be depressing like that. Enter an extreme teamwork opportunity for organizations that are willing to place a premium on how they manage the paradox that teams supply both the hurdle of—and the solution to—psychological fatigue.

Energy Executables

When speaking to groups about this topic we hear two hasty deductions:

1. "Oh, you're talking about the wake-up call new employees or new promotees receive when they get a taste of what is really involved in a coveted job they've finally been handed the reins to."

2. "Are you telling us that change-the-world idealism of fresh-out-of-college twenty-two-year-olds is something that shouldn't wane over four decades of nine-to-five repetitiveness? That we should just keep our eye on the big picture and everything will be roses?"

No. But with a pinch of yes.

The first statement we address by clarifying that we use membership seeking as one example, a considerably salient example. The shift in focus from pursuing rewarding *experiences* of work (a way you want to live your life) to tending to unpleasant or unthrilling *obligations* of work (a way you don't want to live your life) happens constantly throughout a person's career. Attending a conference, participating in an off-site training program, going on a retreat, taking a vacation or mini-sabbatical, writing a proposal for an exciting initiative, rotating project teams, scrapping an old mission statement, unveiling a new logo or new product . . . the list is extensive of revitalizing moments teeing up potential "letdowns" upon returning to the office or getting back to the stack of everyday responsibilities on your desk.

The second inquiry makes us chuckle. It paints for us an image of fluffy motivational speakers giving rah-rah advice that audiences enjoy despite only functioning as a fleeting pick-me-up. We've all attended seminars like that. They can be rousing to listen to, but frankly they're no more than an expensive shot of caffeine. "Just think about the big picture" is clearly not the answer. You have to take care of annoying, time-eating energy suckers.

Both deductions are important. They poke directly at the source of the opportunity for renovating how your team tackles minutiae and the buildup of nine-to-five drudgery that leads to slumps, stagnation, and premature career decline (as well as a midlife crisis—more correctly labeled an "energy crisis").

Practices we see from company to company to company follow comparable tracks: manage the flood, manage the burden on employees' shoulders, manage division of labor and assignment protocols, manage punishment and reward systems for completing the tasks that nobody wants to do, manage human resources policies and programs for coping with stress.

It's all managing work and managing people. What the greatest teams do is *manage energy*.

That doesn't mean lots of vacation to recharge the batteries. You might be surprised to learn that the friskiest teams (classified as groups high in both enthusiasm and productivity) have the largest collective pools of uncashed leave. Competitors dangle a half dozen weeks of annual personal days as incentive to recruit all-stars. Teams that are kicking ass don't. Their vacay package is nothing special; people don't use it

anyway! While opponents treat fatigue as a singularly physical construct, throwing sick days at all versions of the issue, great teams understand there is a psychological side to the equation for which nourishment
isn't "turning off" or getting away. It's the same reason that giant law
firms struggle to get the best out of brilliant young attorneys who had
no trouble enduring—and thriving on—ridiculous sleepless stretches
in the library as grad students.

Google is a standout case. Year after year ranked at the top of
America's most desirable companies to work for (by each of the biggies: *Fortune, CNN,* and *U.S. News & World Report*), Google provides
no more than the age-old standard two weeks' vacation for new hires.
People are banging down their doors to try to get a job there. What
Google does provide is an enviable trove of tools helping employees
bring more energy to the office versus that energy's becoming diffused across town—first-class dining facilities, a health clinic, massage therapy, gyms, fitness classes, commuting buses, laundry rooms,
dry cleaning, haircuts, carwashes, and more. Says executive chairman
Eric Schmidt:

"Let's face it: programmers want to program, they don't want to do
their laundry."

With the opportunity to use energy more efficiently, Googleans put
more of it into their work, take fewer sick days, and are generally happier. We need not detail the resulting billion-dollar impact on the company's share value.

Google employees aren't dashing for the door when the clock strikes
5:00 P.M. They aren't jockeying to get on corporate junket A-lists. They
don't circle on their calendars as many trade shows and tech conventions as they can locate for excuses to be out of the office. They'd rather
not be out of the office. As a result, they are less subject to the seminar
version of the Silver Screen Con.

So sequester people at headquarters? Do away with off-sites and vacation? No, and no. We're not saying that. Family trips to Dinosaur
National Monument are fantastic—when stimulated by excitement to
bring your child's science report to life. Likewise, training, networking,
and information conferences are great from a pedagogical perspective.
They foster growth and development, in addition to ensuring that your
folks aren't operating in a vacuum. The keys to obtaining convention
and retreat benefits without the psychological hitch: A) Handpick programs specifically for content objectives that mesh well with core team
challenges at home (or take vacations as family adventures, not anti-

work rebellions); B) Send the *whole team*! Few experiences are more counterproductive to creative sugars than to be sent off to an event, get your tires pumped up with a vision for change, and then return to a sea of cubicles in which everyone is caught up with their own to-do pile, too busy or too distracted to process your new ideas. Dumping a bunch of effort into cornering colleagues, endeavoring to twist their arms to try out-of-the-box suggestions, is a formula for spikes in psychological fatigue.

Go in the opposite direction of your competitors. Seize the advantages psychological fatigue presents, particularly in three areas: training, minutiae, and routines. We do so by using three executables:

Executable #1—Three Musketeer Road Trips

Reduce your organization's promotion (usually unintentional) of the psychological phenomenon called escapism—mentally tuning out. Escapism is reinforced, for example, when training programs, conferences, and retreats are used as methods of reward or for breaking up the monotony (sourcing external energy). The upsides are transient; the downside is a Silver Screen Con–style energy zap. Stop it! A simple fix in the direction of generating extreme teamwork is to use off-sites less (thus taxing employees with travel less); use only those that help with and are focused on specific challenges your team is facing, and when you do use off-sites, send your whole team so the unit stays a unit. Go mobile together in Three Musketeer fashion!

In addition to tending to the potential contrast of away-from-the-office activity, managing energy instead of managing people also means attending to contrast within the office. By this we mean the natural, internally motivating character of big projects versus routine busywork. Once again, an elimination or escapism approach is ill advised. Keeping attention firmly focused on the exciting peaks is a surefire strategy to lead in a prophetic dead elephant. For those unfamiliar with this analogy, imagine the ten-ton beast wandering into your conference room, keeling over, and dying. Now imagine everyone avoiding the conference room, shutting the blinds, not scheduling any meetings, pretending as if there is no elephant. What would happen as time passed? The carcass would start to rot. It would start to reek. Good luck making it as long as a couple weeks before the situation becomes unbearable (or perhaps we should say unelephantable).

"I've arrived at a decision to send all our staff on a team-bonding course."

© Business Cartoons

Ignoring, or mentally putting on the back burner, blocks of least desirable duties—in other words, going through the motions—eventually builds up a similar stench, though in overall attitude rather than odor. The unnoticed-at-first fumes can propagate an energy-draining atmosphere for long periods. Error rates tick up . . . personnel costs tick up . . . subtly, so little action is taken to stir the environment. Psychological fatigue builds. More employees take more sick leave. Insurance bills climb. All because of a seemingly sensible, yet subconscious, consensus to put as little effort, conversation, and attention into menial tasks as possible—to conserve energy for the most strenuous parts of the job, critical quarterly-earnings demands, or emergencies.

Risk of disaster builds as well. Speaking of emergencies, did you know that very few mistakes are made during the most critical phases of surgical procedures? The greatest percentage of doctor miscues occur during the simplest steps in the OR. Our marvelously insightful friend Dr. John Jane, who saved Superman actor Christopher Reeve from his spinal-cord-severing horse riding accident, describes brain surgery as: "Eight hours of sheer boredom with fifteen minutes of sheer panic sprinkled in." The sheer panic window, when each incision and each stitch is life or death, is the strongest espresso known to man. So much juice is coursing through your system, says John, it's impossible to be unalert or inattentive.

"That's when it's the very easiest to be on your game," summarizes Dr. Jane. "In those instants, every person, piece of equipment, and procedure aligns to help you do your best."

When wading through the least critical parts of an operation, when nothing is really at stake: all the heavy lifting is complete and successful; rock and roll is cranked up on the stereo; doctors are chatting about the pro-am golf tournament they played in last weekend, paired with Tiger Woods; nurses and support staff sign out to handle post-op paper-work . . . that's when something is accidently skipped, or a piece of gauze is left in someone's skull, or a tiny, tiny little bleeder goes unnoticed.

Comments John, "The things least likely to kill you—those are the things that kill you."

The same philosophy exists at the Johnson Space Center in Houston, where our astronauts prepare. Says Alan Pope, one of NASA's crew training chiefs, "Space is a lot of nothing. That includes a lot of nothing time. We care most about how pilots function *then*. Landing the shuttle, on the other hand, is hard enough that we don't worry about our pilots in those moments at all."

It's no accident (sorry for the pun) that NASA, at its prime, was considered one of the most extreme teams on the planet, arguably one of the toughest teams in any industry to join. Incredible cohesiveness resonates between polar-opposite tough-guy naval aviators and IQ-busting physicists. It's the stuff of Help the Helper legend. Walking on the moon is a walk in the park for teams like that.

John Jane's team, incidentally, is also noted for tough-to-crack entrance requirements. They've been the number-one neurosurgery program in the United States in both hospital hours logged *and* residency applications. Med students know the reputation; they know they are in for a grueling nine years. They can't wait to sign up! They also know the team they're joining has a stellar patient success rate. They're going to be part of something special which, in large part, is thanks to "special" being defined as viewing the minutiae of medicine as a point of pride.

"Our residents rave with one another over stitches they put into a hoof while practicing in a pig cadaver lab. I can't think of anything more mindless than placing your six-millionth suture in a cold, dead oinker. So what do we do? We make it as mindful as you can imagine. We turn the exercise into a world championships of suturing."

John's stitching story reminds us of another friend of ours, Terry Davison, an uncommon breed of engineer. University of Waterloo, Harvard, and University of Virginia educated, Terry played baseball in the Toronto Blue Jays organization before reuniting with his love of science. His unique combination of backgrounds has positioned him to be able to dexterously transition between the lab, the clinical research world, the consumer front, and the boardroom. But his rare breadth of multidisciplinary talent, believe it or not, isn't the most lauded trait in his worth as an incredible team asset.

Davison is office-renowned for shaking up dull air. At midday, just as his colleagues' morning Starbucks drips are wearing off, he'll slalom cubicles in his boxer shorts. He'll scream "WOOHOO!" at the top of his lungs when he succeeds—succeeds at sending off an utterly innocuous e-mail! He gives everyone outlandishly crazy nicknames. You might be tempted to think it's because he's a clown. Far from it. He's as cerebral as God makes 'em (save for maybe his brother, Tim, a Ph.D. on the cutting edge of chaos mathematics, nicknamed Stan P. Metallbauer, who's off-the-charts smart).

Terry's secret is turning celebration on its fanny. The less significant the occasion, occurrence, or accomplishment, the bigger a deal he makes of it.

Elucidates Davison, "Everyone will stop work, pick their head up out of their little world, and applaud a product launch or a promotion or hitting annual sales targets. My team doesn't need me then. They need me when those things are off the radar screen, when the days are blending together meaninglessly."

Though he's a fantastic chapter 3 Front of the Jersey model (the kind of talent you should covet stockpiling), extreme teamwork doesn't require employees as unique as Terry. It does require, however, that you value, encourage, and support *actions* like Terry's. It requires that you attack "going through the motions" with deliberate attention.

Terry's grooming as an elite outfielder taught him a vital lesson in this regard. Playing the outfield is more like brain surgery than most people realize. You stand relatively idle for the three-plus hours of a ballgame with maybe one or two crucial balls hit at you all afternoon. If your mind wanders a millimeter before Mr. Rawlings rockets your direction, you don't pick up the spin quite as fast, you're one step slower. That's all it takes for a runner to get an extra base and score, which in a one-run game is win or lose. What made Terry sharp, why he was the best at getting great jumps, wasn't something special he did in the ninth inning with the bases loaded. It's what he did during warm-up, before games even started. When outfielders loosen up their arms, playing catch, they do a lot of grab-assing, joking around, and telling tall tales of the previous night's escapades. It's textbook going through the motions. Terry is anything but antisocial. He's a blast to trade classic baseball conversations and humor with. But when he prepared his cannon, he prioritized preparing his mind. He'd purposely exaggerate his footwork, pick out tiny, specific laces to aim at in his throwing partner's mitt, and pretend each toss was the toss that would bang someone sneaking to stretch a double into a triple. For Terry, an instrumental purpose of warming up was making sure to *not* be going through the motions. He'd rehearse a deliberate sort of thinking to prevent the boring frames in baseball from causing a future error.

Terry would get along famously with Dr. Jane and Dr. Pope. His practices in baseball have carried over to his corporate success and help explain why he has such an unusual amount of energy. Colleagues think he's ten years younger than he actually is. The way he treats "unimportant" duties makes him highly impervious to slumps. Follow his lead!

Executable #2—Kill the Dead Elephant

Increase the prestige in your organization of doing small, unrewarding, and odd jobs. Ask yourself, what acts go the least noticed? Give them notice. What operations do people not realize are getting done? Give them realization.

How do you do that? We're confident a number of excellent strategies already come to mind. A clever method to add is to suture pig hooves like John Jane's residents or play catch like Terry Davison. In other words, identify one or two tasks your team must do that are like warming up your arm in baseball—necessary, but needing scant attention to complete satisfactorily. Enrich their practice by being playful with them, even turning them into championship tournaments. That might seem silly, but willingness to be silly is in fact a characteristic of world-class performers and teams, as is detail orientation when everyone else is taking the details for granted.

Of course, no matter how good you get at flipping the script on elements of work that ordinarily contribute to psychological fatigue, the office isn't going to be all smooth sailing and Hollywood drama. We're human. We're going to get caught up in our silos. We're going to get stuck going through the motions, running on the treadmill, staring at the wall.

Extreme teams size this up favorably. As we've been discussing throughout the book, extreme teams do not look to superstars, or superstar patents and products, to beat the market. They get their competitive advantage by helping people, helping in ways adversaries are not. Recall the machinery that escalates psychological fatigue's potency: A) self-perception is low, that is, we tend not to be aware of the signs of it in ourselves, and B) ego is high, that is, we tend to think help is not needed. Bingo. Help the Helper cultures jump on both by jumping on things that get too routine.

And when it comes to egos and routines, sports take the cake. Athletes are a notorious lot for fastidious, precious, untouchable pregame routines. Interrupt them and you're burnt toast. But that's just what Portland assistant GM Tom Penn did in 2007.

In Memphis to contest the Grizzlies, the Trail Blazers were on a cold streak. Players were tired, caught up with their individual struggles. So Tom, a board member of St. Jude Children's Hospital, after touring the medical facility, decided an extra push of Help the Helper was needed. He decided, as he says, to "break every rule of basketball." He canceled the normal shootaround players use to get ready for a game. The guys were going through the motions. Despite anticipated pushback (potentially cries of bloody murder) from abandoning the usual, comfortable routine, Penn instead took the team to visit with the sick kids at St. Jude.

"I'm not sure I can pick out the right words to describe my pure emotions," Tom shares. "I was sad, I was happy, I was mad, I was angry. I had more joy in my heart that day than many, many days. Just seeing the kids, seeing them overcoming, seeing them show unbelievable toughness and unbelievable unselfishness . . . life-threateningly ill, yet cheerfully engaging *us.*"

Two things happened: (1) Interrupting a routine that had become worn and reinforcing of negative habits clicked on awareness. (2) Witnessing how these children battled excruciating conditions with smiles on their faces was a humbling experience; it put NBA egos aside. How easy would it have been for any of the kids to resent millionaire athletes in premium health who have no idea what it feels like to go through wrenching illness? The kids gladly welcomed their input anyhow, regardless of whether it would really do anything concrete to improve their prognosis.

An awareness increase and an ego decrease—not coincidental with what disarms psychological fatigue. Penn saw an area of performance that had become too routine, that was sucking energy, and he nailed it. Not by rest or escapism, though. A children's hospital isn't the place you go for mindless unplugging. The solution was to go at it head-on.

Said Tom at the time, "See how these kids get after the tedious toil of daily treatment with conviction and determination? That's how we're going to take care of *our* work."

A different team showed up at FedEx Forum that night, not walking through pregame warm-ups as a check-it-off exercise or a mandatory step before playing, but as if the simple ball-handling drills were crucial passes in the final seconds of the evening's contest. Forty-eight minutes later the Blazers snapped their skid—on a gutsy buzzer-beating shot.

One of our mentors, John Rassias, would be proud. John is a world-renowned professor of French and Italian at Dartmouth. He's the inventor of the Rassias Method, a philosophy of teaching foreign languages that centers on the experience of conversation instead of parsing grammar, memorizing vocabulary, or writing phrases over and over in workbooks. Taking a class with him is like being in the middle of a Broadway smash every single day. John shows up in outrageous costumes. He does back flips and hops on desks, making wild gestures and adding his own vocal soundtrack of explosions and superhero *Whams* and *Splats*. Peek through a door when he is teaching and you'd think he was a drama instructor. His concern is getting students engaged. The whole while, dialogue is in French or Spanish. And he doesn't care if students make grammatical errors or stumble over pronunciation. He encourages it, actually. He incorporates corrections into the act, as part of an exciting storyline.

Rassias's brilliance is understanding—and vividly communicating—that speaking in another language is an exercise of personal and emotional expression; it's an act of art. To be maximally effective, it needs to be rich; it can't be dry or scientific. It can't and shouldn't be perfect. Mastering another tongue *does* necessitate repetitive rehearsal and it does take a large volume of hours. John makes sure, though, that this repetition is never boring. He makes sure routines don't become routine. No one gazes at the clock in his classrooms. What is a very difficult thing for many people to accomplish, which they shy away from or are embarrassed to try in public, is a "can't wait to go play" experience with Rassias.

That's why he'd love the Tom Penn Blazers anecdote. It's his passion to take disheartening, bland, rote routines and make them as unroutine as possible. Penn's work happens to be with highly paid athletes, with high stakes. Rassias's happens to be with regular college students, in an arena with no dire career stakes. It's immaterial where on this continuum your team is housed. What matters is whether or not you're paying attention to routines the way Penn and Rassias do.

Executable #3—No Routine Routines

Eliminate what we refer to as the Down and Defeated: people struggling because ineffective or energy-sapping routines have become habits. They're practicing those routines without realizing it. They're not asking for help. Step in like Tom, or like our fictitious colleague coming to the plate with a divide-and-conquer team babysitting plan. Help the Helper cultures manage energy by knowing teammates' routines, not leaving them to chance, watching for junctures where they might get stale, and then being willing to grab the baton.

Praise and Progress Conferences

When tackling psychological fatigue, when going head-on at monotonous areas where errors or subpar performance is apt to crop up unnoticed, it may seem overly obvious to state (but we'll state anyhow): the approach should be one of infusing enthusiasm. We're continually shocked by how many organizations address the issue as a negative. Roy Williams's maxim "If you act enthused, you will be enthused" is widely missing.

The business of medicine provides fertile ground for Roy's message. Curiously, a common practice among medical centers is holding regular Friday intraoffice meetings called Morbidity and Mortality Conferences. The abbreviation "M&Ms" isn't to draw a candy metaphor. They're certainly not sweet. M&Ms are weekly reviews of adverse outcomes in which staffs assemble to rehash circumstances, X's and O's, autopsies, and legal ramifications of patients who died or are dying. Talk about depressing. Imagine the hub of your collegial interaction constantly being malpractice suits and grand losses. Not the substance of a psychological fatigue–free working environment. Is the high rate of physician burnout at these institutions truly a surprise?

Now compare that with the routine Verizon started a decade ago. An expanding number of divisions within the corporation are instituting a standing Friday get-together that they've named Praise and Progress Conferences. One by one they go around the room, each person stating a piece of praise for something a coworker is doing, then reporting an element of progress that is being made. The verbal offers need not be monumental. As we've learned, it's generally praise and progress of a nonmonumental scale that is most needed in groups.

UNKNOWN

Come together, share together, work together, succeed together.

Independent of economy ups and downs, Verizon has remained committed to this program. Correspondingly, the company continues to climb America's Best Place to Work charts every year. They've been steadily picking off competitors, too. With 108.7 million subscribers, Verizon is now the most successful wireless provider in the United States.

Mightn't you prefer Praise and Progress Conferences over Morbidity and Mortality Conferences? What might you achieve if you found just one team process that you could shift from an M&M nature to a P&P nature?

Return with us to this chapter's opening paragraph. People *want* to do their best. Coming up short isn't a cognizant choice. We now know the monster hidden in the bushes, picking the pockets of conscientious employees—pockets of energy. Ordinary teams can become extreme teams by collectively standing up to this monster called psychological fatigue. *Collectively* is the key word.

Ask yourself, ask your teammates, when you look at belonging to the group, do you see a platform for getting ahead in the corporate rat race? Or do you see an opportunity for people to help keep the psychological fatigue monster away from one another? The latter is what programmers love about Google, surgeons love about working with Dr. Jane, engineers love about teaming up with Terry Davison, pilots love about training at NASA, students love about learning French from John Rassias, and salespeople love about Verizon.

Do your teammates love this about you? Are you willing to manage work less so you can stoke your teammates' energy more? Prefacing our next topic, are you willing to go as far as scheduling *more* time-consuming meetings in order to help make this happen?

YOUR TURN!

Seeking Experience Versus Fulfilling Obligations

To recap: Hollywood can light us up with the same inspiration we have when we're in law school working toward standing up for the little guy or when we're in medical school preparing for an envisioned life of curing sick children. Walk out of a theater or practice your craft for twenty years—and energy easily wanes. The extreme type of teamwork comes to the rescue when teammates help one another manage energy, rather than obligations or procedures.

1. Conferences, off-sites, and other work-related travel can have an undetected downside of "outsourcing" energy renewal or fostering escapism. Identify one program that promotes escapism and fix the approach!

Name one out-of-office meeting that you can A) insource, B) ax, or C) take a Three Musketeers approach and send *everyone*.

---

2. The Catch-22: focus heavily on what you do well—that is, the tasks that give you energy—and you're more apt to make mistakes or miss something in the mundane components of your job; focus on reducing those errors and being a "details" champ, and you'll likely squash energy. How do you get better at this juggling act? Be like Terry Davison or John Jane; convert just one otherwise unappealing duty into a teamwide March Madness, complete with a bracket, scouting reports, seeds, the works!

Write it down: what is one mindless area of work you're going to develop into a championship tournament?

---

3. Performance routines are paramount for consistency. But they can become stale or lose effectiveness without notice as a result of the habitual comfort there is in practicing them. Be a leader by staying attuned, by making sure your team's routines don't become routine!

What is one highly effective, energy-imbuing routine your team is using that you are going to make it a point to recognize *today*—and protect moving forward?

_____

_____

What is one stale, Rassias-spirit-needing routine your team is using that you can refresh or eliminate *this week*?

_____

_____

4. Be what we call a Pillar of Positivity. Have you ever noticed that the most positive person in an office is usually the most motivated or most productive? Help your teammates by bringing that kind of energy to them. Be the embodiment of this anonymous quote:

"Enthusiasm is contagious. Let's start an epidemic."

What are five things—they don't need to be big—you are going to do to be *super* positive (*genuinely* so) this week?

_____

_____

_____

_____

_____

6.

Invoke the 30-Minute Rule

An H2H Culture: Bucks Information Age
Communication "Efficiency"

Plastered on the Flint Tropics' locker room wall: *E. L. E.*
"Everybody love everybody!" shouted owner-player-coach
Jackie Moon in *Semi-Pro*, espousing his team's core operating principle . . . and brushing aside the fact that his business was soon to fold.

Aptly portrayed by Will Ferrell, that was leadership in the days of the original ABA—bell-bottom and turtleneck, afro and sideburn sporting start-ups, hocking appliances to stay afloat, chasing an ethically compromised promise to double franchise value by merging with the NBA. Executives assumed they could secure their future with wide-open rules and flashy style, highlighted by the introduction of the slam dunk. They ignored player, manager, and referee grumbling about inadequate arenas. They offered brightly adorned, tie-dyed halftime shows to address sparse crowds—while fans migrated to television. An average of three years per club was all it took for thirty-five of the thirty-nine teams in ABA history to disappear.

Basketball has come a long way from the swinging seventies. So has communication.

We now have an entirely new American Basketball Association, sixty-five teams and expanding, playing in six countries, vying with multiple "minor leagues" (including the NBA's own D-League) for ticket-buying eyeballs. We also now have tweeting, texting, and IMing. Athletes are bigger and faster. Corporate conglomerates are bigger; the pace of business is faster. With pressure to win escalating in parallel— swelling salaries for MVPs, shortcuts to profit such as performance-enhancing drug use, creative stadium financing and taxation, statistics and technology eclipsing the human element, growing foreign influence—hoops, it can be said, like much of professional sports, provides a mirror of competitive commerce.

So it's quite enlightening to examine the outliers—sports franchises that are steroid free, figuratively *and* literally. The real lessons to be learned don't come out of Yankee Stadium. They come from organizations that must earn it the hard way, and do . . . without the drugs or the dollars; without the free agents or colossal coliseums. Such case studies are the very definition of best practices. And they are found in places like broom closets that double as boardrooms for the managers who succeed, without ethical compromise, in today's economy, in today's American Basketball Association.

ABA teams don't get No. 1 draft picks. They are tasked with turning grassroots potential into results, a mission for which they have scarce resources. They play second fiddle, even to college basketball, for fan support. Marketing is relatively fruitless, on a *regional* scale, forget ESPN. Players are motivated to jump ship, hoping to pick up with an NBA-affiliated squad. Survival hinges on finding a way to get the most out of performers, both on the court and in the front office, without really anything to offer—certainly not the massive contract incentives or red carpet treatment commonly associated with life in pro sports.

In 2001, KP was staring this very problem right in the face. A hometown hero at the helm of the ABA's Kansas City Knights, he had clout and connections. He'd pooled all the basketball talent he needed to win. Yet his team was underperforming.

"I was frustrated because I didn't feel like we were playing up to our ability. There were a lot of underlying issues I didn't know about. I could smell them. I could taste them. But I couldn't get to them."

Less than two weeks into the season, team leader Donny Marshall left to join the New Jersey Nets. No one was talking championships in the locker room. No one was really talking at all.

"It was after a win, actually. I went home stewing. Like many coaches do in these situations, I wanted to use the next practice to run the hell out of 'em. Something wasn't working. It's all I'd had on my mind since opening day. Then it hit me like a sledgehammer. I'd logged a lot of time thinking about it. My players had to be logging a lot of time thinking about *something*. I've got to just open it up."

Elite athletes are pretty intuitive when it comes to their coach's mood. The Knights showed up in the gym, heads drooped, expecting three hours of gut-busting gassers. They stood around in a circle instead.

"I want to implement a new rule," KP began. "I just want to see how it goes. It may go well. It may go poorly. But I'm willing to risk it. And if you guys are willing to risk it and work on it, then I think it could be something good."

A look of surprise washed over the team's faces.

"The rule is . . ." Kevin said, making up a name for it right there on the spot, ". . . the Thirty-Minute Rule. If you've thought about something and you have an issue, or I've thought something and have an issue—thought about it for more than thirty minutes—then we owe it to the team to bring it to each other."

Not a peep. Kevin thought he'd laid an egg.

"I didn't know what else to do. Nobody responded; nobody opened their mouth. We just went into our usual routine. We had a decent practice but nothing out of the ordinary. Then it happened. The very next day I got two calls on the telephone, both from players. The first was an issue you might expect, all about basketball. One of my guys was bothered that he wasn't getting many minutes. He thought he should be playing more. So we sat down after practice and ended up talking for hours. Some things we agreed on; some things we disagreed on. Most important, it gave me an opportunity to tell him I appreciated his input. We looked at his situation together and tried to come up with a solution that he felt good with and I felt good with, and we moved forward. The other individual brought something to me that was so far removed from basketball that I probably never would have realized its impact. It was a personal issue. He was uncomfortable on the road with his roommate. He was a family man and he wanted to go to bed fairly early, around ten o'clock. His teammate wanted to keep the TV on and chat on the phone 'til two-thirty or three. It sounds obvious, but you know how that goes. So we rearranged room assignments and he ended up playing a ton better."

GENERAL COLIN POWELL

The day soldiers stop bringing you their problems is the day you have stopped leading them.

The Knights finished the season by reeling off 24 straight wins to capture the ABA crown—a record that still stands as the longest string of consecutive victories by any Kansas City professional sports franchise.

Engage, Engage, Engage

Frustration with playing time is an age-old conflict between athletes and coaches; the same conflict exists between bosses and their employees regarding staffing, project assignments, promotions, travel, R&D priorities, product pitches, and presentations. Sometimes you've got to get comfortable with the fact that you have different assessments of talent or skills from players/employees, especially when egos are involved. So you'd be wise to have an established process for developing that kind of comfort. Otherwise snowballs turn into avalanches.

The first player wanted additional minutes. We worked on it. We tried to help him. Did it come to a complete conclusion and he was absolutely thrilled? No. What it did was make me aware of the issue and his particular needs, make him aware of my issues and particular needs, and we were able to come to a sort of agreement, an improved understanding of each other. It wasn't perfect. But it was workable and it transformed the problem from something bottled up, not communicated—a permanent performance killer—into something more temporary, under construction, moving forward.

Rex Walters, a fellow University of Kansas Jayhawks product and now head men's basketball coach at the University of San Francisco, was one of the Knights' outspoken veterans in 2001. KP inquired of Rex: Why had no one come to him with concerns prior to instituting the 30-Minute Rule, even those that clearly affected performance? Why no equipment upgrade request or small defensive shift suggestion? Nothing.

"You were a great player. You know the game better than anyone. We assumed you knew what issues needed work," Rex stated bluntly.

Rex and KP have been the best of friends ever since. They now speculate that without the 30-Minute Rule, they might have ended up usurping Roman writer Pliny the Elder's generally credited status as propagator of popular mythology that ostriches hide their heads in the sand instead of acknowledging threats.

In reality, there has never been a scientific observation of danger-ignoring behavior by ostriches. It is just a fable. Most likely, in penning his *Naturalis Historia*, Pliny the Elder was documenting how these birds gobble up dirt and stones to aid digestion. Their unique, abrupt neck movement can appear from across the plain as if they are slamming their heads into the ground. And flightless birds are, of course, considerably more vulnerable while they're eating. For the most part, it's simply a humorous business metaphor. Rarely do organizations perish by deliberately disregarding threats to the bottom line. Failure to effectively address issues happens far more unwittingly, as was occurring in KC before Kevin took action.

"There you are!! I've been looking for you!"

Or all too often, it's the guise of communication itself that causes problems to go unidentified, undiscussed, unsolved. Consider the case of an elderly couple. Grandma is cleaning the kitchen, overfilling a hefty garbage bag. Grandpa is in the breakfast nook with their grandson, Thomas, watching *60 Minutes*, the television volume up to max.

"Pa, would you take this trash out to the street, please?" Grandma calls across the room.

Grandpa gives no signs of a response so she raises her voice sharply, "PA, I WANT YOU TO TAKE THE TRASH OUT!"

Still no reply. Grandma turns toward Tom and says, "He never listens to me! Every time I need his help he does this; he just ignores me!"

Tom tries to explain, "I don't think he can hear you over the TV, Gram."

Grandma walks into the breakfast nook, right up behind Grandpa, and shouts, "I ASKED YOU TO DO ME A FAVOR. TURN THAT INFERNAL MACHINE DOWN AND GET YOUR LAZY BONES OUT OF THE CHAIR!"

Flinching, suddenly noticing Grandma, he looks at her and then Tom with a startled expression.

Tom attempts to remedy the situation. "Gramps, Gram would like you to take the garbage bag outside."

"Oh, okay," Grandpa says, promptly getting up.

Now completely furious, Grandma mutters, in a manner that is anything but subtle, "You'll listen to Tommy, but you won't listen to me. I don't know why I've put up with you for the past forty-five years."

Grandpa frowns intensely in confusion, his feelings bruised as he heads to tend to the trash.

Perhaps Grandpa's hearing aid is damaged or his son gave him a gift of upgraded technology that he doesn't realize must be reprogrammed. Perhaps Grandpa suffers from more advanced hearing loss that's never been diagnosed. We can confidently hypothesize from tone and language alike that these two have had plenty of similar exchanges. Their emotions are clear; there's no shortage of expression. But positive change will never occur without an intersection of the right timing and the right approach, without the pair, as Stephen Covey says, "seeking first to understand"—without their priority being to fully attend to a conversation.

Which brings us back to tweeting. And George Bernard Shaw rolling over in his grave. Shaw quipped:

"The single biggest problem in communication is the illusion that it has taken place."

Such an incredible plethora of communication tools is at our fingertips these days. We can send a Google message to thirty colleagues simultaneously while reviewing straight-to-our-inbox RSS news highlight feeds and chatting, walkie-talkie style, on our Bluetooth headsets. All the while we can be trading text messages "w/6 dif ppl, in r/t BTW," firing off a proposal via e-mail, getting pop-up alerts about business transactions, and keeping tabs on our network via streaming Facebook wall posts. To make sure the world (and our boss) knows just how industrious we are? We open a Twitter account and sync it up to Google . . . and Facebook . . . and LinkedIn . . . *and* our cell phone, with a GPS tracking app so our every trivial movement is broadcast automatically, in convenient 140-character cheeky sound bites.

Is anyone listening?

Really listening.

Technologists claim that this downpour of devices is bridging the world divide, strengthening communities, fostering relationships. Sociologists point in the opposite direction. Research is revealing that the more we use and rely on digital interaction, the *less* we know about people in our lives and the less cognizant we are of interpersonal variables. More information. Delivered faster. The illusion of connectivity. The illusion of productivity.

Therein resides the secret sauce of the 30-Minute Rule. In a business climate that encourages glancing at your BlackBerry 24/7—"one sec, honey, I gotta shoot off a quick text"—the 30-Minute Rule makes us pause. It is all too easy to be sidetracked by the flood of messages coming and going from the ether, assuming bountiful communication is in execution. The other definition of execution may be more deft. What we achieve in volume we lack in depth, in substantive integrity, in *engagement*.

As the Knights' title path teaches us, talent without engagement will flounder. Minor yet significant details will be missed. Small problems will become stealthy deterrents. But get that same talent engaged . . . *Jumanji!*

Fruits of the 30-Minute Rule

We didn't have hard currency lying around in KC to incentivize employees for problem solving, for taking ownership of obstacles, for resisting the influence of the Internet age toward cursory relationships. For that matter, we didn't have much in the way of alternative currency either. It goes with the territory of leading in the ABA. Offering trust and respect, however: no other recompense needed.

In addition to providing a system for distinguishing all the trifling chatter that floats around an office from matters truly in need of attention, in addition to creating a platform for critical discussion, the

30-Minute Rule is its own intrinsic reward. We could contentedly rest on the value of providing you with a tool to counter the downside of communication on steroids. Except we've witnessed the 30-Minute Rule accomplish so much more:

- Creating Trust Downline; Creating Trust Upline

- Growing Awareness; Generating a Culture of Mutual Respect

- Engendering Real Engagement

- Relieving Pressure; Relieving Tension

- Allowing People to Let Go and Move Forward

- Putting Focus on the Important; Taking Focus off the Unimportant

- Keeping the Small Stuff Small

- Eliminating Anyone's Feeling Like an Island or Feeling Unsupported

- Bringing People Together; Building Relationships

- Giving Voice to Ideas; Generating Solutions; Building Consensus

- Allowing Healthy, Productive Treatment of Disagreement

- Reducing Corner Cutting

- Providing a Safe Environment for Personal or Sensitive Matters

- Making People Feel Like Valued Members of a Special Team

Help the Helper managers strive, doggedly, for these things. If all they receive from their direct reports is a flow of quarterly statistics and sales contracts, no matter how lucrative, they consider themselves a failure. The payoff they want is the list above. So, like us, they are willing to go to lengths others would deem absurd to gain the fruits associated with the 30-Minute Rule.

When the San Antonio Spurs came knocking on KP's door, attempting to charm him away from the ABA, they didn't need to pitch hard at all. Media that reported on the front office move assumed, as most people would, that the splendor of returning to the NBA did the quick trick. That wasn't the fuel for Kevin at all. What was unique about the Spurs, which unquestionably led to their dynasty of titles, was that the organization was more akin in culture to European basketball than American basketball. It's often noted that teams in Europe act like families. Teams in the United States act like businesses. The Spurs were a family.

In many NBA organizations, the executive staff and the on-court staff don't intermingle much. Sound familiar? In many corporations the C-suite is on an entirely different floor in the building from the front-liners. Not in San Antonio. General manager R. C. Buford and head coach Gregg Popovich don't just visit frequently. They *hang out* together. They have dinner together almost every night. Sharing in the breaking of bread is as important to them as signing the right free agents and staying under the salary cap. They invite their secretaries and interns. Their families and children join in. They talk about life. They laugh and cry. They let down their guards.

They also can't help it; they regularly stumble into chatting about work. They don't mean to. It happens. They're passionate, passionate men when it comes to both family and hoops. The union of family and hoops is special time. And when they reflect on this dining habit (which is what the majority of European clubs do and hardly any American clubs do), they admit: they actually get *more* work done at dinner than they do in the office. The work is meatier (whether steaks are ordered at their restaurant of choice or not), incorporates greater breadth of input, and is highly team-centric. It's therefore more effective.

That's why Kevin said yes to the Spurs immediately.* Signing on with an organization that has meetings of the R.C./Coach Pop nature: a no-brainer for Help the Helper–minded performers. We urge you to keep that in mind when you contemplate how to recruit and retain the best.

Shortly after KP uprooted to Portland the team found itself in a nail biter of a race to get free agent Hedo Türkoğlu. Türkoğlu had played with Orlando the prior five seasons. They loved him. He was tough, unselfish, everything the organization was about. He was NBA elite mustard in the teamwork department. Trouble was, a dozen other teams wanted him. The Blazers' front office burned the candle at both

---

*Kevin was actually cut by the Spurs at the end of his playing career. Why didn't it deter, in the least, his love for the organization? Because Pop, who was an assistant coach at the time, went out of his way even back then in meeting scheduling. He took the time to visit with KP to help Kevin make the transition a positive learning experience. He could have taken the "easy" way out, emotionally speaking. He could have just put a pink slip in KP's locker. Pop instead sat in the gym with Kevin for hours, selflessly giving of himself to help KP use the situation to his benefit, and to find confidence in the process.

ends for weeks in negotiation, hustling, jostling for position. It came down to the wire . . .

The Toronto Raptors snared him.

Long faces and nth-degree moping around the office characterized Portland's suites the following morning. How did they handle the loss? Pritchard picked up on a lesson he'd learned from Buford and Pop. He invited everyone, organization-wide, over to his house.

"It evolved into a *great* day," reflects Kevin. "It was one of the most spirited meetings we'd had through the entire process. We all ended up going swimming . . . and being reminded of what made our team such a special team."

I Object, Your Honor!

Yes, following through on the 30-Minute Rule means devoting time—focused, nonmultitasking, other-demands-can-wait time. Time for open, attentive dialogue. Time for team dinners, even!

We know what you're thinking.

"More meetings? You're asking me to schedule *more* meetings? My day planner is already triple booked; I have a stack of papers on my desk that shuts out sunlight; I can't remember the last time I had a date with my wife. When am I supposed to fit in another meeting?"

You may not want to listen to this, but if you're that swamped you're doing some things inefficiently. Chances are, teamwork (or lack thereof) is one of them. Or you're allocating too many hours to inconsequential communication. If you find yourself balking, an organized strategy for acquiring constructive criticism might be what's lacking. The good news is that the 30-Minute Rule assists with all three. It spreads out responsibility *and* equal measures of commitment, illuminates tasks you can eliminate, and provides you with valuable performance enhancement feedback. And it helps you accomplish what made Rudy Giuliani so successful.

In the wake of 9/11, Giuliani was walking through downtown New York with the mayor of Boston, a reportedly high-strung guy. (Hopefully that doesn't incite a Sox-Yankees riot.) The two were on their way to support their staffs who'd stepped up as volunteers to comb the Trade Towers wreckage for survivors. En route, they passed by a tiny bakery. The proprietor was cleaning ash off his shop's windows. He halted his desolate task. He invited the men in for a cannoli.

"No. We don't have time," said the mayor of Boston. "We have to get to ground zero."

Giuliani was sympathetic to the mayor's heartfelt anxiety to get to their destination. Nevertheless, his gut told him to act otherwise. He accepted the invite and tugged his compadre into the bakery.

"Let's slow down. It's important to see and hear what the world is giving you."

No question, it might be perceived (or misrepresented by paparazzi) as a politically negative thing—stopping for a dessert at such a tragic time. Giuliani's resistance to giving in to perception in an effort to stay focused on what matters most (such as this poor shopkeeper's needs, and the reflection it offered on the plight of people in Manhattan from all walks of life) is a lesson we should all learn from him.

We know where you're coming from, too. The plea of the busy is very real. Initial resistance to the 30-Minute Rule, resistance to eating up time (and cannoli) during stressful periods is actually highest among the most conscientious employees and bosses.

"Everyone is going to be calling me, constantly!"

Conjuring up a vision of overload is enough to make anyone dig in their heels. Or go Pliny the Elder on you. But that's why it's called the *thirty*-minute rule, not the five-minute rule or the two-minute rule. A considerable usefulness of this tool is that it reduces noise generated by the ease with which people can use technology to zip off messages, complaints, opinions, and mental diarrhea. Not every issue needs to be brought up. Far too many are. Especially when leaders have an open, more caring, and personable nature. Is it any wonder that so many folks in authority positions come across as cold?

Instead of leaving discussion to chance, or to the squeaky wheel, or worse, resorting to a certain degree of callousness or corner-office insulation, the 30-Minute Rule supplies an operative filter. It's not just "talking about stuff." By design, the point of conversation that triggers a 30-Minute Rule meeting must be a topic that's been on one's mind steadily, repeatedly, cumulatively, for longer than half an hour.

And if you still end up inundated with requests?

That alone is a golden piece of data. There's a reason so many issues have gone unresolved, been buried, or avoided. It's a sure indication that your organization is underperforming or is a pressure cooker waiting to burst. So ask yourself: would you rather have remained ostrich oblivious? Or are you excited about the insight, thrilled to start scaling this new mountain so you can find out what your people are truly capable of achieving?

What If Nobody Buys In?

A bigger risk is people *not* engaging. Well, perhaps we shouldn't use the word *risk*. If you implement the 30-Minute Rule and nary a soul puts it into practice, disappointment or discouragement would be more appropriate descriptions of the outcome. You have a team that's short on real commitment.

One could say nothing gained, nothing lost. But that would be inaccurate as well—as inaccurate as it is a bastardization of the cliché. Quite a lot, actually, is gained in this scenario. You glean considerable insight into the variables discussed in chapter 3. Who's on the bus? Who do you have in the trenches with you?

 DOUGLAS MCGREGOR

Most teams aren't teams at all but merely collections of individual relationships with the boss. Each individual vying with the others for power, prestige, and position.

You also create an opportunity to shed light on whether or not your business is being affected by the dreaded Post-Meeting Meeting.

When the doc was in college he competed in both baseball and rugby. Two very different team cultures. Though not because of the games' origins, not because of the home countries and languages of his mates and coaches, not because of the physicality or training demand differences between the sports, not because of rules or traditions. Because of the way communication was organized.

Baseball had the late slot indoors in Leverone Field House in January. It was Dartmouth. It was winter. Snow covered the baseball field prior to opening day.

Preseason practice would be scheduled for 8:00 P.M. But you'd have to get up extra early before class to swing by Davis Varsity House at six or seven o'clock in the morning to double-check the bulletin board in the locker room. Prior to day-of, you never knew when team meetings would be penciled in, or how many there would be, or how long they would be planned to run. Sometimes we'd have to dress out four hours before practice time! Sometimes we'd finish workout at midnight and then have *another* meeting. We wouldn't get to start studying until 3:00 A.M.

A couple of animated team members, Johnny Ross and Johnny Owens, coined the terms Pre-Meeting Meeting and Post-Meeting Meeting (PMMs). They became running jokes.

"We've got meetings to talk about having meetings," ribbed Ross.

Johnny Owens, who also played football, used to tell his gridiron fraternity brothers, "Baseball's not a game for the soft. You gotta handle a ton. You've got the pre-pre-post-pre-meeting, and the pre-meeting meeting meeting, and the post-meeting practice meeting to practice meeting. It's intense, man."

There was so much superfluous organization and instruction that players grumbled nonstop about not getting enough fundamental baseball work done, not to mention being sleep deprived. Overcoaching and micromanaging were topics of much of the locker-room chatter.

"We'd leave Davis House at two in the morning, trudging through two feet of snow en route to Baker Library, and all we'd talk about was how stupid the meeting was we just had."

Rugby had team meetings. Of an entirely different nature. When Coach Nigel Topping—a former World Cup–winning captain of the English national team—arrived, he scrapped coach-led prepractice huddles. He instead held chalkboard sessions once a week, usually on Monday in preparation for upcoming Saturday matches, breaking down scouting reports, plays to be emphasized, etc. If you needed to go over a performance element beyond that, you could approach him individually anytime. All other formal meetings, though, were conducted by on-field leaders, commencing each practice with a forty-five-minute focused chat about needs and objectives while players stretched. That's it.

There was a visceral difference in the conversations between teammates on the rugby pitch versus those of teammates on the diamond. Baseball always seemed to be negative. Talk was mostly criticism and second-guessing lineups or drills. It definitely killed focus during practice. A lot of guys quit. Nobody quit the Dartmouth Rugby Football Club (DRFC). The DRFC was four squads deep in roster size. Everyone was dialed in when it came time to work. And when practice was over, there was no prattling on, no critique, no doubt that the day's mission was accomplished.

It wasn't long before "Post-Meeting Meeting" surpassed joke status. John's academic adviser, psychology professor Dr. John Corson, suggested applying formal study to this contrast of training and competition cultures. A light bulb went off.

"I realized the expression Post-Meeting Meeting had strong human performance connotation."

A PMM, in a nutshell, is when people break from an official assembly while continuing discussion privately—where thoughts tend to end up sequestered. Whether the rambling is good or bad (we find it's mostly the latter, and subconsciously so), it's not known to the whole group and certainly not to the folks at the top. That's significantly counterproductive.

"Our baseball team had Post-Meeting Meetings left and right," John recalls. "We had a losing record. Our rugby team was as close knit as you get. We never had Post-Meeting Meetings. When something needed to be addressed, we addressed it during stretch, with everyone. We were ranked as one of the United States' top five teams my entire career."

If you give the 30-Minute Rule a shot and people don't buy in, chances are PMMs are occurring.

Of course, it is possible that attempting a new program may flop at first, but at the very least it will supply worthwhile color, helpful in assessing future potential or needs of your personnel. You can learn from failure: Who embraces innovation? Who wants to grow personally and professionally? Who sees the benefit of open, transparent, and meaningful dialogue? Answers to those questions show you who has *real* commitment, not just "punching the clock for as many hours as possible" commitment. Again referencing chapter 3, one of the "intangible" traits extreme teams seek to stockpile is real-commitment capital.

So toss asunder worry about employees' disappointing you. Instead, beware the true risk: inadvertently maintaining the status quo. Twitter and text messaging are here to stay. Communication fragmentation is a reality of business in a high-speed, technology-driven world. Is that reality going to make you feel "too busy"? Or is it going to get you jazzed about the fruit-garnering opportunity becoming more and more available as the gap widens—the gap between the style in which the majority of today's workforce communicates and the way people communicate at companies with vivid, performance-propelling, human engagement?

The Kansas City Knights didn't have an NBA payroll, or a fancy sports medicine complex, or their own private jet. They flirted with a perfect season. The San Antonio Spurs act like a European basketball team, prioritizing all-inclusive, family-style team dinners over extra hours in the office. During the current pro sports era in which coach and GM tenure is precariously short, Spurs personnel enjoy tenure that kicks other organizations in the buttocks. As an Ivy League university, Dartmouth Rugby can't traverse the globe recruiting or hand out full-ride athletic scholarships. But year after year the program contends for national championships.* Makeup of these three teams is as divergent from one another as it gets. Yet they share a common bond: priority placed on the quality and depth of interaction exchanged across all levels and ranks.

They share a common bond with the company Evanta. Launched as a small meeting planning firm in the Pacific Northwest, Evanta now coordinates, stages, and operates more than sixty global leadership summits that support CFOs, CMOs, and CIOs within nearly nine hundred of the Fortune 1000 organizations. Founder Bob Dethlefs recognized a conflictual truth: *competition* among corporations generally hinders *communication* among corporations. Industry leaders are hesitant to share best practices for fear of giving away trade secrets, intellectual property, first-mover advantage, or other types of work product. Yet co-operation—just like the cooperation of Larry Bird and Magic Johnson, which raised the entire level (and future) of the NBA—is a necessary ingredient for long-term survival. So Dethlefs set out to create industry best practices programs that would facilitate sharing, trust, and alignment—that would facilitate Bird-Magic thinking in arenas such as finance, marketing, and human resources. Evanta was born.

The first success lesson we should all heed from Bob is the *profitability of sharing* in areas and on occasions where sharing seems to be a risk. Doing so (and aiding others to do so) not only vaulted Evanta into its current, enviable position of being a trusted adviser to the most well-respected senior executives in the world, but it's helped pave the way for Evanta's clientele to generate a combined $12 trillion in annualized revenue.

The second success lesson we can nab from Bob comes from his overall business approach. With so many famous customers, one can imagine how in demand Bob's time is. The volume of e-mail and text messages he receives daily could easily consume his every waking hour,

---

*The reputation launched by Coach Topping has been fostered and grown by another Help the Helper genius: Alex Magleby, former DRFC star and former captain of the U.S. national team, the Eagles. Alex's dedication to communication—and unselfishness and toughness—resulted in Dartmouth's bringing home the 2011 NCAA crown in Sevens.

even if he limited his communiqué to a one-sentence max. He doesn't. He writes old-fashioned, handwritten notes. He makes personal phone calls. Do his demanding clients get impatient? No, their loyalty is ever strengthening. Bob also starts every day by gathering his employees together for a powwow. To delegate duties and pile on the overflowing work? No way. He takes the time (as his inbox beeps and flashes) to listen to and then commend each team member on elements of progress nearly all bosses we've studied tend to overlook or consider unimportant. Prioritizing this Help the Helper-style communication is one of Evanta's secret sauces. Bob is happy to divulge it to you; he is the embodiment of leading by sharing.

Interestingly, the rise of all four (the Knights, Spurs, Big Green rugby, and Evanta) happened in veritable light-switch fashion. Success tracked each organization's establishment of tactics for encouraging people to connect in more than just a surface or Facebook wall post manner. Certainly, wins don't always cascade as quickly or voluminously. But these case studies beg the question:

What gains, big or small, will *you* see in a short period of time if you spend less time communicating in digital fashion and more time taking the hit for your team to hold meetings of personal depth?

Implementation: Agree or Disagree, but Unite

Picture us abruptly standing up at our desks, snapping our pencils in half, and tossing this manuscript across the room. No, not pulling a Bobby Knight (though many of his outbursts were calculated). Rather, for dramatic emphasis in reminding you that great leadership is based on the foundation: make the complicated simple. To borrow from The Home Depot's advertising slogan (and acknowledging that there is a pretty darn good reason why The Home Depot is crushing other teams in its industry, a reason we bet you can guess): Stop reading. Stop analyzing. Start doing. The benefits of the 30-Minute Rule await.

> **LAUNCH STEP:** Identify one person with whom you want to develop a better, more engaged relationship—a colleague, a client, your boss, an employee, your spouse, a friend.

> **INVESTMENT STEP:** The two of you must make a promise. Vow to each other that you will follow through. When you have

thought about an issue or obstacle or idea solidly, repeatedly, for thirty minutes, schedule a sit-down meeting. No phone calls, no Skype, no "banging it out" over lunch or coffee. Make sure to mind a couple crucial keys to success:

1. Before meeting, reaffirm that the objective isn't for someone to win and isn't to nail a perfect solution. Agree or disagree, but vow that you will find a way to unite.

2. *Listen.* Be determined to fully understand what the other person is feeling and where he or she is coming from.

3. It's okay to table an issue. Sometimes you'll come up with a quick and easy strategy (like switching travel roommates). Sometimes you'll simply obtain clarification or share critical, insightful information. Sometimes you'll identify "back to the drawing board" steps and schedule another meeting. Measure success by increases in *engagement* and *understanding.* Having those as metrics is what will ensure that you progress toward extreme teamwork.

Get your feet wet. We're confident that you'll figure out how to tweak and customize the 30-Minute Rule to fit your and your business's personality. Once you do, move to your direct reports or one of your project teams. If it doesn't make sense to go downward, go one up. We've never met a decent boss who'd turn this opportunity down. Bosses who show hesitancy because they feel inundated with requests? Sure, that's a possibility. But that doesn't mean they're bad bosses. Likely the 30-Minute Rule is exactly the excuse they need to afford a more effective filter. Any boss with a particle of leadership talent knows how essential productive communication is and will love that you're taking initiative in such a critical area and looking for methods to further invest yourself in the company.

You say you work for someone who'll spit back a categorical "no" to a thoughtfully crafted, baby-step approach for testing a performance enhancement tool? You'd better ask yourself then, "Is this the person I want for a leader, mentor, and role model?"

Press yourself to ponder: what do you risk by keeping your head down, by *not* suggesting a new tactic?

Whether it's upline or downline, your sales team or your CEO, trade

"What we need in this organisation is
more personal contact."

© Business Cartoons

this chapter's promise with them. You owe it to the ambition of having a Help the Helper culture; you owe it to one another personally.

It doesn't matter if you're in a partnership or a member of a staff of ten thousand. The 30-Minute Rule is effective when implemented with targeted working groups. It's about depth and quality of engagement, not instituting company-wide policy. So start small. Once the performers in your charge commit to this plan and experience the benefits, they will apply the 30-Minute Rule to *their* direct reports. In this way, the 30-Minute Rule grows organically, as any good strategy should. Over time, you'll see a trickle-down effect spreading to everyone.

And *that* is a sign that an organization's culture is on the way to becoming award-winning.

Now go do it!

YOUR TURN!
The 30-Minute *Promise*

To recap, research shows that the speed and ubiquity of communication technology today is actually an impediment to relationship building. You therefore have a tremendous extreme teamwork lever in working hard to counter "digital dialogue." Yes, that might mean scheduling *more* meetings. Trust us. The returns are more than worth it. Give it the good ole college try. Be like Dartmouth rugby coach Alex Magleby in that regard. He shows us all what slowing down communication can do; he wins national championships over mammoth budget powerhouses like Texas and LSU—at a school that can't give out a cent of athletic scholarships, not even to cover the cost of books!

1. Have meetings like R. C. Buford and Coach Pop.

Whom will you take to dinner or invite over to your house to watch a ballgame *tonight*?

_____

Whom will you take to dinner or invite over to your house to watch a ballgame *next week*?

_____

Whom will you take to dinner or invite over to your house to watch a ballgame *the week after that*?

_____

2. Make the commitment to develop the type of communication that the Kansas City Knights fostered.

Whom will you make a 30-Minute *promise* with?

_____

Eat Obstacles for Breakfast

An H2H Culture: Has the Kind of Toughness That
Just Might Surprise You

I f you want to build an extreme Help the Helper organization, you
need to make *true* toughness a paramount priority. You need to be
like Navy SEAL Eric Greitens and Trail Blazer scout Michael
Born, whom we'll introduce you to in this chapter. You need to:

Be authentic and real with your teammates

Be emotionally rich with your teammates

Be willing to fail with your team's fate in your hands

This chapter will explain why and how, getting at the ingredients of
special teams which people often shy away from. We set the table by
taking you to February 3, 2008. . . .

Super Bowl XLII is one hour away from kickoff in Glendale, Arizona.
University of Phoenix Stadium is loud, packed to the gills. Hordes of
New Englanders have trekked out of the snow, out of the deep freeze,
cross country to the desert in hopes of witnessing the second perfect season in NFL history. The sole squad to do it was the Miami Dolphins,
running the table in 1972 with 14 unblemished wins. The Goliaths—the
New England Patriots—warming up on the turf, are in uncharted territory, 18-0. They are confident, prepared, focused, ready to go. The

Davids sit huddled in a cramped locker room beneath the arena—the 12-point-underdog New York Giants. They are holding hands.

Tears well in their eyes.

This is a team Hall of Fame commentator Chris Berman refers to, in the gruffest, grittiest of voices, as *The G-Men*—quintessential tough guys, in the quintessential tough-guy sport, led by the quintessential tough-guy coach, Tom Coughlin. They are moments from battle. Players are on the verge of crying.

What is going on?

Hold that thought.

BRUCE LEE

Notice that the stiffest tree is most easily cracked, while the bamboo or willow survives by bending with the wind.

Earth-shattering it is not to point out that adversities and gut checks are part of the territory of striving for excellence. We've never heard of an exceptional accomplishment that didn't involve clearing hurdles, bouncing back from mistakes, and scaling a mountain or two. The Wright brothers crashing, Michael Jordan cut from his high school basketball team, John Grisham's first novel rejected by sixteen literary agents and twelve publishing houses, Einstein expelled from school, Winston Churchill's public-speaking-preventative speech impediment, the Ford Edsel—a mere spackling of history's famous failure stories. Individuals with a fortitude, a perseverance to overcome the odds, separate themselves from the pack. As do teams with a *collective* courage. Again, not an earth-shattering statement. How that courage is defined and fostered on exceptional teams, however, *is* noteworthy. We've found it contrary to the sort of toughness most people assume is required to win at the highest levels.

Toughness Defined

When we're out on the scouting trail, scouring for Help the Helper–caliber athletes, we've been known to remark, "Toughness is like pornography; you know it when you see it." We get chuckles and nods. But there's more than glibness to our simile. When watching performers under pressure project an aura of toughness, all you are seeing is the physical, surface representation. Few have the depth we want to recruit. Forgive us for the phraseology, but much of toughness is, also like porn, only skin deep—lacking true substance. Based on appearance, it's easy to be fooled. Which is why we log so many hours looking under the covers (get your mind out of the gutter), examining resilience beyond its stand-tall, walk-tall framework.

We talk with former coaches, classmates, ex-girlfriends, gymnasium janitors. We watch endless footage of game tape. We gather piles and piles of data. What we don't do, in the process of inspecting psychological variables, is rely on pencil and paper tests. To understand why, it's useful to take a minute to consider the relationship between emotions and performance, as well as a little of the history of assessing emotion, to explain how organizations miss the mark.

Rewind one hundred years.

On the brink of entering World War I, faced with a sudden influx of 2.8 million draftees from a broad swath of citizens (including a large number of recent European immigrants who, it was postulated, might have conflicts of interest), the U.S. Army deemed it necessary to develop quick tests of aptitude. American Psychological Association (APA) president Robert Yerkes and Columbia University psychologist David "Wex" Wechsler were commissioned for the job. They set to work adapting what was then the only standardized measure of intelligence, the Stanford-Binet IQ scale, so as to differentiate "officer material" (A-grade) from those earmarked general infantry from rejects (E-grade). What they wrestled with in the process gave rise to a still ongoing debate regarding the use of general intellect in forecasting human performance. IQ makes intuitive sense when it comes to predicting marks in school. But does it adequately encapsulate the propensities that distinguish fine soldiers? The soldiers destined to become generals?

Wechsler thought not. He devoted his life to moving forward the notion that intelligence is more than a singular trait or capacity, blazing a trail to incorporate noncognitive factors in assessing the power of the brain. His groundwork led to today's most widely used psychological inventory, the Wechsler Adult Intelligence Scale (WAIS). He paved the way for Howard Gardner's breakthrough theory regarding multiple intelligences. He lit the critical lamp to be mindful of cultural biases in human testing.*

As the twentieth century progressed, so did acceptance of the idea that IQ is a fairly limited construct. Significant human behavior insight emerged out of studying mental ability from a multidisciplinary standpoint. Social science advances, however, were largely academic. It took *New York Times* journalist Daniel Goleman's bestseller in 1995, *Emotional Intelligence*, to put a more evolved view of "smarts" on the mainstream map.

Goleman tallied the research up to that point to propose that emotion is equally as influential as cognition in success, particularly leadership success. From a substantial media pulpit he argued that the reason so many high-IQ people fall short of their potential in business (relative to fields like mathematics or physics) is that they fail to grasp the role emotion plays; they take too analytical an approach to jobs with sizable degrees of human interaction. Feelings, taste, personality, sensation, sentiment, disposition . . . all fulcrums of human interaction. It follows that an intelligence of these mechanisms in an office environment, in the marketplace, would be valuable for achievement. Goleman labeled it "EQ." He broke it into four emotional competencies: self-awareness, self-management, social awareness, and social management. He suggested everyone receive as much career training in these areas as they do in the technical aspects of their work.

Though backed by eight decades of theory progression by eminent scholars (Wechsler, Gardner, et al.), it was a bold claim in the realm of business where, as in professional sport, toughness is considered an essential quality.

"Maintain a poker face."

"Never let 'em see you sweat."

In baseball, we've heard a corollary countless times: instruction given to pitchers to "be stoic on the mound." Roger Clemens made famous the strategy of holding his glove up to cover his mug so opponents couldn't see his expressions. Hitters would see only his eyes staring them down with deadpan determination. He was the model of stoic. His 4,672 strikeouts and record-setting seven Cy Young awards were presumed to be the result. Until all the clear, the cream, and the

---

*Of fascinating note: Wex, as early as 1939, railed against "quotient" measures as a less valid methodology. Corporate America hasn't listened to those objections as it's rolled out Q after Q. IQ, EQ, SQ, KQ . . . what's next?

needles malarkey was exposed by Congress. We're certain Goleman would agree; the Rocket's boosters were probably not EQ seminars.

Syringes, though, aren't lying around coffee-room counters in the worlds of sales, finance, advertising, trading, accounting, and such. Caffeine generally suffices as the performance enhancement (PE) drug of avail. So it's not entirely surprising that Goleman's ideas caught interest. He cleverly presented EQ as a performance tool. Like athletes, executives are looking for advantages wherever they can find them. It didn't hurt that *Emotional Intelligence* hit bookshelves and talk shows at a juncture of rapidly growing psychotropic medication popularity in the United States. Diagnosing children with ADHD in order to prescribe drugs for better concentration in school was gaining acceptance. The practice spilled into escalation of work-related depression and anxiety reporting, adults seeking meds to help them work.* Methylphenidate (Ritalin) and fluoxetine (Prozac) and their cousins were beginning to be viewed in high-pressure professions as steroids of sorts for the brain. Culturally tracking toward a trendiness of "happy pills"—mucking with mood as a manner of modulating human capacities—made the soft-skill strategy of emotional training all the easier to swallow in traditionally hard-skill-centered domains.

Time magazine was quick to splash "WHAT'S YOUR EQ?" across the cover (October 2, 1995), tagging *Emotional Intelligence*, after barely a month on the shelves, one of the twenty-five most influential management books ever written. *Harvard Business Review* chimed in, listing Goleman's HBR sister article, "What Makes a Leader," as one of its top-ten all-time must-reads. The notion that managing emotions is not only a learnable business skill, but a skill differentiating who can lead effectively from who can't, seemed to hit an overnight tipping point.

Five million copies later, an industry that sprouted up in response to a groundswell of demand for corporate lectures, workshops, and training products hasn't shown any signs of slowing. It's safe to say, our population more than caught up with Wex's initial deduction in investigating how to measure the predispositions of draftees: cognitive intellect isn't the differentiator among the elite, the officers—especially when it comes to handling adversity, such as the rigors of war.

---

*From 1985 to 1999 the annual number of prescriptions written for attention deficit issues in kids increased by a whopping 327 percent. Keep in mind, *doubling* the volume of drug use would've been a 100 percent increase! Today, Americans pop *three times* as many psychology-related pills as do our European counterparts.

More than caught up; it's worth repeating. Management surveys indicate that greater than 65 percent of American corporations now include a facet of emotional intelligence in hiring and promotion decisions, as well as in staff development programs. The military tests EQ. So do professional sports teams. The NFL Combine, which serves as the final major-stage screening prior to the draft, at one point topped seven hundred questions in psychological testing. Sabermetrics proponents love it . . . Moneyball of the mind. Mental toughness in black and white.

Aha! That's what the New York Giants were doing. Fearful, worried, emotionally strained, they were participating in a pregame EQ tune-up class, trying to flip around their EQ scores in preparation to take on Goliath.

Um . . . no.

It turns out that emotional intelligence doesn't hold water as a championship predictor. Research scrutinizing the efficacy of EQ has yet to provide any empirically reproducible evidence that emotion management correlates with business outcomes. Probes comparing Combine exam scores to on-field game production show a near zero relationship. And while the findings of scientific journal articles may be lost on GMs and head coaches, busted signing bonuses are not.

Take Drew Henson, for instance, the third baseman converted to quarterback whose pro sports lore is notching the NFL's highest EQ total. Henson played two seasons for the Yankees. He collected *one* major league hit. Deciding he was better suited for football, Drew retired from baseball in 2003 to join the Dallas Cowboys. He earned his way to a start on Thanksgiving Day, 2004 . . . only to be yanked after completing just four passes in a half, replaced by joint-creaking, forty-one-year-old Vinny Testaverde. Henson never started another game in the NFL, despite having shots to hook on with the Vikings in 2007 and Lions in 2008.

Or take Ryan Leaf, for example. Fill-in-the-bubble sheets prophesied him to be the better bet—better makeup, more of a leader, said EQ consultants—than the other guy teams were fawning over in 1998, a southern bumpkin with a slow drawl to match named Peyton Manning. The San Diego Chargers traded two first-round picks and a three-time Pro Bowler, Eric Metcalf, in exchange for a *one-slot* draft board move to get Leaf. They lavished him with a $31.25 million deal, containing an $11.25 million windfall up front, the day he signed on the dotted line. It was the largest sum ever paid to a rookie at the time. Leaf proceeded to throw two touchdown passes amid fifteen interceptions in ten games that season. Worse still, he overtly blamed his teammates for his performance woes. If you had to tab it with a number, Ryan would probably receive a 0 on a Help the Helper 1–10 Likert scale. The Chargers had to eat his contract, kicking him and his acidic locker-room outbursts to the curb in what ESPN promptly touted as the number-one biggest flop in the history of professional sports.

So what gives? EQ captures the talent to read and understand emotions, control them and stay fixed on goals, empathize, influence teammates, and manage conflict. Good stuff for being an unselfish leader. Good stuff for knowing how to support your colleagues through difficult periods. It would seem like emotional intelligence is a holy grail for measuring Help the Helper ingredients. Clearly, that is a common conclusion. We thought so, too. In the late nineties we ventured down the path of implementing EQ. We stumbled upon an interesting dichotomy. The subset of our population who scores highest on understanding and managing emotion, who have the most adept capability to teach others how to use their emotions to succeed? Psychologists. The profession least welcome in pressure-packed environments—locker rooms, pre-op, fighter plane hangars, concert backstages, homicide squad rooms? Psychologists.

Doc recalls his first year in graduate school. A coach requested that he visit with an athlete going through a slump. The athlete had no say in it.

We were instructed to meet in the library. It was ridiculous.

The second we sat down the kid asked, "You gonna psychologize me?"

"I knew instantly I wasn't going to be much help. Not because of some kind of resistance to the subject matter or lack of brain power. Those are the obstacles everyone assumes get in the way of athletes' working on their mental games. Nope. We needed to tackle what this young man was doing minutes before competition, when coaches were breathing down his neck, when teammates were counting on him to lead, when challenges were glaring at him. And we were going to accomplish that sitting passively at a desk, surrounded by books, whispering? Good grief."

Examples like this bring up misconceptions about how elite performers handle emotions. Namely, that the tougher a surgeon or attorney or executive is, the better they are at keeping emotion out of the equation (and, many infer, the more they get divorced). The misconception is also that psychologists (or spouses) pry into vulnerabilities and insecurities too much, that perhaps a high EQ is being too touchy-feely. In academic circles, it's called the "curse of emotion"—a hypothesis that people too sensitive to their and others' feelings won't be able to make difficult decisions that carry emotional knocks with them, such as firing an employee, or pushing a colleague out of a comfort zone. Back in the seventies, when the NFL climbed on the old-fashioned IQ bandwagon to assess cognitive capacity relative to "thinking" versus "nonthinking" positions, Pat McInally, a wide receiver and punter from Harvard, ripped off a perfect test score. He was picked up in the fifth round by the Cincinnati Bengals.

"Being smart . . . it cost me a couple rounds," jests McInally.

Pat says it tongue-in-cheek. He knows that while research doesn't show a positive intelligence to thriving-from-stress correlation, there's not an *inverse* relationship, either. There are plenty of greats with high IQs and EQs. There are also psychologists (admittedly a tiny pocket of them) who get hugs and high-fives every time they walk into a locker room or firehouse or military base. And there are the Giants crying. . . .

It seems we're at an impasse. On the one hand, we know how vital toughness is in beating the odds. Companies in every industry recognize it. We know EQ gets at some of the key ingredients—controlling impulses, managing emotions to facilitate focus, propelling teammates. Yet, on the other hand, the movement to measure and train these specific skills hasn't produced systematic or sustainable performance enhancement, at least not in the theater we ultimately care about: building a team that takes down the biggest opponents, being the *best*.

The impasse forced us to rethink toughness altogether. The more we examined it, the more we realized that the importance of emotional intelligence is the importance of *how* it's addressed. We realized that analyzing emotion, processing it, turning it into a cognitive exercise, doesn't jibe with how emotion plays out in the heat of battle. World championships, stock market IPO launches, breaking the news to someone that they have cancer, closing arguments to prevent the innocent from going to jail, inking deals with new customers—they are all emotionally rich activities. To excel, you must be engaged in positive, passionate, channeled ways. *Emotionally* engaged. That's a far cry (to keep hinting at the Giants) from intellectually engaged. A flint sparked when we stepped back enough to notice that the vast majority of EQ trends and tactics center around exams, seminars, workbooks and the like, a host of tools that try to put the round peg of toughness into the square hole of testing and training. There's a mismatch between how toughness is thought about, how it's defined, and how it's most effectively executed.

Goleman himself is fond of qualifying, "A misinterpretation started nearly the moment *Time* put EQ on the cover."

All the thinking is gumming up the works.

Doc Eliot's sister, an acclaimed relationship psychologist in Massachusetts, draws a parallel to the fashion by which their father, Rick, coached generations of junior skiers with Olympic potential:

"Dad was as well versed in ski technique as anyone on the planet. He knew the physics down to every angle. But he taught that way only a small fraction of the time. Other coaches would instruct the heck out of arm swing and hip involvement and foot position. Dad would take kids to hang out with great skiers, like Bill Koch.* You get so much better, so much faster, skiing behind a legend than you do cognitively studying a legend. Your brain gets out of the way."

Your brain needs to get out of the way to excel in applying emotion to performance, too.

That's why we don't pencil-and-paper it when it comes to Extreme Team toughness. We love having high-EQ guys—as long as they get there organically instead of deliberately, instead of artificially governing their way through emotion manipulation. Nobody wants a teammate to manipulate their, or anyone else's, feelings. The reason psychology thrives in our locker rooms is that we don't make it a scientific or "therapeutic" regime. We don't roll out the couches. Our teams elevate because, instead of attending yet another workshop, we attend to the philosophy:

Toughness is not emotional control; it's emotional authenticity.

Toughness Distinguished

Why is this so important? Why is this far more than just semantics?

Because, as we've witnessed in our careers over and over again, the toughest athletes, those who find a way to come back and beat you when a contest appears already sealed, who rise above the greatest of adversities, those like Joe Montana or Wilma Rudolph or Greco-Roman wrestler Rulon Gardner or surfer Bethany Hamilton, learn to tap a re-

---

*Koch is the only American ever to have won an individual Olympic medal (Lake Placid, 1980) in the sport of cross-country skiing.

markable well of resiliency, one we haven't come up with a statistic for yet. It's a well from the heart and soul, not the brain.

In that regard, they share a kind of kinship with the men and women whom oncologists label "spontaneous remissions." Spontaneous remissions are cases of late-stage cancer patients—tumors spread throughout the body, brain, liver, lungs, beyond all hope of treatment—who one day walk into their doctor's office, a curious glow in their eyes. Scans reveal no masses. Cancer has vanished. Poof, gone as if in a puff of magic smoke. They were handed a life sentence, laughed at it, and kept on truckin'. Actuarial tables are but a passing joke to them.

It's not mythology, any more than slow-mo again-and-again sports upsets are Disney fiction. It's not DNA either. What connects these folks isn't an off-the-charts pain threshold or an unbreakable constitution. When spontaneous remissions are poked and prodded by physicians, blood assays are that of purely average human beings. Just as Montana and company rank as middle-of-the-pack in strength, speed, you name it. Their hardiness comes from a much deeper well.

Naturally, doing what we do for a living, we've been on a mission, pardon the expression, to get to the bottom of this well. Here's what we've discovered distinguishes people whose toughness drives extraordinary accomplishments.

I. The Toughest People Are *Real*, with Faults, Imperfections, Quirks, and Weaknesses

Jim Valvano is probably the toughest man we've ever known, right up there with the best leaders in history, in or out of sports. If you've never listened to his 1993 ESPY Awards acceptance speech, *stop reading right now*! Fire up YouTube and watch it. Valvano delivered his famous "Don't Give Up; Don't Ever Give Up" oration as he was dying, hardly able to walk to the podium, having to periodically pause to catch his breath from the toll bone cancer was taking. He could have politely excused himself from having to appear onstage. Not a soul would have blamed him. He'd never hide his frailty from the world, though. It wouldn't have even occurred to him. Healthy or sick, happy or sad, Jim was the ultimate role model of an authentic person. His words from that night, which can't possibly be worn out:

"You should have your emotions moved to tears . . . if you laugh, you think, and you cry, that's a full day. That's a heck of a day. You do that seven days a week, you're going to have something special."

ALEX KARRAS

It takes more courage to reveal insecurities than to hide them, more strength to relate to people than to dominate them, more "manhood" to abide by thought-out principles rather than blind reflex. Toughness is in the soul and spirit, not in the muscles.

Jim could have used the captive national audience that night—the famous figures in the crowd who ended up bawling, like Lou Holtz, Coach K, and Joe Namath—to deliver a full discourse on cancer activism, pushing hard publicly to raise money for his foundation. He could have been all business. Instead he spent the precious opportunity sharing stories of career mistakes and failures. How he screwed up his first big pregame pep talk at the helm of Rutgers basketball. Jim understood one of the most critical lessons of toughness: *Don't be a superhero.* Leading a team through challenges is not about demonstrating thick skin. It's like self-confidence. As we instruct our clients, "If you have to tell someone you're confident . . . you're not."

Valvano understood that toughness is not a solo act. You only have so much fortitude. It's a condition of being human. It's going to wane or be absent on occasion. Your team is the ultimate source—your family, your friends, your officemates, your employees. Being emotionally transparent with teammates so they can help you, so they are more apt to be transparent, too, allowing you to help them in return . . . *that's* a loftier level of toughness. If you strive to always present a bulletproof front, you prevent the wealth of resources around you from knowing when and how to contribute. Your effort to be strong actually reduces the strength of the group. It's *team EQ* that provides the ultimate well depth.

Concluded Valvano at the ESPYs, "People think I have courage. Courage is my family."

We feel this simple utterance is so vastly important that we'll repeat, in call-to-action form: be the loftiest level of tough; be emotionally transparent with teammates so they can help you; help them by encouraging them to be emotionally transparent in return.

Oh how we wish Jimmy V had made it to spontaneous remission. He passed away within two months of the ESPYs. It's valuable to note, even the greatest come up short. They are completely at peace with that. They don't shy away from it—yet another element of toughness excellence. And why Valvano is still with us. KP fondly remembers Coach V's recruiting verve, which didn't ebb one iota despite Kevin's committing to Kansas.

"We were chatting in the rec room at my house, where my family had a pool table. It was a pool table from a billiards hall that my dad bought, that was once owned by Al Capone. Capone's signature was underneath. Coach V loved it. It was an Italian thing. He took it as an omen that I should play college ball for him. When I told him I was going to be a Jayhawk, he grinned, motioned to the table and told me he'd play me for it! We played all day long. I don't know if I've ever had that much fun. He ended up pulling out the win. He just winked at me; he knew I was going to Kansas anyway. He wasn't going to let that stop him from treating me like family."

To this day, we flip on "Don't Give Up; Don't Ever Give Up" regularly, sometimes weekly. We highly recommend you do so as well. Or pick other clips that bring you to tears and make them part of your toolkit. Make it a habit to send emotionally powerful video segments to colleagues frequently. Share them with customers. Open important meetings with them. Let them—and your tears—fly.

II. The Toughest People Hug, Get Silly, Get Scared, Rejoice, Weep . . . in *Public*

Autumn 2000 was the doc's first semester at Rice. The transition proved to be extraordinarily educational.

Teaching accolades from the University of Virginia would mean little to new students. A track record in professional sports might create a little buzz, particularly among athletes, but it wouldn't suffice for holding fifteen weeks of attention. It was nice to have the recommendation of the baseball coaching staff. The Owls had manufactured a formidable program and, as championship organizations do, they acknowledged that they could use help. Coach Graham ardently encouraged his players to enroll in org psych classes. But we all know how far an authority figure's pushing goes in engendering inherent buy-in. Personal trust needed to be established before any credentials, lessons, or mentoring could have an impact.

The doc's signature course, Introduction to Performance Psychology, was scheduled to meet twice a week. Rather than lecture both days, half the available instruction time was forgone in favor of small group discussions—gatherings for relationship building, a chance to get out of the mode of being a professor.

"I wore workout gear to the discussions, ratty sweatshirts and tattered baseball caps. I encouraged Q and A to be a bit of bullshitting around. The application of letting down my guard with students would serve their best interests far more than would extra instruction, problem sets, or pop quizzes."

Still, there was an artificial authority layer that hung on. Final exams approached. Lectures had finished; review sessions were all that remained of course meetings before the holidays. And then it happened.

"It was late. The student masses had left for the evening. Four baseball players stayed behind, probably for some brownnosing points in case I relayed attendance to Graham. They happened to be the team's four studs. First-rounders. Nails. They liked to BS about baseball. I was more than happy to chill with them. But I had this tremendous pocket of gas swelling up. I was holding it in. It was getting intolerably uncomfortable. I considered calling it a night. These were guys I hadn't been very successful at developing any kind of authentic relationship with yet. So I decided to let it go. Boy did I let it go. It could very well be ranked the loudest, most impressive fart of my life. BOOM. In an instant I was no longer Dr. Eliot, no longer an 'adult' at arm's length. It was an instant that set the stage for everything I was able to accomplish at Rice."

Who would've thunk it? A fart. The foundation of trust that led to packed-house classes (late in semesters when most classes experience an attendance drought), teaching awards, and more weeks as the nation's No. 1 ranked baseball school than any other Division I program—for a decade—a veritable dynasty of conference championships and College World Series runs.

Jimmy V would be very proud. It's one thing to be real, to let those close to you see all your peccadilloes. It's an even better measure of toughness to be unreservedly real in public, to be human, to be okay with being fallible in the vision of people you want to impress. Be a hero like Jimmy V and find occasions in public, occasions when you would normally be self-consciously reserved, and free it up; let the world really know you!

III. The Toughest People Are Willing to Offend or Disappoint

Can we really top a gas explosion to explain willingness to be offensive? Unlikely. We would, however, like to share the story of Michael Born. Mike played college basketball at Iowa State and would drive up to

Kansas each year when school let out to play in the Lawrence summer league. Summer league is notoriously rough. Fouls are seldom called, it's run and gun, and courts belong to the local players. Jayhawks dominated. It was their turf.

Mike was a scrapper on defense. Excuse the vernacular, but he was a dick to play against. Not in a character flaw way; in the sense that he was hardnosed, relentless. Plus, he was from a rival Big Eight school. KU players wouldn't let him into the games.

Born stayed anyway. He didn't care that his style of play was unpopular. It's who he was as an athlete. He wasn't going to pretend to be someone he wasn't, as easy as that would have been, in order to gain admission into some basketball games. Lawrence was *the* place to be if you were a college basketball player in the summer in the eighties. The best talent, the best competition, the best scouts watching. And scouts, of course, were watching for "good fits." It added up to tremendous pressure on Mike to conform to a public image of what a team player was supposed to look like. He held on to his commitment to be authentic.

The hometown boys eventually let him in. His mettle was proved by his honesty to his character. He could've given everyone what they wanted. He could have done what nearly every player does, which is be concerned with what is written on his scouting report. But then the league's players wouldn't have gotten to know who he really was. They wouldn't have had an opportunity to form a brotherhood that still lives on.

"To this day," shares KP, "when we get out for some pickup, we try to kill each other. We fight like brothers."

Some say Mike's approach cost him an opportunity to make it to the NBA. We say it extended his career. He's been winning professional basketball championships as a coach and executive for twenty-plus years now. His alacrity for being authentic, for being okay with making wrong decisions—as long as he's sincere and competitive about it—makes him a vast resource of toughness for an organization. At multiple junctures in KP's career when KP felt he needed more toughness, he brought in Mike.

Born is a true asset because colleagues know, without a shadow of a doubt, that he's strong enough to make mistakes. Big mistakes. That's a mark of someone special. The Blazers wouldn't be where they are without teammates like Mike.

IV. The Toughest People Are Willing to Fall Flat . . .
in Front of Millions of Fans

Remember ABC's *Wide World of Sports*? Remember the opening reel contrasting the thrill of victory with the agony of defeat? Vinko Bogataj was the agony of defeat, the ski jumper wiping out at the start of every broadcast in a spectacular flurry of equipment, snow, and limbs. Ordinary performers would sooner quit than have their legacy be of famous failure. Vinko loves it. He knows a thing or two about the kind of toughness revered by the best athletes in history.

"Every time I'm on television, I crash," Bogataj told an audience at an ABC Sports celebration gala. Muhammad Ali promptly asked him for an autograph.

If you're worried about embarrassing yourself in the eyes of your brethren, if you're worried about tarnishing your reputation, what you're doing is putting up a barrier to deeper team cohesion. Take a page out of Vinko's book.

That's what KP did. He pulled a Vinko after the Trail Blazers suffered the worst loss of his tenure. It was 2009. The season was creeping up to the playoffs. Portland was on the bubble and they'd just handed away, on their own hardwood, 114 points to the Philadelphia 76ers. Nary an employee was firing on all cylinders.

INDIAN PROVERB

I had no shoes and complained. Until I met a man who had no feet.

"We were bemoaning some pretty awful performances. It was one of those days when *everyone* was complaining about something. I'll tell ya, I was the main culprit. So I signaled for a huddle. I told my staff it was carte blanche for thirty minutes: lament, bitch, as much as you possibly can. Have at it. Turnover to assist ratios, refs, ticket sales, migraine headaches, late buses, unwashed towels . . . all fair game."

An incredulous gaze bounced back at him.

"I'm a pretty positive guy so I guess they thought I was a bit out of my gourd."

KP had to kick it off.

"You know what? The cafeteria crew dished up Swedish meatballs for lunch this afternoon. They sucked. I *hate* Swedish meatballs!"

That broke the ice. Floodgates let loose. The conversation reinforced that it's okay to not always be at your best. It's okay to have disgruntled, frustrated feelings. Everyone gets down. Everyone gets stuck in bad moods or gets thrown off course by a curveball sometimes. Great teams don't waste energy trying to prevent the natural fluctuations of being human. They embrace them as opportunities for Help the Helper teamwork to blossom. Suppress, bury, or hide your humanity and you're like every other company trying to be tough. Be vulnerable and you can stimulate extreme teamwork. If you can show your "ugly" emotions to your colleagues, you unlock the door for them to help you stretch and continue to expand as a performer.

Thirty minutes flew by. The group gave rousing high-fives to one another. Then KP interrupted, "Let's go shoot some hoop!"

What happened next was an embarrass-yourself instant of eminence. After the rest of the squad was dressed and ready to go, Kevin walked out onto the court wearing every imaginable basketball trinket—wristband, kneepads, elbow guards, high socks, goggles, about twenty headbands anywhere he could fit them. The picture doesn't come close to doing the moment justice.

"Everyone just burst out laughing. We realized we'd gotten into a bad habit of taking ourselves too seriously and being too worried about our fans' booing us, or not coming out to the Rose Garden if we were going to miss the playoffs. We were working not to fail. We had to snap that mood."

The Blazers proceeded to win every remaining game but one, to put a cap on the season and punch their ticket to the playoffs.

Your Internal Compass

We've come to refer to it as having an internal compass: knowing where your toughness comes from, knowing it is distinguished by what you're about, on your worst days, not your records or highlights. In other words, the obstacles life throws at you—faults, failures, occasional idiocy, embarrassments, errors, choking, turnovers, air balls, missing a game-winning shot—don't change who you are or your belief in yourself, and they don't reduce your willingness to be in those situations again, not in the least.

We've found that people tend to confuse the idea of an internal compass with how they generally feel. They equate resilience with always feeling calm, relaxed, sure, worry free. In doing so, they suffer from False God Syndrome: the supposition that top performers don't get nervous, don't have doubts, or don't take punches to their confidence. They look at Dirk Nowitzki or Mia Hamm or Barack Obama and see only cool-under-pressure exteriors. Perhaps the most significant problem of False God Syndrome is that it blinds you from paying attention to how all-stars handle mistakes and misses. Dirk and Mia and Barack do stupid things. They cough it up. We advise our clients to stop compiling a library of observations and memories of great performers when they're at their best; start compiling data on what they do when they're at their worst.

THEODORE RUBIN

The problem is not that there are problems. The problem is thinking having problems is a problem.

Exceptionally tough people like Nowitzki and Hamm and Obama get as many butterflies as you do. We'd even wager they get more butterflies than you. What separates them from the pack is not an ability to make butterflies go away. They *want* to be nervous.* They don't hide it from their teammates, trying to project bravado as the counter to adversity. They know the answer to the secret little question we've been discussing in this chapter. They know: how confident will my teammates be if they see I am filled with nervousness and see that it—genuinely—doesn't alter who I am; if they see I *like* it? They share a love of obstacles and adversity with their teammates like Dennis Rodman did. Rodman, arguably the best rebounder in NBA history, always said: "I don't feel like I'm helping my team until I start feeling bruised."

---

*Though beyond the scope of this book, it's important to briefly clarify the physiology of nerves. Butterflies, dry mouth, a racing heart rate, chills, and the rest of the sensations that kick in when stakes rise are yields of the body's sympathetic nervous system maximizing blood, oxygen, nutrients, and hormones for the task at hand. When you feel your nerves, it is a signal that you have more juice at your disposal, allowing you to perform at a higher level. The best performers are well tuned in to this; these feelings give them a confidence boost. For more information about how to leverage these gains, visit www.overachievement.com.

Greats like Dirk and Mia and Barack also know that if they are transparent and authentic about their emotions, on the days when they struggle with worry or doubt their teammates won't be kept in the dark; they'll be able to swiftly and effectively help. And knowing *that* makes it all that much easier to get after it yourself. It's self-perpetuating *team toughness*.

One of the indicators of an internal compass that we specifically look for, in fact, is a *desire* for obstacles. Wanting the biggest challenges is wanting the chance to cultivate more team toughness. It's why Help the Helper cultures promote extreme practices.

Like the Navy SEALs. We strongly recommend that you pick up a copy of Eric Greitens's autobiography *The Heart and the Fist* (Houghton Mifflin, 2011). In addition to Tom Brokaw's calling Greitens his hero, Eric is a Duke graduate, Rhodes Scholar, gold-medal-winning boxer, humanitarian Ph.D., and SEAL. Whew. You've gotta pause for a breath in the middle of reading his bio. It's tempting to revise our statement about Jimmy V being the toughest man we've ever met. Eric will be the first to tell you, though; he doesn't have freakish DNA that makes him different from you and us. He doesn't have a crazy thrill-seeking fondness. What he does have is a thirst for the most real, open, vulnerable, unprejudiced, unwavering friendships one can muster. So when Hell Week rolled around—typified by stories of soldiers stranded in the wilderness, no exit in sight, having to pee on one another to stay warm enough to survive— Eric smiled. Bring it on. His family was about to grow.

Of course you don't need to go to SEALs' lengths to develop extreme team toughness. But you do need to push yourself and your coworkers to have the best internal compass in your industry. Accomplishing that means putting yourself in situations that test true toughness—that test, to reiterate our chapter opener, is of your willingness to:

Be authentic and real with your teammates

Be emotionally rich with your teammates

Be willing to fail with your team's fate in your hands

You need to strive for these distinctions of toughness. Ask yourself, frequently, "How authentically real am I being with my coworkers? How emotionally rich am I being? Have I honestly been willing to fail recently?"

Stoicism, control, and superhero status don't cut it; they limit access to the depth of resourcefulness a team can provide to its members. *This* is what the New York Giants knew.

With a hot-start season on a nosedive, eking out .500 ball to sneak into a Wild Card slot, the odds of going the distance were stacked against them. But instead of rah-rah, "tell everyone we're great, there's nothing to worry about" messages as the team embarked on their play-off run, Coach Coughlin, thanks to an introduction his assistant coach Mike Sullivan facilitated, gave the locker room to Lieutenant Colonel Greg Gadson.

Gadson, a U.S. Army vet who had both legs blown off by a roadside bomb in Iraq, resisted at first.

"I'm not a hero; I'm a regular guy who was in the wrong place at the wrong time."

A kick in the rear end of authenticity. Perfect. Tom asked Greg to just tell his story, be real, get the guys' efforts off trying to be anything other than who they are as people.

"I told them that they play for an organization with a rich history, but, in the end, they play for each other," Gadson recounts. "As soldiers, we fight for our country and our flag, but we also fight for our brothers, the guy on the left and the guy on the right of you. You forge a bond that can never be broken. I told them that the same soldiers that I trained were the ones who saved my life. I'm alive because of them, and I'll be forever grateful."

He got a standing ovation. The Giants made him an honorary captain, scooting his wheelchair out to midfield for the coin toss of every playoff game. And when Corey Webster—a cornerback saddled with a scouting report of being "too soft"—intercepted a Brett Favre pass in the closing seconds of the NFC Championship to put New York into the Super Bowl, he didn't keep the football as redemption or as a trophy case symbol that he wasn't soft. He gave it away. On the spot. To Colonel Gadson.

Two weeks later the Giants were in Arizona, gearing up for their biggest fight. Gadson didn't need to give a pregame speech at all. He simply rolled into the locker room, and was swarmed in embraces by fifty-three grown men with tears in their eyes.

The rest, as they say, is history.

The G-Men took the game to the wire, defeating perfection to be enshrined Super Bowl XLII champions, one of the great upsets of all time. The monstrous ring now on Greg Gadson's finger is footnote bling, in a nod to the value of learning what a true internal compass is all about—an internal compass that doesn't wait to feel all warm and comfy to take the big shot, an internal compass that's thrilled to be human, an internal compass that enjoys the most difficult days as they are paths to the kind of emotional richness sharing that separates the rarest of teams.

YOUR TURN!
The Hard Is What Makes It Great

Be the toughness leader of your industry—the real, team-vaulting version of toughness. Help your teammates make their internal compasses guides for the kind of communication and relationships that propel truly amazing groups like the Navy SEALs (groups that know, and help one another remember: the fear of getting hit and thus shying away from adversity is *far* worse than actually getting hit).

1. Be like Jimmy V! Don't try to be a superhero. Be strong because you are a real, authentic, rich-emotioned person. Laugh, think, and cry every day.

What are five clips, articles, photos, or videos that you will share with colleagues and customers, like Jimmy V's "Don't Give Up; Don't Ever Give Up" ESPY speech, which bring out your most passionate emotions?

_____

_____

_____

_____

_____

2. Learn to embrace nervousness as your body's own, natural performance-enhancing drug.

What is one thing that gives you butterflies—that will make you smile now that your toughness is not eliminating nervousness but rather enjoying the boost of juice, and enjoying sharing that boost with your teammates?

_____

3. Being like the New York Giants and Tom Coughlin means being tough enough to cry in public.

What are two things at work that you've been avoiding, putting off, or flat out not doing because you're worried about how you'll be viewed, or you're afraid to fail, or you're concerned that people you respect won't think you're tough?

_____

_____

When will you do them?

_____

4. The toughest people we've ever met, like Dr. Eric Greitens and Mike Born and Vinko Bogataj, have incredible relationships around them because they pursue family and friend and coworker bonds, not based on success, but based on what the relationships are about at low points.

What is one thing you vow to share that people close to you don't know about you yet?

_____

5. Be like us. Take a hit to show your team that it's okay to be embarrassed, to be human—and that it's a source of extreme teamwork.

What are the five crazy pieces of clothing, or crazy excess pieces of equipment, or other crazy-purpose items you will show up to an important upcoming staff meeting with?

_____

_____

_____

_____

_____

Measure the Immeasurable

8.

An H2H Culture: Picks Up Where Moneyball
Leaves Off

Now that you know the core variables for developing extreme
teamwork, it's vital to walk through the best strategy for
keeping tabs on those variables, keeping them front and
center as priorities. Every great team monitors their cohesion and
chemistry to ensure they stay faithful to their Help the Helper culture.
They know, however, that the practice of monitoring can itself hamper
teamwork. This chapter rolls up our sleeves on what to do about the
potential conundrum.

You could couch much of our discussion to this point as centrally
relevant to increasing human capital. As we've been discussing, the collective energy, resourcefulness, and resilience of Help the Helper cultures produces greater output. But it would be a mistake to take a
heavily econometric approach to identifying, tracking, and assessing
the elements of extreme teamwork. Looking at people, and likewise
teams, as commodities is fundamentally flawed.

How so? First, it's not nice. Which we say only partially in jest. Consider an analytics conference we attended a few years back. Experts
were lined up to touch on a wide range of topics regarding measurement of human factors in sales, communication, hiring, and the like.
One of the more fascinating keynotes concerned posture and facial

expression. The speaker was a former FBI interrogator. He went into depth teaching the audience how to discern eye shifts—the direction one's eyes move depending on how one is processing information. He explained how to tell if a person you are talking with relates best to visual, auditory, or kinesthetic cues. He explained how to tell if a person you are talking with is being honest or lying. The content was very interesting and he was a dynamic, humorous presenter. The most insightful take-home, however, came post-speech. A complimentary cocktail reception was scheduled. Usually, at these events, attendees are abuzz with conversation about the hot lectures. Networking abounds. Everyone wants to shake as many hands as they can. But after listening to the FBI agent, nobody wanted to chat. No one wanted to make eye contact with anyone!

The same phenomenon arises when you try to score the qualitative dimension of work. People get self-conscious. They often avoid the behaviors you are trying to track, or deliberately display what they think you want to see. The validity of your measures is compromised since what you are measuring is less than natural or fully genuine.

It's the same reason personality inventories are terrible predictors of performance (as we referenced in the chapter 2 footnote contrasting David Robinson with Dennis Rodman). When filling out tests during a job interview, applicants tend to color in the bubbles they presume will aid in getting them hired.* Imagine you are sitting in a classroom at the NFL Combine as a football player who has a shot at getting drafted in the first round. Seven figures are at stake. You are taking a psychological exam that scouts and GMs will scrutinize. The test booklet asks:

TRUE or FALSE. When my dog misbehaves, I smack him.

Do you just be as transparent as you can? Or do you pause to contemplate what the brass wants to read? Does "TRUE" illustrate that you have the testosterone capacity and assertiveness necessary for han-

---

*When we explain to organizations the pitfalls of pencil-and-paper psychometrics, we hear a common preliminary objection. Referring to Gallup's StrengthsFinder or the Myers-Briggs, folks tell us, "Personality tests have served us well; they are very helpful." We don't disagree. We recommend StrengthsFinder . . . as a *communication* tool. Exams of this variety are a boon to employees' better understanding one another. Remember, seek first to understand. As instruments for predicting who will outperform whom, however, they are rife with problems. Use StrengthsFinder or Myers-Briggs (or others, as long as they have a depth of independent, double-blind research trials validating them) to support the 30-Minute Rule efforts, *not* to support Front of the Jersey hiring efforts.

dling a 275-pound linebacker charging at you, wanting to clean your clock? Or does "TRUE" throw up a red flag that you might have emotional regulation problems or are at risk for off-field trouble? Did league attorneys insist this question be added as a result of the criminal activity that got Michael Vick thrown in jail!?

There is no way for score talliers to know how you'd *really* act. Bubble sheets have no way to reflect degree of honesty. Some people will be straightforward; some people will try to beat the test. Some will overthink it. Some will breeze through as fast as they can. Net-net: test reliability is out the window. The more you turn performance contributions such as taking initiative, helping, toughness, and unselfishness into numbers, especially numbers that affect Christmas bonuses, promotions, or employee files, the more your team will push back. You'll drain away the ingredients of extreme teamwork.

Which brings us to the second flaw of commoditizing people, a trend spreading through sports and business alike: quantifying human capital. Recall the background we outlined in the introduction. Thanks to number crunchers like Bill James and forward-thinking teams like the Oakland A's, the sports world is beginning to recognize that traditional notions of talent—genetic gifts in the realm of size, strength, and speed—don't offer much in the way of data to differentiate good athletes from those who will become superstars. Geoff Colvin could well have included reference to Billy Beane in his bestseller, *Talent Is Overrated*, to put an exclamation point on his thesis that those who rise to the top do so not on inherent ability, but on the way they practice their craft. We surmise that he didn't because he's as disappointed as we are. Disappointed that the modish Moneyball pursuit, especially in its application to business performance, is turning out to be merely replacing one set of statistics with another.

Of course, we're only marginally disappointed. We're happy to continue stealing the competitive advantages that live beyond statistics while our opponents devote disproportionate hours and dollars to spreadsheet jockeying.

Reiterating an earlier statement, we don't shun sabermetrics. We absolutely incorporate analytics into our performance evaluation operations. But we intentionally limit use; we make sure to keep a very conscious awareness that human capital quantifications are inextricably linked to outcomes. On-base percentage may be far superior to batting average when calculating correlations to runs scored and team wins. But it's still measuring results. As we mentioned at the start of the book, OBP doesn't illuminate the *source* of performance; it doesn't provide any intelligence regarding what *caused* that OBP. Relying on performance data like this requires that you just *assume* something positive was going on to generate good numbers. We don't like to assume. We don't like to make performance decisions in an ad hoc fashion (particularly when doing so relegates us to the company of average companies, as we discussed in chapter 3). That's a surefire formula for getting fooled from time to time. We're not fond of getting fooled.

"Our sabermetrics guy has confirmed that last year's team that went 60-102 was bad."

www.CartoonStock.com

In his treatise on the A's, Michael Lewis tells the story of Scott Hatteberg, the washed-up catcher with a blown-out elbow whom Beane resurrected. Hatteberg was a major league OBP leader. His inability to throw didn't matter; it was his propensity for getting on base that lent greatest bearing to team success. Scott is presented, for excellent reasons, as a prime example of Moneyball effectiveness. What surprises us is the lengths the book (and movie) goes to elucidate Scott's process—shrinking the strike zone, going deep in counts, putting pressure on pitchers, not allowing circumstances to distract him from his focus—yet, overwhelmingly, masses of readers conclude that on-base percentage is the secret sauce. It's not, which we applaud Lewis for attempting to explain, albeit to deaf ears. The secret sauce, for Scott Hatteberg, was *patience* at the plate.* Patience is the *source* of Hatty's success, the cause of his high OBP.

Would you like to join us in being fooled less than our competitors, avoiding ad hoc errors, reducing the magnitude to which performance reviews cause employee tension? Then join us in shifting from exploring human capital in terms of outcomes to exploring it in terms of sourcing.

Contrast Scott Hatteberg with Milton Bradley. On paper, they're twins. In reality, they're chasms apart.

Bradley is an eleven-year major league veteran who's played for eight different organizations. Why so much franchise hopping? He consistently posts eye-catching statistics in categories sabermetrics geeks love. Most years he's been among league leaders in OBP, ranking number one in all of baseball at getting on base in 2008. Not coincidentally, teams that have picked him up are teams making heavy use of analytics—the Cleveland Indians, Los Angeles Dodgers, Seattle Mariners, and, you guessed it, the A's! But seemingly as frequently as he reaches first, he explodes. He's got a fierce temper. He smashes bats and tosses water coolers. He's not what you'd call a clubhouse guy. He regularly leaves the stadium when he's pulled out of a game instead of sticking around to support his teammates. He has yet to last in the lineup for two full seasons with any one team.

If you can't help but fawn over numbers, here is a particularly discerning portrayal of Bradley's career:

Team	Finish in Season w/Bradley	No. League Teams	Finish in Season Before/After Bradley
Expos	14, 14	16	3
Indians	9, 12	14	Playoffs
Dodgers	14	16	Playoffs
A's	9	14	4
Padres	14	16	4
Rangers	9	14	4
Cubs	8	16	Playoffs
Mariners	14, 13	14	7

---

*Quite enamoring is the account Lewis relays of legendary Red Sox hitter Jim Rice's publicly humiliating Hatty for not swinging at more first pitches when his first-pitch batting average was .500. The *source* of that .500 BA was patience, i.e., *not* swinging at too many first pitches! This is a perfect illustration of the errors ad hoc metric reliance can generate. Even Hall of Famers like Rice make this mistake.

Each of these organizations ultimately assessed the wrong information to determine Milton's potential contribution to the team. They saw a high OBP, calculated the human capital of that OBP (runs and wins), juxtaposed it against the cost of his salary to gauge asset market value, and signed him. They didn't assess the source of Bradley's productivity: his fierceness, his unrelenting selfishness, and the chip on his shoulder. Those traits can compel a performer to work his ass off and to get on base a whole lot. The critical misstep is that organizations haven't assessed how the source of Bradley's productivity would affect other players, nor what to do about it. They lost money. Worse, Bradley has proven to be a bit of a cancer in the locker room that detracts from his team's ability to foster a Help the Helper culture.

© Randy Glasbergen
www.glasbergen.com

"Both job candidates are equally educated, equally experienced and equally qualified, but one can play *Layla* on his armpit!"

Our goal is absolutely not to speak ill of Milton. He has the potential to turn it around. Our goal, rather, is to highlight the fact that commodity production thinking blinds organizations and prevents them from A) identifying the *sources* of team success germane to their current circumstances (versus looking at the outcomes of those sources), B) hiring and rewarding team members who are good at those sources, and C) continually working to attend to, teach, enhance, and develop those sources once team members are onboard. Bradley *could* end up being a feel-good story, one for the Disney history books . . . if an organization is willing to make some significant extreme teamwork moves.

Removing Limits

The strategy we've discovered to be considerably bountiful is to work *with our people* to cultivate indices directly relating to sources of performance. We collaborate with our team to identify focus targets that have the highest likelihood of leading to great outcomes, specifically those most conducive to our teammates' helping one another be the best.

Swimming provides an excellent backdrop by which to explain how we do this. To get to the top, one must endure long, grueling training sessions, rising before the sun, staying at it well after friends in other professions have gone home for the day. Though on a team, a majority of the time you are in your own lane, concerned with your individual effort. Payoff comes rarely; your preparation is in hopes of peaking at a national or world championship, which happens once a year. If you're an Olympian, your work is geared for one shot at glory every four years. In some respects it's very similar to taking a start-up company public, the R&D curve of designing a new pharmaceutical and obtaining FDA approval, or preparing a class-action lawsuit. Small milestones certainly exist along the way, but the extent to which your team has to put their heads down and toil laboriously against resistance is substantial. Meanwhile, competitors are hard at work trying to outpace you. And there are plenty of experts weighing in on your progress and competitive market standing. "Fans" study your stock value daily, hourly.

Swim experts will advise you, in the sprints, if you're not tall you can't succeed. Races come down to the touch. At the wall, reach is everything. Women who compete in the 50-meter freestyle . . . they tower, six feet plus.

Mandy Mularz is five foot six.

As an academic standout at Rice University at the turn of the millennium, Mandy was smart enough to do the math. She swam for a small school program with no history of success in the sport. The Owls hadn't ever come close to the top twenty-five. They were members of the WAC, a conference not stocked with swimming and diving talent, nothing like the kind of push-you-to-your-best proving grounds that pools in the Pac-10 and SEC provided. They didn't even have any divers; they had to forgo all scoring in that component of meets. One might confidently suppose that Mandy didn't opt for college in Houston in quest of aquatic achievement. One would be wrong.

Mandy chose Rice because she didn't just want to win races; she wanted to do something special—extreme team kind of special. Doug Boyd, the head coach, was a former U.S. National swimmer and considered to be one of the top sprint coaches in the world. He got it. While all the metrics-hungry recruiters in the country had written Mandy off—too short, too academic—Boyd saw guts. And he was assembling a group of others with guts, who weren't trapped by notions that facilities, conference forte, and physical attributes determine success. Mandy wanted to be around those sorts of athletes. She didn't want to be part of a swim factory that replaced the human in the equation with splits, blood lactate, and meters. She also wanted to chase a career as a doctor. The big programs wanted their athletes to enroll in the easiest classes, putting school at the bottom of their priority list so as to be maximally dedicated to their sport. Once again, the "experts" chimed in: you're either a straight-A student or a champion athlete; you can't be both at the highest level. Mandy wasn't willing to buy that. She wanted to be part of a program that would help her be great in all facets of life, not limit her. And she wanted to encourage her teammates to do the same.

The table was set. Help the Helper leadership . . . Doug Boyd, check. Help the Helper hiring . . . Mularz and a cast of Front of the Jersey swimmers . . . check. Help the Helper enthusiasm for obstacles (a big one in this case given the Owls' nonexistent swimming and diving prowess) . . . check. The next piece of the puzzle was Help the Helper evaluation. Lap splits and meet finishes are, of course, important. But Rice had a mountain to climb, so those measures would be deflating at first. Plus, they are not at the source of swimming fast; they don't tell you if you are on an optimal path. A sprinter, for example, can shed a hundredth of a second or two—eternities in the 50 and 100—by changing diet patterns, losing a bunch of body weight, so she has less drag in the water. If the pounds lost are in muscle, however, the corresponding loss of strength will haunt her come championship meets when a week of competition, heats morning and night, takes a toll. There are myriad ways to get a swimmer to improve splits that won't hold up over the course of a season. Relying heavily on numbers increases the probability of veering slightly off course without knowing it—getting self-fooled, as we call it. Once you arrive at the national championship (or client pitch meeting, FDA submission, IPO launch, etc.) you can't go back to correct having been off course.

So the Owls scheduled an intensive training camp prior to the 2001 season. The entire squad packed up for San Diego to celebrate New Year's together, to get after it in the pool for a week with zero outside interferences, and to dig into their team process. As it turns out, one evening was all it took.

Lounging in pj's at the seaside Catamaran Resort, we threw the measurement question at the girls:

"How will you know you're a success this year?"

Mandy volunteered, "I'd like to take home a WAC title."

Her teammates nodded in approval, to which the doc inquired, with a Columboesque air of curiosity, "How about an NCAA title?"

"Um, I dunno . . ." Mandy hesitated in response, like someone who hadn't considered the idea before.

We urged her on by clarifying, "The girl who's gonna win the national championship this spring in the fifty free . . . what split is she going to post?"

"Probably twenty-three, maybe twenty-two high," she said, referring to seconds on the clock.

"And how fast can you swim fifty meters?"

"Um . . . well . . . twenty-three."

A moment of silence overtook the team suite. The girls stared at one another with a "holy shit" expression. All the coaches kept quiet, letting the mood sink in. It was impossible not to smile. After a long pause, we continued. It was the teachable moment we were hoping for, complete with requisite emotion. We shifted from numbers to sources.

"What would it take to swim that twenty-three at nationals?"

Mandy contemplated, before thoughtfully responding, "I'd have to really get up on top of the water."

What she meant was that she couldn't grind out that speed, merely swimming as hard as she could. Bull-like effort would create a lot of wake, most notably on the turn when a swimmer has to head back into the wave following the competitors. Smaller swimmers are more adversely stalled by a big wake. Also, being shorter in height translated into less water she could chew up with each stroke. To compensate she'd have to be quicker, lighter in her movements, a tactic a big haus couldn't invoke.

"And I'll have to have a superclear mind so I'm *way* looser than those girls from Auburn and Georgia," Mandy added, her tone already sliding into an excited timbre, hinting of *possibility* beating out *probability*.

That did it. The team committed to spending the rest of training camp working to get on top of the water and to clear their minds. Coach Boyd helped them devise systems and drills for practicing those approaches. He worked tirelessly helping them figure out which cues, day to day, they could look for to provide feedback that the source of their performance was a quiet brain and an efficient tempo. The team also wound up implementing two more measures:

1. They kept tabs on motivation. The fervor of the training protocol Doug laid out for them meant heavy weight training of a nature swimmers weren't used to, combined with interval work in the pool that would make mortals cringe. Powering through it—effectively—meant continually picking up one another's spirits. They decided the best measure was frequency of high-fives and vocal acknowledgments of teammates' exertions.

2. They tracked the overall attitude at the beginning of every practice. When work is fun, you can endure more. They kept a log of fun-demonstrating behaviors at work start. And whenever a day came along when getting into the water was less than a thrill, they all lined up on the edge of the pool and did simultaneous belly flops. OUCH! But boy did that stimulate their mood. It worked so well, in fact, that they made it the cornerstone of their prerace routine. Other teams couldn't believe what the Owls were willing to do; it added an intimidation factor.

Fast forward to Sunday, March 18, 2001. After many a day on which the scoreboard didn't offer rewards for their labor, the Rice Owls were still measuring how well they were getting on top of the water, clearing their minds, high-fiving hard work, and belly flopping. Except, they were also departing the Long Island Natatorium, site of the 2001 NCAA swimming and diving championships, as the *eighth best* team in the country.

Mandy didn't capture the 50-meter freestyle crown. She did, however, set two Rice school records. And her confidence was blooming knowing that she had two assets other powerhouse sprinters did not: (1) a way to beat their analytics, and (2) a Help the Helper team. In 2002,

Mandy returned to the NCAA finals, a little girl no "expert" thought would amount to more than middle of the WAC pack, making back-to-back nationals appearances. Twenty-three seconds would have been a laudatory achievement. She touched the wall at 22.17. She broke the American record.

She also vaulted to the top in her other aspirations. She went on to ace medical school. She's now a leader and exemplary Help the Helper ob-gyn physician at the University of Florida—a school that completely overlooked her as a swimmer!

LEWIS B. ERGEN

The ratio of "we's" to "I's" is the best indicator of the development of a team.

Uncanny are the similarities (though we're not in the least bit astonished when considering what we've learned about the source of extreme teams) between Mandy and finance professionals with the longest track records of sustained market dominance, like Warren Buffett. And our dear friend, Tony Apollaro, the Flower Mound, Texas–based version of the Oracle of Omaha.

For starters, winning as an investment banker, especially at the start of one's career, requires routine nights at the office running analyses and drawing out projections until two o'clock in the morning. Due diligence to ferret out diamond-in-the-rough deals can make a swimmer's training look like an afternoon at the beach. Tony's endurance is as steadfast as you can get. He'll crunch numbers until even possums have gone to bed. Then get up at four in the morning to do it again.

Exactly like Mandy, Apollaro opted for a path that "experts" scoffed would make it impossible for him to become a leader in the field. He chose a small, relatively unheard-of firm (to casual CNBC watchers, anyway), Quad-C Management, in out-of-the-way, rural Charlottesville, Virginia. To many, a young professional's not being on Wall Street is akin to being a five-foot-six sprinter. But also exactly like Mandy, Tony didn't just want to win races—that is, make money. He wanted to do something truly special with his skills and intellect. He wanted to build a team of people helping other people achieve *their* wildest dreams. He wanted to do copious charity work. He wanted his career to be more than a collection of charts in an annual investment prospectus. He was committed to a vibrant, engaged, extreme team of a family, not a collection of hired servants looking after estranged kids in a mansion of a house.

Quad-C chairman Terry Daniels, investing's version of Coach Boyd, got it. While the majority of banks would key in on a missing mono-grammed power tie, Daniels saw in Apollaro remarkable Front of the Jersey passion, someone who wouldn't get stuck in the all-too-common investment pitfall of overreliance on financial reports. Apollaro, just like Buffett, has the personal interest to go an extra mile (or marathon) to understand his companies at a deeper level than their books, to understand businesses at a human level.

Patterning Rice swimming's turnaround doesn't stop there. Tony and Terry put their brains together to identify more meaningful performance measures. In their investment prospects, of course, but more important, in *themselves*. We aren't at liberty to discuss the financial details of Quad-C's $5.5 billion worth of successful transactions. We can unequivocally say, however, having countless times visited Quad-C and now Tony's recently launched firm, the Varsity Financial Group: in addition to outstanding economic achievements, the spirit, attitude, and quality of work life at those headquarters flat out trumps those of any other finance office we've known or studied.

Which brings us back on point. You want to be an incredible performer or an incredible organization, so you tally the dedication of a swimmer or an investment banker. The question is: is the majority of that time and effort working with your teammates (helping them, and them helping you) to keep your eyes on the *source* of exceptional performance, just as Mandy did and Tony does? Or is the majority of your time and effort spent focused on outcomes? We recommend that you periodically pause, step back, and ask that of yourself. The latter, assuredly, will occupy most of your competitors. Will you be the former?

Eyes, Ears, and Numbers

Great teams put copious resources into assessing "intangibles" throughout the hiring life cycle. As we saw in chapter 3, they go beyond recruiting to full-fledged scouting. The special teams take it a step further. They apply "intangible" assessment *after* team members are assembled. They work to continuously measure variables such as

Scott Hatteberg's patience and Mandy Mularz's clear mind. And then there are the truly exceptional extreme teams. They bring it full circle, "measuring the immeasurable" to evaluate evaluation, or as we say, evaluate the evaluators.

Scouts, recruiters, HR directors, hiring executives, interviewers, headhunters, third-party review consultants, managers conducting annual reviews—none of them get it right 100 percent of the time. In industries like professional sports, evaluating accurately 50 percent of the time is outstanding. Putting your finger on the source of performance is extremely tough. There's a reason most companies put few dollars into this, or don't even try. There's a reason we call the variables "intangibles." But teamwork being difficult to pin down on paper does not mean you can't get better at measuring it. You just have to be willing to put assumptions aside. You have to be willing to score your scoring system. Check your pride at the door. You might find out you're not initially great at it, or you might be using weak indices, or the people who see through to intangibles hiding behind statistics might not be who you surmise.

Take Jason Filippi, for instance. He is what many folks would label a "nerd." He's not built like an athlete. He's socially awkward. He wears stereotypical Coke-bottle glasses. In 1999, he and his brother, Adam, created a European scouting service to feed data to the NBA, fueling conjecture that his success scouting basketball players must be because he's a sabermetrics guru.

For five years his reputation for bull's-eyeing athlete assessments escalated. The Trail Blazers decided they'd seen enough positive statistics. No sense in sharing with the other children if they didn't have to. In 2004, they brought Filippi on staff full-time to run international scouting.

Committed to evaluating evaluation, committed to going beyond analytics to determine the success of the Blazers' efforts, KP flew across the pond to go on the road with Jason. It would have been faster, simpler, and cheaper to tabulate the statistics of players Jason promoted, comparing his reports against their output to calculate Jason's +/- track record. But it wouldn't teach the organization about what led to positive and negative decisions. And it wouldn't promote extreme teamwork.

The organization wanted to learn from him. And to be honest, everyone wanted to see how he did it. With those glasses, he couldn't see! Scouting is hard enough as it is. To scout without being able to tell players apart . . . amazing.

KP connected with Jason in Croatia. The plan was to compare notes and compare processes on a player they were vetting, Ante Tomić.

"We got to the arena and Jason started introducing me around. He knew everyone. We had seats in the president's box because Jason knew the president personally. It wasn't like he'd made a bunch of phone calls in advance to work out arrangements. It was like everybody was an old high school friend of his. George Clooney he is not. But, man, was he dialed into the network. He knew little details about people—their favorite phrases, their pets' names, you name it—details you only discern if you care enough to really *listen* to people's stories. Natural charisma, no, but he maintains incredible, real lines of communication. He even knew the guy who operated the gym's lights."

They settled in to watch pregame warm-ups. But all the players had shooting shirts covering their uniforms. Onlookers couldn't see any jersey numbers or tell one player from another.

"I turned to ask Jason which guy was Tomić. Jason wasn't there. I looked around. Jason wasn't chatting with the president or picking up a snack. One of the other VIPs nudged me, pointing toward the center of the court."

There he was. Filippi was walking out onto the floor!

Minutes before a game was about to start, Jason didn't ponder twice. He walked right through the middle of the players, walked up to Ante, grabbed his sleeve, and started yelling back up into the stands.

"THIS IS HIM! THIS IS THE GUY!"

He had no fear whatsoever. When you think about it, that's a pretty damn good skill for a scout to cultivate. Scouts are going to make mistakes. Most get their self-identity wrapped up in how many first-rounders they successfully peg. They'd be too afraid to put their reputation on the line to walk out on the court like that. Jason has 'em all licked.

Perhaps more telling was Tomić's reaction. Pregame is sacred. Players despise being interrupted when they're getting locked in. Yet Ante didn't mind at all. He nodded, gave Filippi a pound, and went back to work. Jason knows that understanding the source of a performer's success means you have to go further than just watching him or her perform.

He's become a master of a methodology research scientists have shown generates the greatest validity: triangulation. Triangulation is the union of three distinctly different sets of data to look for overlap. When three different sources and types of information agree, you have significant confidence that you're getting to the heart of a matter.

In our organizations we abbreviate it EEN: Eyes, Ears, and Numbers.

EYES = What you see, *and expressly what you don't see*, when you are observing performers. The eyes are targeted to scanning for patterns and tendencies in human interaction.

EARS = What you hear when you talk with people, what converges when you gather as many diverse personal perspectives as you can.

NUMBERS = Both industry-popular sabermetrics *and* documents or records detailing performance qualities that you can rate, rank, and organize graphically.

EEN gives us a common language that is not valuable merely in scouting and hiring. It provides a common language to sustain the conversation about sources of performance. We can then efficiently triangulate one another. We check and triple-check our assumptions regarding analytics. It allows us to understand why any given number, for example PER, happens to reflect correctly for one performer (Scott Hatteberg's OBP, for example) and not for another (Milton Bradley's OBP, for example).

Triangulation also accomplishes two essential Help the Helper–promoting objectives when it comes to measuring performance.

BRUCE COSLET

Everyone is needed, but no one is necessary.

First, triangulation necessitates teamwork. You're not just triangulating information; you're triangulating the people involved in collecting the information. By definition, it's an engaging process. As we mentioned shortly after commencing this chapter, evaluation can raise a host of negative reactions, worries, concerns, and pushback that deters chemistry. The more you strive to measure the immeasurable, the more you need everyone's help. The more you elicit everyone's help, the more you are replacing hesitation with initiative taking, the more you are promoting an extreme teamwork culture. Give it a try. And have some patience. It's a self-fulfilling prophecy waiting to happen.

Second, triangulation helps you and your team become more attuned to the human side of data. When you're consistently bantering back and forth with colleagues about what causes particular numbers, you watch more, listen more, and sit in front of spreadsheets less. You get more connected in the field. You notice gold-nugget subtleties such as our discovery that the odds of scouts' predictions coming true hinge far more on *how* they report findings—their body language, nonverbals, and confidence—than on the actual statistics of those findings.

And when you watch and listen to a greater extent than you calculate and evaluate, you grow as an extreme team leader—and *un*leader, as we'll peel back the layers on next. . . .

YOUR TURN!
Thought of the Day Trickledown

You can't measure everything. In fact, if you try to measure every-thing, you'll end up tying yourself in knots. You'll likely end up not measuring anything worthwhile at all. One of our principal pieces of advice to you to gain an assessment advantage is to first define: What are you about? What is your team about? Don't put performance measures in front of performance character. Then, just as crucial, once you've defined what you're about, *make every decision trickle down from that*. Instead of trying to evaluate every hot, sexy metric, make your performance and your team's performance more fundamental; evaluate how well you're executing what you are about!

1. In our studies, we've come across an incredibly powerful tool for gaining feedback on how well you're executing who you are and what you are about. It's called the Thought of the Day Trick-ledown. Every so often, launch the workday by, very first thing, gathering your immediate team. Make it a short meeting. The purpose: give them a thought of the day—a phrase or quote or idea or life lesson you feel poeticizes what the company is about in sock-it-to-'em fashion. Then return to going about your usual routine. As five o'clock rolls around (or the next day or at the end of the week), stroll around the company and spontaneously catch people. Ask them, "What's the thought of the day?" Have they heard? Did it impact their work? Did they pass it on? See how far the thought has traveled. Do a flow analysis. Did it stick; did it make it out of your direct reports; where did it die off? Did it cross divisions? Did it resonate with certain folks and not others? Take random samplings. Even ask customers and clients! We've found that an *incredible* wealth of insight percolates from this exercise. We highly recommend continuing it periodically into the future.

What is the Thought of the Day you will infuse this week?

How far did it travel? What did you learn?

_____

_____

One note: Do *not* use the Thought of the Day Trickledown as a method to figure out whom you're going to fire in upcoming lay-offs. In no way should it be punitive.

2. Be like Scott Hatteberg and Mandy Mularz. Evaluate yourself and your teammates by going to the *source* of great performance.

What are two causes (not outcomes) of your being at your best—two focal targets, for you, that lead to your best work?

_____

_____

What are two causes of one of your teammates' being at their best—two focal targets, for them, that lead to their best work?

_____

_____

3. Be like Jason Filippi and become a master at triangulation. Rather than digging deep into one type of metric, look for data that overlaps and agrees across three different types of metrics.

What is one qualitative variable that will help drive your organization to develop more of a Help the Helper culture?

_____

What are three different pieces of data (your version of EEN) that you will collect to triangulate your assessment of how well your team is doing on this variable?

Eyes:

_____

Ears:

_____

Numbers:

_____

9.

Act Like an *Un*leader

And Once You Sow the Seeds for an H2H Culture:
Get Your Sorry Butt out of the Way!

As we were debating the manner in which we'd like to bring this book to a close, a thought struck us like lightning: given the choice, we'd rather have a teammate scoring 5 (or less) on a 10-point scale of ability and 10-plus on engagement in the organization versus a teammate scoring 10 on ability and 5 on engagement. That's central to the way we won in Portland and Tampa—central to how we can thrive in an über-competitive marketplace without the personnel budget of the Lakers or Yankees, and without the sabermetrics budget of the Knicks and the Red Sox.

Prioritizing engagement in the Help the Helper traits and behaviors we've covered so far allowed us to do another significant performance enhancer:

Trust.

If you make it your mission to help people be more engaged in extreme teamwork, folks will start coming to you with solutions instead of problems. Initiative taking will flourish. Motivation and leadership essentially become moot points. And that then opens the door for you to be a conveyor of freedom rather than a manager of responsibility. It means you can be an *un*leader.

Freedom Versus Responsibility

When we talk with business owners about what holds their companies back, atop their improvement wish list is the same grumbling we hear incessantly from teachers and coaches coast to coast. Responsibility, responsibility, responsibility.

"If my staff would step up and take more responsibility, it wouldn't be a pugnacious struggle to hit our numbers every quarter."

Project managers complain about having to do too much handholding, constantly on their employees to get after it or focus. Teachers complain about students' not asking questions. Coaches complain about their players not giving their all in practice or not taking it upon themselves to do individual work. Pick any authority-subordinate pair. You'll find a similar pattern of grievances. Physicians complain about their patients' not adhering to therapy or healthy diet recommendations.

"KP and Doc, ya got any good tricks to hold people accountable?"

We sure do. *Cut it out!*

Consider the educational process that typifies the vast majority of college courses. A professor, a thought leader in a particular field, designs a program of study on a particular topic. He writes a syllabus, mapping out the semester—meeting schedule, attendance policy, objectives, content outline, assignments, exam format and dates, grading—and distributes the document on the first day of class. From week to week he stands at a podium lecturing. He projects bulleted PowerPoint slides on an overhead screen or walks through models and equations on a whiteboard. Pupils furiously scribble notes, copying down everything he orates or diagrams. He makes up quizzes, deciding what subject matter is important to grill them on. He sets finite office hours; he has a lab to run and the university is counting on him to win grants so extra time for undergraduate interaction is limited. He conducts supplemental review sessions to inform class attendees what information they should concentrate on studying (that is, memorize) for the final exam. When all is said and done, he calculates a bell curve, anointing most students with Bs and Cs, an A+ or two, and perhaps a couple Fs.

Educators do an exquisite (albeit subconscious) job of fooling themselves into thinking that learning is up to their pupils. Functionally, it's really not. At least, not in scenarios of the ilk described above. With structures like that, who has all the power? Who has all the "answers"? Clearly, the professor. He's the one up front, controlling the curriculum and work flow, doing the lion's share of the talking, setting the rules, and of greatest significance, evaluating.

The FAQ students ask professors without a close second anywhere in sight:

"What do I have to do to get an A?"

It's a telltale example of giving up responsibility. Though it *sounds* like a pupil inquiring how to do excellent work, how to get ahead, how to be the best, it's rarely a query with the impetus of initiative taking. It's actually (again largely subconscious) keeping the onus on the instructor and/or the lesson plan (1st and/or 2nd Order Teamwork). If a student follows directions and fails, it's easy for him or her to deem the prof or plan at fault. The student didn't have to take responsibility; he or she did as told.

When the doc is teaching, he doesn't put grading formulas in his syllabi. He doesn't even mention the word grade. And when, invariably (it's nearly impossible to get through a semester's inaugural lecture without its rearing its ugly mug), he's barraged with "the" request, he frustrates the heck out of undergrads.

An arm is raised. "Dr. Eliot, I can't find grading instructions in the syllabus. Could you go over that, please?"

"Nope."

That completely catches them off guard. Grading has become such a standard plug-and-play element of school. There's usually a capacious pause to try to process the denial. Then a tentative, "Um . . . well . . . how can we earn an A?"

Smiling, the doc says, "I have no idea."

Doc admits, he loves to leave it at that and watch a room full of kids who crushed the SATs do mental gymnastics. Of course, he's pressed for clarification. At which juncture he explains that high marks are received for figuring out how to get high marks. In other words, it's up to the students to take ownership, to identify knowledge acquisition methods and motivations and metrics that work well for them, not up to their professor to assume and dictate how to program their learning.

The objection, often coming from fellow faculty (a fact insightful in and of itself): "But professors know the material better than twenty-year-olds. They are scholars; they make a living learning. They know the chiefly effective tools for garnering information."

Really? Who are we kidding? Ninety percent of college classes are memorization and regurgitation, long forgotten by graduation.

Courses showered with rave feedback, with standing room only enrollment (enrollment maintained through the dog days of a semester), with lessons impactful well into alums' careers, have a key commonality:

"The professor [or substance] was inspiring!"

Are people inspired by rules on a syllabus? Hardly. People need to engage their minds and emotions to be inspired, which doesn't happen by following a prescription. The success or failure of a prescription is in the hands of the prescriber. Not unlike computer engineering. The success or failure of a computer program is in the hands of the programmer. When a spreadsheet doesn't spit out what we want it to, do we blame the spreadsheet? All too normally, yes. It's an enlightening reflection of our society's characteristic approach to responsibility. But spreadsheets, like computer programs (even AI) don't have a personal say in the game. They're just along for the ride. Which is exactly what occurs in education when teachers provide students with a syllabus outlining "success." It's programming. Students are along for the ride. Responsibility remains with the syllabus and with the teacher.[*]

Famous profs don't program.[†] They pour their energy into getting *out* of the role of authority. They ask more than they answer (yes, even in hard sciences; that's how enthralling chemists, for example, make chemistry exciting). They stir curiosity. They speak *with* you, not *at* you. They make college a team game. They find ways to dole out aspirations, not assignments. They know a cornerstone principle of this chapter: *There is a strong positive correlation between freedom and responsibility.*

Not freedom defined as the absence of obligation or the opportunity to blow off work. Those are what we call freedom *froms*. Freedom from oppression. Freedom from deadlines. Freedom from bills, or traffic, or headaches. There is another type of freedom, one that engenders *increased* responsibility. It's what we call freedom *to*.

Ask yourself, in meetings and conference rooms and performance

---

[*]And the complaints continue. "Students procrastinate too much." The reality: they've been given deadlines; they're heeding those deadlines and putting their stock in them. "Students don't think out of the box." The reality: their textbooks tell them what to think. "Students don't ask good questions." The reality: they know they'll be told the solutions.

[†]A library of legendary teachers can be accessed thanks to a visionary company, The Great Courses, Inc. (www.thegreatcourses.com). Bear in mind, though, audio recordings lack the dynamic Help the Helper acts we're discussing in this book, so please don't be disappointed that famous profs aren't as effective on CD or DVD as they are in person.

reviews, who does all the talking? Who sets the agenda? Who's doing the evaluating? Those individuals are like professors. They have a larger fraction of the freedom *to* decide the process. They therefore have more of the freedom to determine the outcome. And the one who most determines the outcome is the one who is most responsible—who most takes responsibility.

This relationship working against employee engagement generally stems from the best of intentions, and without awareness. Managers and VPs and bosses have a wealth of training, experience, and knowledge. They work hard to leverage those resources and resourcefulness to steer their team. What they don't realize in doing so is that the self-determination of people around them is caught up in the mix. Freedom *to*s diminish. Complaints about lack of accountability increase.

Undeniably, an occasional student or employee comes along who takes the bull by the horns, who snatches freedom *to* regardless of how much is provided or environmentally available. It's not typical. Waiting until these gems populate your team is leaving responsibility to chance, or pinning it on a few unique personalities. It takes more time and money to pluck these people out of the workforce pool than it does to switch: switch from wanting accountability measures to developing strategies for sharing more freedom-*to* responsibility with your current team.

Here are three strategies you can start implementing today. We'll fill in further color on each as the chapter progresses:

1. Nuke the perception that those in positions of authority have all the answers. Tap the power of saying "I don't know. I'll find out."

2. Quit doling out fathoms of feedback.

3. Flip the authority-subordinate relationship upside down. Act on the principle that people won't give you their all until they know how much you care.

Overtraining

Ever notice that elite runners—Olympic marathoners or the gal who wins your local 10K year after year—rarely have an iPod strapped to their biceps? They don't need a distraction to make arduous tasks like wind sprints, twenty-milers, or hill repeats pleasurable. They don't depend on music for their motivation.

"Yeah, but they actually *like* running."

That's an illuminating response we catch, especially from people who do a fair volume of jogging in an effort to stay in shape.

To those folks, our immediate retort is: "Why are you running then?"

We get it. There's bountiful joy to be gained at the intersection of heart-pumping tunes with heart-pumping exercise. Ourselves, we love cranking up the V on some AC/DC or Eric Church and ripping up a workout. But we're not training to win the Boston Marathon or to snag middle-distance gold at the next Summer Games. And we'd have equal amounts of fun working out if the jukebox was broken.

On a personal level, our emphatic point is to pursue challenges that you don't need a crutch to survive—the challenge itself is a creature you enjoy putting your thoughts into. There is an incredibly diverse menu of fitness activities at your disposal—rock climbing, racquetball, kayaking, hang gliding, kite surfing, roller skiing, figure skating, mountain biking, spelunking. We could carry on listing all day . . . without having to dip into traditional sports and games. There has to be *something* you fancy the same way exceptional runners do running, where the exertion itself is the feeling you're pursuing rather than having to have music supplying the feeling.

Phrased another way, discover activities that, for you, have their own vibrant sense of freedom *to* (fill in the blank according to your passions) instead of freedom *from* (belly fat or feeling lethargic or self-consciousness wearing a bikini). The more fitness becomes an expression of freedom *to*, the more vigorously you chase it, the more intense your participation, the higher it climbs on your priority scale, the more responsibility you are taking for your health without knowing it and without its feeling like it's a chore or a necessity to demonstrate to your insurance carrier that you're accountable enough to qualify for a lower premium.

It's the best preventative medicine we know for the condition of overtraining—briefly: decline in productivity, stamina, outlook, etc., as a consequence of too hefty a workload.

We don't intend to belittle overtraining. It's a very real and very serious concern. In our experience, though, it tends to be misdiagnosed. Sagging performance more often results from underinvolvement of the soul than it does from overinvolvement of physiology. The latter happens to be easier to quantify so the former is explored too infrequently by trainers, HR directors, and family physicians. We'll tell you this: every performer we've ever known, who outshines expectations, ratchets up a disproportionate ratio of time to toil. They bust their ass. It may look like overtraining. But they don't *feel* taxed. Additional freedom *to* begets additional capacity.

Enhanced capacity should be of interest to every team. Alas, we see authority figures attempting to squeeze another drop of juice via accountability. That *will* escalate the likelihood of overtraining. Performance is better enhanced by giving performers impetus and opportunity to look inside—in other words, to invest in themselves and the team rather than in directives or metrics. Stated practically, champions gain an edge by reducing their reliance on technology, specific techniques, and formulae (record holders aggressively so). The more they rely on those things, the more the responsibility for their success hinges on external things. And that doesn't jibe with commanding greatness. Michael Jordan, for instance, was legendary for showing up each preseason with a new facet to his game, including distributing the basketball. He didn't rely on leaping ability or a particular move to the basket; he wasn't going to let his career be constrained by a singular skill or a playbook.

Since a decent portion of our workweek can feel like a marathon, let's stick with the running analogy. Contemplate the unusual story of Ryan Hall. Hall, a standout Stanford track and cross-country athlete who overcame serious injury his junior year to win the NCAA 5,000-meter national championship as a senior, turned pro in 2005. He signed on with prominent coach Terrence Mahon to chart a career as a long-distance specialist. Ryan then proceeded to ripen rapidly, stringing off victories. In 2006 he captured the 12K national title and then broke the U.S. 20K record with a swift 57:54. In 2007 he won the Houston half marathon, clocking in at 59:43, setting the North American record—the thirty-eighth-fastest half marathon in history up to that date. As an encore, in London he notched the fastest marathon ever by a United States–born citizen, 2:08:24. He then set the U.S. Olympic Trials record to cap the season. In 2008, as the Games approached, he appeared on the cover of *Runner's World* as one of our red, white, and blue glory boys. He strode to the tape in the lead pack—top ten in Beijing.

Ryan cruised through 2009 and 2010. Everything seemed to be going his way, as he steadily marched up the world rankings, emerging as a legitimate threat to the preponderance of African superstars who've dominated the sport for decades. Until the headlines hit. As 2010 came to a wrap: HALL SPLITS FROM LONGTIME COACH MAHON.

The running world was abuzz. Didn't Hall and Mahon have a tremendously successful formula working? What happened? Was there a philosophy shift or tabloid-worthy rift? Did Ryan's recent withdrawal from the Chicago and New York marathons, with newspapers citing fatigue, factor into the unexpected twist? Was he hurt? Was he suffering from overtraining—too many races, too many miles?

None of the above. Indeed, Hall and Mahon had a system going that produced results. They worked well together. They were good friends. Ryan, however, was grappling with a situation we find common for general managers in every industry. You can be world-class at developing skills, you can keep accumulating all the right pieces, but it just never comes together. The oomph it takes to reach number one doesn't click in. You don't win the big one. U.S. and North American titles are nice, but Hall's sights were on bigger prizes.

Confounding the change in fans' eyes, and attracting the reproach of analysts, Ryan didn't convert to a new coach. In an event hinging on the minute manipulation of blood oxygenation, pace splits, glycogen tracking, and lactate threshold, he's no longer banking on a person to manage it all. Nor is he banking on a particular paradigm. He's adopted "faith-based coaching." Essentially, that means he wakes each morning to his faith, his feel, and his fellow runners to determine how to maximize his work that day. From a freedom-responsibility relationship perspective, it means he's invigorating the responsibility of his own body and belief system rather than handing the responsibility to another person. Ryan feels that the low motor he was experiencing at the close of 2010 had a lot to do with training and prerace strategies being too programmed. Under that regime he'd only ever be as good as the program.

Can he be labeled "out there"? If you must. Does it equate to his snubbing advice or being uncoachable? Not at all. In fact, he's expanded to a broader, team-based philosophy. A number of counselors now make up a multidisciplinary support system he taps, who all bounce ideas off one another. It includes his wife (also an elite distance runner) plus massage therapists, chiropractors, nutritionists, strength coaches, pacers, physiologists, and others. He consults with them only occasionally, though. He doesn't lean on them to set plans or instruct him in what to do.

Since making the transformation, Ryan's taken another leap forward. No American had ever posted a sub-2:05:00 marathon. At the

2011 Boston, Hall snapped the barrier, punching the dial at 2:04:58. Of note, the race winner, Geoffrey Mutai of Kenya, only managed to outstride Hall . . . by breaking the world record.

Comments Mutai, "Couldn't have done it without Ryan."

Hall's new team style is paying dividends beyond his own individual stopwatch readings. His wife Sara is also quick to draw attention to his renewed vigor, a renewed love of the sport that translates into more productive workouts. More freedom *to* equals more responsibility, equals more gains, equals more fun. Ryan agrees (courtesy of the *Los Angeles Times*, January 12, 2012):

"Since taking this giant leap of faith, life has been really exciting. My dad always says that happy feet make light feet, and I have certainly experienced this to be true. The happier I am in my day-to-day living, the faster I run."

Overcoaching

Wait! Are we secretly providing an excuse to rail against the boss, to ditch division managers, VPs, and such? We hope not. We're trying to emphasize, albeit strongly, a hidden disadvantage of talented, brilliant, well-meaning, go-getter leaders. It'll bite you if you're not vigilant. . . .

Do you remember Sparky Anderson? He was the first MLB manager to win a World Series in both the National League (1975 and 1976 Cincinnati Reds) and American League (1984 Detroit Tigers). As a player, he enjoyed only one season in the bigs, hitting a quiet .218 with no home runs. His God-granted gift was not swinging the lumber; it was teaching. Jack Kent Cooke, owner of the AAA Toronto Maple Leafs, the squad with whom Anderson played minor league ball, spotted how Sparky would take young players aside, mentoring and tutoring them. Cooke saw a knack. He convinced Sparky to give up playing in favor of managing.

Without the cachet of all-star appearances or a lengthy major league career, Anderson's foray into coaching was as quiet as his former batting average. His teams won four minor league titles in four consecutive seasons (1965–68). Nary a reporter commented, save on the back pages of small-town prints in the nooks of neighborhoods where he was coaching—Asheville, North Carolina, and Modesto, California, for example.

Bob Howsam didn't need newspapers to notice. Founder of the Denver Broncos, Bob was the brains behind the creation of the American Football League (AFL), which successfully competed against the original NFL, forcing a merger and evolving into what is today the AFC. Howsam also established baseball's Continental League. An official game was never played in that league, but Bob's vision compelled MLB to expand from sixteen to twenty teams in 1961. Upon expansion, the Reds offered Howsam their president's seat, which he graciously accepted, subsequently building the 1970s Big Red Machine dynasty. He defers credit.

"The best leadership move I ever made was hiring Sparky and then getting out of the way," Bob recounted at numerous functions.

After a solitary season as a major league assistant coach, tending to the third-base box for the San Diego Padres, Anderson was nabbed by Howsam to take the helm of the Reds. The *Cincinnati Enquirer* stamped atop its sports section: "SPARKY WHO?"

But 102 wins later, and with an NL pennant in his inaugural MLB managing campaign, Sparky was finally a household name. No doubt about it, the man could coach. He deserves his resting place in the Hall of Fame tenfold—*because he didn't much care for managing!* Anderson was the modern-day Rodin *Thinker*. A typical ballgame would feature him sitting on the bench, legs crossed, virtually motionless for three hours. Reserved and grandfatherly, he would sit with his palm propping up his face as he quietly studied the action. You could attend a whole homestand and not see him emerge from the dugout. Many a fan wondered if he was napping.

"Is he actually doing anything down there?"

Ah, how off base that train of thought was. But we certainly understand its source from Anderson's public appearance. Compare it with the prototypical persona of a coach, particularly a college or high school coach. Pacing the sidelines, barking instructions, rallying the troops, providing constant feedback. There are scores of good coaches like that. They win games. They get contract extensions. And then there are the Sparky Andersons and Tom Landrys and Phil Jacksons. There is a reason why all those high school coaches are in high school and Sparky and Tom are in the Hall of Fame. Phil will join them in enshrinement soon enough.

A young man named Sammy Kahn supplied us with an instructive lesson on this topic. Sam was what baseball scouts call (as they do Carlos Peña) a five-tool player. He could get on base, hit the long ball, throw his leather around, pin a baseball on a dime at home plate from the outfield, and swipe bags—hit for average, hit for power, field, throw, and run.* Boy could he run. But he was relegated to the bench as a junior at the University of Virginia when the doc arrived on campus as a graduate assistant coach.

Doc probed Dennis Womack, the program's head coach in his fifteenth season, "What's Kahn's story?"

"Oh, Sammy? Fantastic kid. Love him. But ties himself up in knots. A guy throws some good heat and it gets in on him. Can't pull the trigger," replied Womack. "You know the head game. Maybe you can help him."

Johnny Psych (or JP), as the players called Eliot, had his first project on the team. He stayed late the next day to watch Sam get in some extra cuts after practice. Pulling up a stool behind the cage, he sat and watched. Ten minutes went by. Twenty minutes. Thirty minutes. Finally Sammy paused between pitches.

"Coach, you see anything?"

"Yeah. Your swing looks good. It's hungry. You're getting great wood on the ball. I'd relax your hands just a touch, though. Nothing big. Just a little tweak. Just think 'loose,' man."

Kahn returned to taking hacks. Doc returned to watching. Another thirty minutes rolled by without exchange. When Sam finished up his work, he grabbed his water bottle and a towel and they headed down the hill from the field to University Hall, where the locker rooms were located. As they walked, Sam made a remark that turned out to be a defining moment in his college career.

"JP, you're not like any coach I've ever seen. You don't say much. I mean, you're not correcting everyone all the time. I hit for an hour and you said *one* thing. I really appreciate that. Thanks."

You see, Sammy's troubles in the batter's box stemmed from an overly diagnostic mind. He was slow to get his hands started because he was too busy thinking about the nuances of counts and mechanics and situations. He was what you'd call a classic case of paralysis by analysis. It wasn't that Eliot's approach to hitting was anything unique. As a rookie coach, he simply picked out the best role models he could find to interview and study, like Sparky Anderson, and copied what seemed to be their most efficacious strategies. Strategies like watching silently enough to notice Kahn's underlying issue. The ubiquitous practice of

---

*Since working with Sammy, we've come to label "complete" performers seven-tool players. The sixth tool is skill at the mental game. The seventh tool is skill at Help the Helper teamwork and leadership.

offering feedback after every swing—adjustments, praise, the entire gamut—inserts a two-pronged obstacle: 1) It overcontributes to the amount of information a performer has to process; 2) It siphons a segment of a coach's brainpower away from a full depth of observation.

Sammy and John started working BP together every day. And each afternoon it was the same. Sammy would tear off a couple hundred swings. Doc would sit back and watch, tossing out suggestions or reinforcements only when absolutely necessary. Mostly they just enjoyed their time together, bullshitting about school and girlfriends and other sports. It gave Sam permission to stop thinking so much. His hands softened.

Two weeks later Coach Womack put Sammy back in the starting lineup versus Coppin State. Twenty years and counting, players from that team still use the expression "Coppin Stating" to describe unreservedly destroying an opponent. Sammy went 4 for 4 with a three-run home run *and* a grand slam!

We recently caught up with the pitcher who got the W in that game, now a successful business owner. When we inquired how this former pitcher's company was doing, he said:

"We're Coppin Stating 'em, JP!"

The take-home shouldn't be that coaching is negative or that highly vocal managers are putzes. We've found that a distinct portion of the most vocal also happen to be the smartest. A tough thing it is, for certain, to know a trade forward and backward, to have a wealth of insight, and *not* integrate it all. "Overcoaching" shouldn't be spoken in the same breath as "bad coaching." We'd wager that 99 percent of the substance of overcoaching is good stuff, from a content perspective. From a leadership perspective, it's the difference between good and exceptional. It's what separates an industry's Sparky Andersons, Tom Landrys, and Phil Jacksons from their peers. There are scores of product managers, floor managers, sales directors, and staff chiefs with the potential of Sparky, Tom, and Phil. There are only a handful tapping that potential—by *tabling* some of that potential!

Failure to achieve performance breakthroughs, like Sammy Kahn's, is seldom due to lack of direction or lack of motivation. It's generally either A) too much overeager desire to drive success, or B) too much hesitancy to turn people loose. In a nutshell, it's a leadership expression of the sentiment: "I have a ton of experience; I can prevent the repetition of our company's past mistakes; I can make a difference; I can teach my folks how to get ahead."

Super. But are you willing to do so in the manner of Sparky Anderson?

Youth sports today is an epidemic example of people in positions of authority not saying yes to this question. Kids go from the last bell at school to practice to private lessons to tutoring to homework to awake two hours before school starts the next morning to fit in some more private lessons or personal training or extra tutoring. Families that can afford it load their children with individual $100 an hour instructors. That's on top of participating in multiple "select leagues" which layer on extended seasons, national travel, and regular incorporation of fancy biomechanics testing equipment. Parents have read Malcolm Gladwell's *Outliers*, touting ten thousand hours of practice as the differentiator of world-class skill mastery. They are tallying, daily, the hours in smart phone apps!

It's all with the aim of helping their kids be the best they can be, of course. But burnout rates are rising. As is Prozac usage. There isn't a proportional increase (population adjusted) in the supply of supremely talented athletes (or musicians, or scholars, or sales executives). Meanwhile, criticisms fly that kids today are less responsible, unmotivated, don't take initiative, don't think for themselves, or lack problem-solving ability.

Experts wheel out the overtraining verdict. Interestingly, if you examine child activity patterns from the 1970s, you find that kids logged an equal number of hours engaged in athletics. In the seventies, however, it was in the form of sandlot—mothers yelling and pleading to come in for dinner, kids staying out until it was too dark to see— games. Volume of work is clearly not the problem. Gladwell is right, practice *is* a variable influencing success. Dr. John Jane's neurosurgery residents, Coach Pop's basketball players, Doug Boyd's swimmers, Danny Meyer's waiters, General Schwarzkopf's soldiers, Google programmers—all trounce their competitors in time-card stamping; none burn out or quit. The crucial difference is not extent of effort. It's extent of coaching.

Let us reiterate. Overcoaching is not bad coaching. It's just not three-dimensional coaching.

1-D = Teaching and Feedback

2-D = Listening and Learning

3-D = Giving Freedom *To*

Organizations that develop extreme teamwork thrive on three-dimensional coaching. They have bosses, GMs for instance, out taking tickets, doing all kinds of jobs—and having a blast at those jobs. They are learning, not just leading. In the process, they are removing the clutter. They are helping their team be less encumbered. And goodness, how it trickles down.

On one occasion we witnessed a sports team president huddle his folks together to talk about helping. He announced that he was going to do better at his job by getting out of the office and touching everyone who walked into the stadium that day. Moments later, one of the team's middle managers called together all the ushers and had the *same chat*. What's even more positive, in the midst of the game an usher noticed a fan accidently knocking over his freshly purchased cup of beer. The usher raced off to the nearest vending counter, grabbed a couple sodas and hot dogs, and brought them to this fan and his son.

Trickledowns like this are so much more likely when you get out of the way, when you approach leading in a three-dimensional manner—when coaching is a bit less concerned with X's and O's and a bit more concerned with "beyond Moneyball" variables, such as self-actualization, helping, toughness, unselfishness, taking initiative, team confidence, and emotional authenticity.

To enhance *these* elements of teamwork, look to leaders less for answers. Curtail the flood of feedback. And reverse the authority-subordinate relationship. . . .

The Sherpa Mentality

In Tibet, the word *Sherpa* means "Eastern People," referring to an ethnic group living in the rockiest region of Nepal, the Himalayas, where Mount Everest rises. Their culture, combined with their terrain expertise, combined with their unique physical adaptations, makes Sherpas elite mountaineers. Some foreigners who ascend K1 and K2 gape in awe at the towering packs Sherpas can lug, while carrying children *and* carrying on routine conversation. Others ramble on about Sherpas' off-the-charts nitric oxide production or cold tolerance or hearts that can process glucose or lungs that increase in efficiency at low-oxygen altitudes. We're partial to their unfailingly cheerful smiles and ever positive attitudes. Ultimately, it's the whole package that makes Sherpas revered worldwide as symbols of hardiness and wisdom.

COACH DEAN SMITH (TO MICHAEL JORDAN IN HIS FRESHMAN YEAR AT UNC)

If you can't pass, you can't play.

Our dear friend Larry Domingo was the one who brought Sherpas to our attention. He'd shun the recognition, but Larry is the guy who put Precor's elliptical machine concept on the map, guiding the corporation's sales division to become a market-share-commanding forerunner of the fitness industry. LD is a voracious reader; he buys endless streams of books for his staffs. He's a data hound. He also enjoys fine wine and collects luxury watches. A run-of-the-mill executive he definitively is not. When he had the reins at Precor, a run-of-the-mill sales team they definitely were not. Both human and machine got more bang for their buck than could be found at any other exercise equipment company. Because they invented a secret engineering sauce? Nope. Because they made smart bets and controlled costs? Nah-uh. Because they hired marketing geniuses? Wrong again. Larry, of course, works hard in those areas. But what separates him from the pack is his tenacious determination to get behind every single person in his charge. It seeps into his team. They all have a tenacious determination to get behind their clients.

LD calls it the Sherpa Mentality.

"When a climber shows you photographs of scaling Everest, there are always snapshots of their group hoisting arms and ice picks in celebration at the top of the mountain," relates Domingo. "There's never a Sherpa in those pictures."

What he's referencing is the contrast in mission between climber and guide. Hikers' goals are to summit, to stake their flag in the mountain. Sherpas' goals are to see to the hikers' safety and survival. And while foul weather can derail climbers, Sherpas stop at no length to accomplish their goals. Barry Bishop, the first American to reach Mount Everest's peak, suffered debilitating frostbite on his heroic 1963 expedition, presenting a seeming impossibility of descent—certain death. He told *National Geographic*:

"Sherpas came to the rescue, a team of four carrying each [climber] on a two-day journey to Namche where we could be evacuated by helicopter. They set to even this grueling task with [inspiring] good humor."

From the instant Larry heard that story, he was determined to be an executive version of a Sherpa. He observed at Precor that a hefty portion of corporate sales activity was wining and dining clients, schmoozing, winning business. He couldn't imagine a Sherpa doing that. Hustling for new accounts didn't serve the customer, it served the company. Larry replaced the practice with a challenge to his team to find loads to carry for customers, just like a Sherpa would. He substituted the word *help* to replace the word *sell* in every company manual, memo, and communication. He started organizing sales meetings for his entire team in which they would work on methods to be trusted advisers to their clients. The team discovered how deeply Larry cared about them. The company took off.

Not long ago, we visited with Larry to chat about how we should tell his story. LD responded in classic Sherpa style. He said:

"You don't need to put me in the book. Put in Dave Zachry, or Brad Baker, or Jeff Hoke, or Dan Toigo, or Chuck Fedorka, or Jarred Willis, or 'DJ' Jones, or Greg Dearholt. They are the real heroes. They're on the front line of sales being incredible Sherpas for all the YMCAs and 24 Hour Fitnesses and Gold's Gyms out there."

He kept on listing. He didn't want to leave anyone out. We absolutely apologize to anyone on Larry's teams whom we didn't include. They truly are all Hall of Fame–caliber Help the Helpers.

Like Sal Pellegrino, who might just take the cake in the category of unselfishness. Shortly after the Precor team launched their practice of converting from selling into Sherpa-ing, Sal learned that one of his customers was lacking a database of its fitness center usage. He knew this owner was worried about making mistakes or underproviding for patrons. She was also overly time-strapped, not affording her the time to gather the data. It's a schlep of an effort, to state it mildly, to compile all the relevant information—exercise machine codes and conditions, the number of miles logged on each piece of equipment, belt wear, traffic patterns through the club, human flow stats . . . all the way to community demographics, membership patterns, and competitor offerings. The only way to gather it all is by hand, going facility to facility. It takes forever.

This owner was already a client of Sal's. He didn't need to earn her business. Database research and construction had nothing to do with his job of selling ellipticals and treadmills. He did it anyway. He saw a load his customer couldn't carry and he took unsolicited initiative to put the pack on his own back. Sal spent weeks driving from club to club building the database. He asked for nothing in return.

Finding ways to help other people succeed is what Pellegrino's all about. Can you see why we love him so much? He's the perfect role model of the advice in the concluding section of chapter 8: first define what you're about and then make every decision trickle down from that. Sal is also a wonderful case study of what we affectionately titled this chapter: being an *un*leader. To that end, to take a few cues from Sal, three Sherpa Mentality recommendations are worth emphasizing.

MARVIN WEISBORD

Teamwork is the quintessential contradiction of a society grounded in individual achievement.

One, Sherpas, literally, take an incredible weight off the shoulders of climbers. It frees climbers up to focus on the success of the venture. As a result, climbers take on and maintain immense responsibility. Might you relish your people being that invested? Then do what Sherpas and Larry Domingo and Sal Pellegrino do. Find ways to remove packs off your teams' (and your customers') backs.

Two, Sherpas are the true, functional leaders of an ascent. They know the best routes; they attend to subtleties in climate patterns that the finest instruments cannot ascertain; they select campsites and position tents; they decide when to press forward and when to break. But they do so from the back of the group, in the shadows. They allow climbers to be the ones out ahead, in the sunshine, with the best view—the first to the top. Have an ascent you'd like to top in your industry? Then follow in the footsteps of LD and Sal and the Sherpas. Lead from behind your team.

Three, the enormous respect for Sherpas around the globe cites how astute they are, how advanced their intuition is, how sage they are. It's not the product of sitting in classrooms, memorizing texts, or taking standardized tests. They don't guide missions by waving directives, circulating policy memos, lecturing at base camp, writing mission statements, or conducting mid-trek personnel reviews. They guide by large measures of watching, listening, observing . . . and listening some more. Might you benefit from a team as wise? Then be a Sherpa like Larry Domingo, like Sparky Anderson, like Phil Jackson.

Even go as far as the doc does in a school setting. At least once a se-mester he invites students to come to the front of the class to imitate him.* If they can readily mimic him to a T (which brings raucous joy to the group) and he can't imitate the kids equally well in return, it's an indication that the authority-subordinate relationship hasn't been flipped upside down enough—the doc is spending too much time do-ing the talking, too much time leading, not enough time watching and listening. He immediately rights the relationship.

Another way of getting at this is to ask of authorities and subordi-nates, "Who knows more about whom?"

The more you are in charge, the more actively you lead or coach, the more you are the source of direction, the less bandwidth you have to learn about your employees; the more they are in an observational position to learn about you. They will be able to imitate you better than you can imitate them. Fix this. Extreme teams are well balanced. And they don't get that way by lounging around a coffee room singing "Kumbaya."

A leader who knows this as well as anyone we've met is J. T. Higgins, head coach of the men's golf program at Texas A&M University. J.T. is comparable to outstanding college coaches in that he's highly person-able; he recruits well. He has impeccable moral fiber (which, unfortu-nately, can be said of fewer and fewer leaders in elite sports these days). He is an excellent fund-raiser, paving the way to build beautiful facili-ties. He's tireless. He's well organized. He involves the community and the team's boosters as family. What makes J.T. super unique is that he's not a golfer. He's not a former PGA Tour pro or No. 1 ranked All-American as a collegian. Nor was he a teaching pro at a swank club or PGA course. He comes to the sport from baseball and basketball. Sure, he can engineer his way around the links. He'll take a five-dollar Nas-sau off you. He does it, though, as an athlete rather than as a polished ball striker. He draws upon team-sport lessons for his success.

---

*Hardly a year into the doc's tenure at Rice, students were already looking forward to the imitation invites. It quickly became a source of class bonding. Two of Eliot's all-time-favorite pupils, Jason Hebert and Dan Dawson, who were cocaptains of the football team, spent weeks preparing, even though John didn't know they knew about his technique. They researched Doc's background, called former class participants, and dug up video. When John finally made the offer, they sprinted down the aisle, dressed in elaborate Dr. Eliot costumes, wearing his sunglasses, the works. It was a display Hollywood casting directors should have witnessed. Needless to say, Hebert and Dawson were stalwart anchors of the Owls' turnaround on the gridiron during their undergrad years.

Critics, particularly coaches trying to recruit against him, attempt to point out that his players are at a handicap. They claim (falsely) that Higgins doesn't know enough about swing mechanics to instruct. It's a handicap, J.T. knows, a handicap other coaches suffer. While his opponents are tied up (as if in a game of Twister) with grip position and hip alignment and all manner of subtle corrections—the technical aspects of the game known for wreaking havoc on the conscientious—Higgins isn't perturbed. He's a pro at staying freed up to concentrate on the big picture. In turn, his players are freed up to compete, to be athletes rather than perfectionists.

He's armed with plenty of golf knowledge. He *could* learn more minutiae. He knows it would rob him of his edge, though. It would interfere with his clarity and resultant priority to be a master in attending to his golfers' fundamental needs, a master in reversing the authority-subordinate relationship, and thereby a master in helping his golfers develop trust and confidence in themselves.

The critics were silenced in 2009.

At the famous Inverness Club in Toledo, Ohio, the Aggies turned in solid stroke play rounds to advance to the eight-team match play national championship. They upset their Elite Eight opponent, No. 2 ranked Arizona State, to reach the Final Four. They then pulled out a win over Michigan, with senior Matt Van Zandt's dramatic victory at the five-slot in the lineup, to get to the ultimate stage. Two teams left standing. A&M versus the Arkansas Razorbacks.

More than four thousand fans surrounded the fairways. Junior Andrea Pavan smoked his match 7-and-6 and sophomore John Hurley dropped a hammer with a 6-and-4 win to give the Aggies two quick points. Alas, despite outstanding play, Van Zandt and sophomore Conrad Shindler couldn't quite close out their contests. The Razorbacks tied it up at two matches apiece. It all came down to the maroon-and-white captain, Bronson Burgoon, head-to-head with Arkansas's best player, Andrew Landry—a longtime friend of Burgoon's from South Texas. Bronson went up one. He went up two at the turn. Then three . . . and four! With five holes left to play, the sweet taste of a national title seemed to be waiting on a silver platter. Until a little bad luck fluttered its wings.

On fourteen, Burgoon's tee shot bounced just into the rough, giving him an impossible lie. Landry found the finest part of the fairway. Three up with four to play. Landry again stripped it down the middle. He pushed Burgoon to two up with three to play. Then one up with two to play. On seventeen, the craziest of awkward stances forced Bronson to chip up short of the green. Andrew remained hot. *All square walking up to the eighteenth tee box!*

What was Coach Higgins doing this whole time? Analysts would've been raking him over the coals and second-guessing his every step. J.T. didn't mind. He's too Help the Helper tough to be bothered attending to analysts. He continued strolling alongside the course, not an ounce of doubt in his mind, instilling bucketloads of confidence in his captain (and his assistant coach, Jonathan Dismuke, who was walking with Burgoon) by *not* coaching.

NORMAN SHIDLE

A group becomes a team when each member is sure enough of himself to praise the skills of others.

Landry didn't waver. His drive on eighteen was picture perfect. Exactly where every pro would tell you to hit it. Bronson pushed his drive right. It came to rest in the deep rough. Buried. The gallery groaned mightily.

Did J.T. panic or rush out to the rescue? Nope! Thanks to his unique-to-golf team-sports training, Coach Higgins is arguably one of the best coaches in the nation at understanding how a group can add to an individual's toughness. He knows the power of trust and how excess instruction can squash that trust, especially during tense moments when huge outcomes hang in the balance.

When Burgoon glanced over, before getting ready to hit his shot out of the rough, J.T. simply nodded his head. It was so positive and confident that we get goose bumps just recalling it. We get goose bumps on top of goose bumps when we remember what happened next.

Landry hit his approach smack in the middle of the green, thirty-five feet from the pin. Thirty-five feet from the championship—if not for Bronson's strength, backed up by Higgins's freeing it up. Burgoon took a colossal whack into the knee-high grass with a gap wedge. The ball flew out. The crowd went mute watching it soar. It landed on the back of the green, somehow with spin. It rolled back toward the pin. It kept rolling. And rolling, as someone in the gallery screamed out, *"Get in the hole!"* It rolled to three inches from victory! Coach Dismuke launched himself into Bronson's arms. The two were so jacked they almost toppled right into a sand trap.

As Burgoon then strode up to the green, Landry conceded the putt. He took his visor off and shook Burgoon's hand in congratulations—sportsmanship at its very finest. And then the entire Aggie family ran out onto the course to mug Bronson.

Freeing It Up

We want you, and your team, to experience this mugging on a regular basis. We want you to have lots of Aggie and Roy Williams–style huggers. We know it's possible because we've lived it. Not just on basketball court and baseball diamond; not just after monumental wins. We celebrate with our friends, and families, and coworkers over what outsiders gazing in might deem the silliest of little things. Why? Because we proactively reinforce with one another that it's the little adjustments, the seemingly inconsequential moments of helping others, that bring people closer together.

We want you to have that mission, too. As we described at the beginning of chapter 1, it's the lifeblood of what makes the special teams in history so special. We know that if you can find one thing—*just one thing*—in this book that you'll be passionate about using to help people, you'll improve someone's life. You'll be on your way to building one of those special teams.

The reason we've written this book is because we've witnessed the tremendous benefits of being committed to Helping the Helper and we want to pay it forward. To share one last story with you, remember Tom Hankins from chapter 3?

During a particularly noteworthy game as student-athletes, with the stands packed, famous scouts aplenty, KP and Hankins were shoulder-to-shoulder in battle together. Tom stole a pass, opening up a two-on-none fast break. Tom could have dunked the ball in ESPN *SportsCenter* highlight fashion, raising the arena roof and popping scouts' eyes. He got to the basket and dished off to Kevin instead, giving him the glory.

A year later, KP was playing in the Kentucky Derby Classic. He had one of the most memorable nights of his career and was named MVP of the famous event. It was because of what he learned from Tom. Early in the game, Kevin stole the ball and raced down the court uncontested. Hankins—and the overwhelming thankfulness he'd felt the year prior—flashed through his mind. Kevin proceeded to lay off the ball to a teammate. His teammate slammed it home to the pleasure of the crowd—and to a feeling of reward for KP that changed his life.

Join us in being like Tom Hankins.

> *"I may never be as strong or as wise as a Sherpa, but I'll always strive to act like a Sherpa."*
>
> —LARRY DOMINGO

YOUR TURN!

Be a Leader, in Your Industry, in the Sherpa Mentality

We hope a tear welled when you read the Tom Hankins story. We cry every time we tell it. That we do is feedback letting us know we are tough and we are unselfish. In fact, the next journey we are embarking on is a large-scale, in-depth study of the toughest people and companies in the world. We'll gather the data and findings for you as soon as we can. In the meantime . . .

1. Be like *all* the incredible Help the Helpers in the Sherpa days at Precor; strive to be a trusted adviser instead of a manager or boss or product director or company.

Who are three teammates you are going to listen to more, carry a pack for, or allow to have the glory—*this week*?

_____

_____

_____

Who are three customers or clients you are going to listen to more, carry a pack for, or allow to have the glory—*this week*?

_____

_____

_____

Acknowledgments

This book would not have been possible without all of the athletes, coaches, and colleagues we've learned from over the years. We're sad that space didn't allow us to include each one of you and your remarkable, inspiring stories in the preceding pages. With every revision of the manuscript we found ourselves grappling with the desire to share five hundred more pages of Help the Helper heroes. How could we leave out Rob Searle's miraculous tennis match, playing on only one leg, defeating the No. 1 ranked player in the country (and the all-pro hug from Coach Ladhani)? Why couldn't we fit in the tale of MLBPAA's Mike Groll pulling a rabbit out of his hat to get Vida Blue to a charity event for kids? Is it really true that we don't have a single John Goff example!? He's one of the most unselfish Help the Helpers we've ever known. Perhaps we need to get our fannies in gear on a sequel. In the meanwhile, though, to all of you who've forever lifted our lives with your wisdom and assists, THANK YOU!

Thank you to our former teammates. There are too many of you to list, but you know who you are. You know all the endless hours of BP, all the amazing passes, all the pick-me-ups you've given us! And an extra distinct THANK YOU to coaches John Emery, Bill Reinhardt, Jo Evans, Nigel Topping, Alex Magleby, John Phillips, Larry Brown, Roy Williams, Gregg Popovich, Dirk Bauermann, Carlo Recalcati, and R. C. Buford.

We owe, as well, a *very* special gratitude to the absolutely world-class team behind this publication: our literary agent, Jim Levine, and his entire staff; everyone at Penguin/Portfolio—Adrian Zackheim, Will Weisser, Jillian Gray, and Amanda Pritzker; our extraordinarily gifted, Monet-talented graphic artist and Web designer, Manny Gonzalez; and our family members (including Terry Davison, John Katen, and Tony

Apollaro) who reviewed draft after draft and continually pushed us to be better. A lineup to beat this collection of all-stars cannot possibly be found.

Three cheers, of the most rousing nature, must go out to cherished friends Brian Kramer, Tom Penn, Bryan Hardman, Bill Bayno, Chad Buchanan, Michael Born, Nate McMillan, Brad Kime, and Lauren Anderson. Three cheers must also go out to agent Warren LeGarie! And to Cheri Hansen for all the sound advice.

The old-fashioned kind of cheer—Huzzah!—must go out to all of the vintage ballists who provide us with regular reminders of what sports and teams are really supposed to be about. Huzzah to Roy Hobbs and Ray Kinsella. "Is this heaven?" Huzzah to Tsui, Moonshine, Stonewall, Boomer, Timber, Jumbo, The Face, Scraps, Tatonka, Cannonball, Freight Train, Hatchet, Daisy, Flip, Pipes, Muffin, Gapper, El Presidente, P. T. Alvarez, Gil "I need a nickname" Sustache, and Pink Whiskers. And, of course, let's not forget a huzzah to the Slick Pickles double-play combo!

Finally, our dearest and most heartfelt thank-you to Larry Bird, Wayne Walden, Dr. Bob Rotella, and Dr. John Corson. Your mentorship guided us in developing careers that have been unbelievably personally rewarding. We think of the help you gave us every time we are able to help someone else.

To *all* of you, our love.

Sources

Introduction

Opening restaurant analogy created by Adrian Zackheim.

Gladwell, M. (2008). *Outliers: The Story of Success*. New York: Little, Brown, and Company.

Smith, D., G. D. Bell, and J. Kilgo (2004). *The Carolina Way: Leadership Lessons from a Life in Coaching*. New York: Penguin Press.

Lewis, M. (2003). *Moneyball: The Art of Winning an Unfair Game*. New York: W. W. Norton.

Ma, F. (2010). *The House Advantage: Playing the Odds to Win Big in Business*. New York: Palgrave Macmillan.

James, B., and J. Henzler (2002). *Win Shares*. Northbrook, IL: STATS Publishing, Inc.

Chapter One: Help the Helper

Hays, G. (2008). "Central Washington Offers the Ultimate Act of Sportsmanship." ESPN: www.youtube.com/watch?v=yaXVk5GBx-s/.

Hartman, S. (2006). "Autistic Teen's Hoop Dreams Come True." CBS News: www.cbsnews.com/2100-500202_162-1339324.html/.

The Hoyt Foundation: www.teamhoyt.com.

Schutz, P. W. (2003). *The Driving Force: Extraordinary Results with Ordinary People*. Irvine, CA: Entrepreneur Press.

Wise, J. (2010). "Who'll Be the Alpha Male? The Brain's Secret Mechanism for Determining Who Comes out on Top." *Psychology Today*, Oct. 4.

Klucharev, V., A. Smidts, and G. Fernandez (2006). "Social Context and Decision Making." *Perception*, vol. 35.

Rangel, A., C. Camerer, and P. R. Montague (2011). "A Framework for Studying the Neurobiology of Decision Making." *Nature*, Jun. 11 (Neuroscience Reviews).

Dash, E. (2011). "Outsized Severance Continues for Executives, Even After Failed Tenures." *New York Times*, Sept. 29.

Meyer, D. (2006). *Setting the Table: The Transforming Power of Hospitality in Business*. New York: Harper.

Chapter Two: Create a Dynasty of Unselfishness

NFL Scores and Statistics: www.pro-football-reference.com/.

Lewis, M. (2006). *The Blind Side: Evolution of a Game*. New York: W. W. Norton.

Takahashi, H., M. Kato, M. Matsuura, D. Mobbs, T. Suhara, and Y. Okubo (2009). "When Your Gain Is My Pain and Your Pain Is My Gain: Neural Correlates of Envy and Schadenfreude." *Science*, 323, 937–39.

Kruglanski, A. W., and O. Mayseless (1990). "Classic and Current Social Comparison Research: Expanding the Perspective." *Psychological Bulletin*, 108, 195–208.

Suls, J., R. Martin, and L. Wheeler (2002). "Social Comparison: Why, with Whom and with What Effect?" *Current Directions in Psychological Science*, 11, 159–63.

Salzberg, S. (1995). "Liberating the Mind Through Sympathetic Joy." In *Loving-Kindness: The Revolutionary Art of Happiness*. Boston: Shambhala.

Sternberg, S. (2010). "College Students Have Less Empathy Than Past Generations." *USA Today*, June 8.

Maslow, A. (1943). "A Theory of Human Motivation." *Psychological Review*, 50, 370–96.

Chapter Three: Hire the *Front* of the Jersey

Keri, J. (2011). *The Extra 2%: How Wall Street Strategies Took a Major League Baseball Team from Worst to First*. New York: Ballantine Books.

MLB Scores and Statistics: www.baseball-reference.com/.

Hatfield, E., J. T. Cacioppo, and R. L. Rapson (1993). *Emotional Contagion: Studies in Emotion and Social Interaction*. Cambridge, UK: Cambridge University Press.

Iacoboni, M., R. P. Woods, M. Brass, H. Bekkering, J. C. Mazziotta, and G. Rizzolatti (1999). "Cortical Mechanisms of Human Imitation." *Science*, 286, 2526–28.

HBO Films (2002 Documentary): *Do You Believe In Miracles? The Story of the 1980 U.S. Hockey Team*.

Colvin, G. (2008). *Talent Is Overrated: What Really Separates World-Class Performers from Everybody Else*. New York: Portfolio.

Harris, G. (2011). "New for Aspiring Doctors, the People Skills Test." *New York Times*, July 10.

Reiter, H. I. (2011). *How the Multiple Mini-Interview Has Become the Better Predictor for Future Job Performance*. Las Vegas, NV: SHRM (conference presentation).

Chapter Four: Ditch the Stick and Ditch the Carrot

The Brookings Institution: www.brookings.edu/.

Constellation Films (1996): *The Ghost and the Darkness.*

Cacciola, S. (2011). "Dallas's Secret Weapon: High Fives." *Wall Street Journal,* June 9.

Keltner, D., M. J. Hertenstein, R. Holmes, and M. McCullough (2009). "The Communication of Emotion Via Touch." *Emotion,* 9, 566–73.

Newburg, D. (2009). *The Most Important Lesson No One Ever Taught Me.* Charleston, SC: CreateSpace.

Newburg, D., and J. G. S. Clawson (2008). *Powered by Feel: How Individuals, Teams, and Companies Excel.* Hackensack, NJ: World Scientific Publishing Company.

Eliot, J. F. (2005). "Motivation: The Need to Achieve." In S. Murphy (ed.), *The Sport Psych Handbook.* Champaign-Urbana, IL: Human Kinetics.

Chapter Five: Manage Energy, Not People

Katerndahl, D. A. (1993). "Differentiation of Physical and Psychological Fatigue." *Journal of Family Practice,* 13, 81–91.

Baumeister, R. F. (2002). "Ego Depletion and Self-Control Failure: An Energy Model of the Self's Executive Function." *Self and Identity,* 1, 129–36.

Williamson, A. M. and A. M. Feyer (2000). "Moderate Sleep Deprivation Produces Impairments in Cognitive and Motor Performance Equivalent to Legally Prescribed Level of Alcohol Intoxication." *Occupational and Environmental Medicine,* 57, 649–55.

Carnegie Mellon University (2008). "Just Listening to Cell Phones Significantly Impairs Drivers." *Science Daily,* Mar. 5.

Arias-Carrión, O., and E. Pöppel (2007). "Dopamine, Learning, and Reward-Seeking Behavior." *Neurobiologiae Experimentalis,* 67, 481–88.

CBS Productions (2000, Episode 8). *CSI: Crime Scene Investigation.*

Battelle, J. (2005). "The 70 Percent Solution: Google CEO Eric Schmidt Gives Us His Golden Rules for Managing Innovation." *CNN Money Magazine,* Dec. 1.

The John Rassias Method: rassias.dartmouth.edu/method/.

Chapter Six: Invoke the 30-Minute Rule

Mosaic Media Group (2008): *Semi-Pro.*

Secundus, G. P. (Pliny the Elder), and J. Healey (1991). *Natural History: A Selection.* New York: Penguin Classics.

Shaw, G. B. (2010). *An Unsocial Socialist.* Florence, Italy: Nabu Press.

McQuillen, J. S. (2003). "The Influence of Technology on the Initiation of Interpersonal Relationships." *Education,* 123, 616–23.

Walther, J. B. (2011). "Theories of Computer-Mediated Communication and Interpersonal Relations." In M. L. Knapp and A. J. Daly (eds.), *The Handbook of Interpersonal Communication,* 443–79.

Bob Dethlefs: www.evanta.com/.

Chapter Seven: Eat Obstacles for Breakfast

Fancher, R. E. (1985). *The Intelligence Men: Makers of the IQ Controversy*. New York: W. W. Norton.

Wechsler, D. W. (1939). *The Measurement of Adult Intelligence*. Baltimore: Williams & Wilkins.

Gardner, H. (1983). *Frames of Mind: The Theory of Multiple Intelligences*. New York: Basic Books.

Goleman, D. (1995). *Emotional Intelligence: Why It Can Matter More Than IQ*. New York: Bantam.

Gibbs, N., S. E. Epperson, L. Mondi, J. L. Graff, and L. H. Towle (1995). "Emotional intelligence: The EQ." *Time*, Oct. 2, 146.

Locke, E. A. (2005). "Why Emotional Intelligence Is an Invalid Concept." *Journal of Organizational Behavior*, 26, 425–31.

Brody, N. (2004). "What Cognitive Intelligence Is and What Emotional Intelligence Is Not." *Psychological Inquiry*, 15, 234–38.

Boyd, W. (1966). *The Spontaneous Regression of Cancer*. Springfield, IL: Charles Thomas.

Valvano, J. (1993). "Don't Give Up . . . Don't Ever Give Up" (ESPY Lifetime Achievement Award Acceptance Speech). ESPN: espn.go.com/video/clip?id=3118760.

The Jimmy V Foundation: www.jimmyv.org/.

Greitens, E. (2011). *The Heart and the Fist: The Education of a Humanitarian, the Making of a Navy SEAL*. Boston: Houghton Mifflin Harcourt.

Eliot, J. F. (2004). *Overachievement: The Science of Working Less to Accomplish More*. New York: Portfolio.

Garber, G. (2008). "Source of Inspiration: Injured Soldier Produces Giant Emotions." *ESPN The Magazine*, Jan. 31.

Chapter Eight: Measure the Immeasurable

Wiggins, D. K., and P. B. Miller (2003). *The Unlevel Playing Field: A Documentary History of the African-American Experience in Sport*. Champaign-Urbana: University of Illinois Press.

Lewis, M. (2003). *Moneyball: The Art of Winning an Unfair Game*. New York: W. W. Norton.

MLB Scores and Statistics: www.baseball-reference.com/.

Tony Apollaro: www.thevarsityfinancialgroup.com/ and www.getinthebox.org/.

Patton, M. Q. (2001). *Qualitative Research & Evaluation Methods* [3rd ed.]. Thousand Oaks, CA: Sage.

Denzin, N. K., and Y. S. Lincoln (2000). *Handbook of Qualitative Research*. Thousand Oaks, CA: Sage.

Chapter Nine: Act Like an Unleader

Rotella, R. J. (1990). "Providing Sport Psychology Consulting Services to Professional Athletes." *The Sport Psychologist*, 4, 409–17.

Newburg, D., and J. G. S. Clawson (2008). *Powered by Feel: How Individuals, Teams, and Companies Excel.* Hackensack, NJ: World Scientific Publishing Company.

The Great Courses Company: thegreatcourses.com/.

Eric Church: ericchurch.com/.

Burfoot, A. (2011). "Ryan Hall, and the Mind of a Marathoner." *Runner's World,* Oct. 12.

Hessler, P. (2008). "Running to Being: The Making of a Long-Distance Runner." *The New Yorker,* Aug. 11.

Rushin, S. (1993). "The New Perfesser: The Spirit and Syntax of Casey Stengel Live On in Detroit Tiger Manager Sparky Anderson." *Sports Illustrated,* Jun. 28.

Sherpa Sales: www.larrydomingo.com/.

Rotella, R. J., B. Cullen, and T. Kite (1995). *Golf Is Not a Game of Perfect.* New York: Simon & Schuster.

Eliot, J. F. (2004). *Overachievement: The Science of Working Less to Accomplish More.* New York: Portfolio.

Index

OVERACHIEVEMENT
http://www.overachievement.com/

**OVERACHIEVEMENT,
THE COMIC BOOK**
http://smartercomics.com/overachievement/

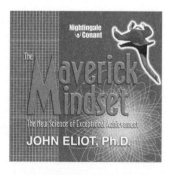

THE MAVERICK MINDSET
http://www.nightingale.com/prod_
detail~product~maverick_mindset.aspx/